Robinson Crusoe after 300 Years

TRANSITS:
LITERATURE, THOUGHT & CULTURE, 1650–1850

Series Editors
Kathryn Parker, University of Wisconsin—La Crosse
Miriam Wallace, New College of Florida

A long running and landmark series in long eighteenth-century studies, *Transits* includes monographs and edited volumes that are timely, transformative in their approach, and global in their engagement with arts, literature, culture, and history. Books in the series have engaged with visual arts, environment, politics, material culture, travel, theater and performance, embodiment, writing and book history, sexuality, gender, disability, race, and colonialism from Britain and Europe to the Americas, the Far East, and the Middle East. Proposals should offer critical examination of artifacts and events, modes of being and forms of knowledge, material culture, or cultural practices. Works that make provocative connections across time, space, geography, or intellectual history, or that develop new modes of critical imagining are particularly welcome.

Recent titles in the *Transits* series:

"Robinson Crusoe" after 300 Years
Andreas K. E. Mueller and Glynis Ridley, eds.

Transatlantic Women Travelers, 1688–1843
Misty Krueger, ed.

Laurence Sterne's "A Sentimental Journey": A Legacy to the World
W. B. Gerard and M.-C. Newbould, eds.

Hemispheres and Stratospheres: The Idea and Experience of Distance in the International Enlightenment
Kevin L. Cope, ed.

Rewriting Crusoe: The Robinsonade across Languages, Cultures, and Media
Jakub Lipski, ed.

Narrative Mourning: Death and Its Relics in the Eighteenth-Century British Novel
Kathleen M. Oliver

Lothario's Corpse: Libertine Drama and the Long-Running Restoration, 1700–1832
Daniel Gustafson

Romantic Automata: Exhibitions, Figures, Organisms
Michael Demson and Christopher R. Clason, eds.

Beside the Bard: Scottish Lowland Poetry in the Age of Burns
George S. Christian

The Novel Stage: Narrative Form from the Restoration to Jane Austen
Marcie Frank

The Imprisoned Traveler: Joseph Forsyth and Napoleon's Italy
Keith Crook

Fire on the Water: Sailors, Slaves, and Insurrection in Early American Literature, 1789–1886
Lenora Warren

Community and Solitude: New Essays on Johnson's Circle
Anthony W. Lee, ed.

The Global Wordsworth: Romanticism Out of Place
Katherine Bergren

For a full list of *Transits* titles, please visit our website: www.bucknelluniversitypress.org.

Robinson Crusoe after 300 Years

Edited by

ANDREAS K. E. MUELLER
AND GLYNIS RIDLEY

Bucknell University | UNIVERSITY PRESS

LEWISBURG, PENNSYLVANIA

Library of Congress Cataloging-in-Publication Data
Names: Mueller, Andreas Karl Ewald, 1972- editor. | Ridley, Glynis, editor.
Title: Robinson Crusoe after 300 years / edited by Andreas K. E. Mueller and Glynis Ridley.
Other titles: Robinson Crusoe after three hundred years
Description: Lewisburg, Pennsylvania: Bucknell University Press, 2021. | Series: Transits: Literature, Thought & Culture, 1650–1850 | Includes bibliographical references and index.
Identifiers: LCCN 2020031145 | ISBN 9781684482863 (paperback; alk. paper) | ISBN 9781684482870 (hardcover; alk. paper) | ISBN 9781684482887 (epub) | ISBN 9781684482894 (mobi) | ISBN 9781684482900 (pdf)
Subjects: LCSH: Defoe, Daniel, 1661?-1731. Robinson Crusoe.
Classification: LCC PR3403.Z5 R5755 2021 | DDC 823/.5—dc23
LC record available at https://lccn.loc.gov/2020031145

A British Cataloging-in-Publication record for this book is available from the British Library.

www.bucknelluniversitypress.org

Distributed worldwide by Rutgers University Press

Manufactured in the United States of America

CONTENTS

A NOTE ON THE TEXT

The twenty-first-century reader of *Robinson Crusoe* has many published versions of the novel from which to choose. Even the reader in search of a critical edition complete with scholarly apparatus has more than one option. In the essays that follow, all quotes to *The Life and Strange Surprizing Adventures of Robinson Crusoe* are from Daniel Defoe, *Robinson Crusoe*, ed. Thomas Keymer (Oxford: Oxford University Press, 2007), since this is a version of Defoe's work likely to be available to most readers. Page numbers to this edition are included in parentheses in the text.

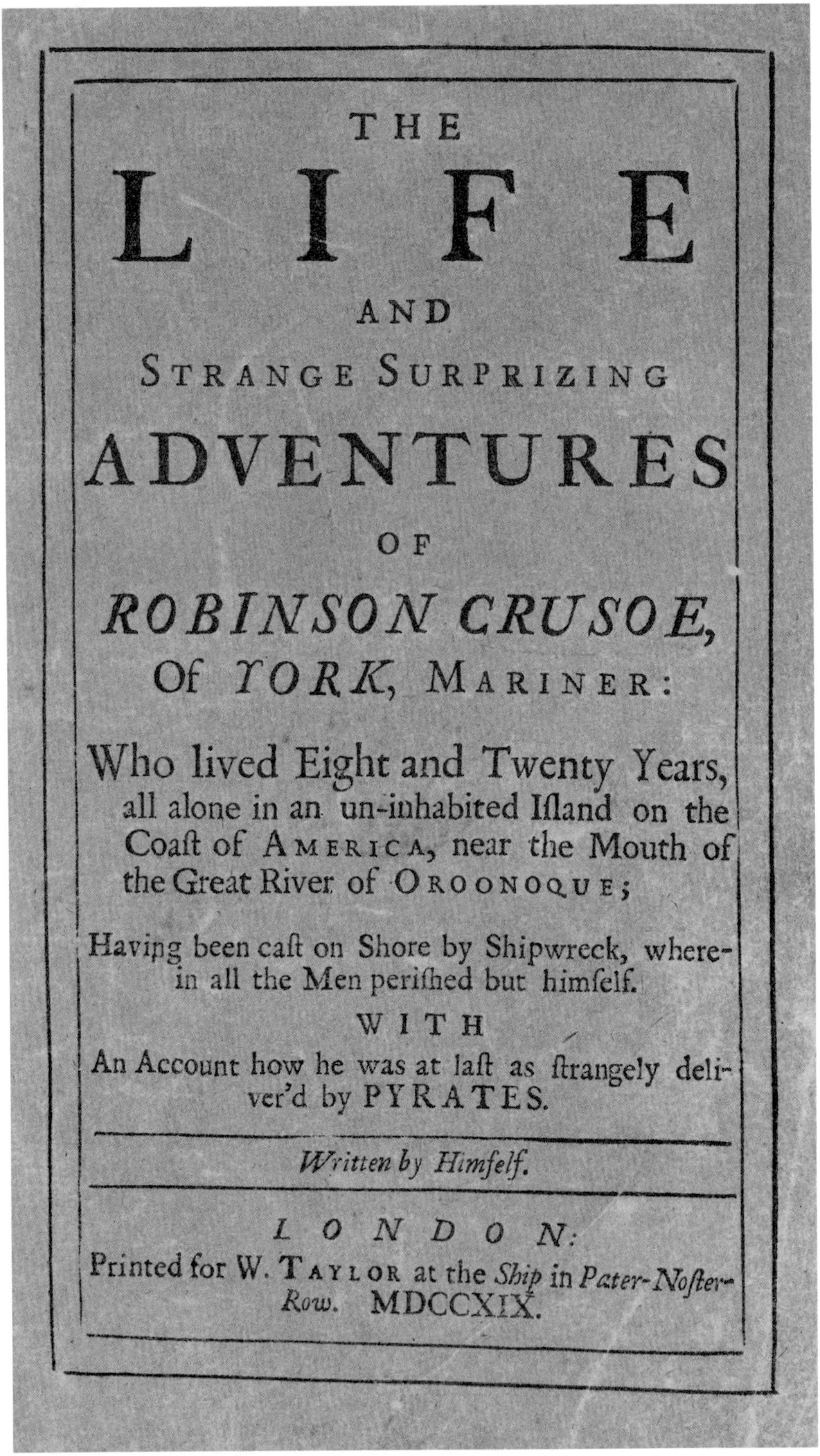

THE

LIFE

AND

STRANGE SURPRIZING

ADVENTURES

OF

ROBINSON CRUSOE,

Of *YORK*, MARINER:

Who lived Eight and Twenty Years, all alone in an un-inhabited Iſland on the Coaſt of AMERICA, near the Mouth of the Great River of OROONOQUE;

Having been caſt on Shore by Shipwreck, wherein all the Men periſhed but himſelf.

WITH

An Account how he was at laſt as ſtrangely deliver'd by PYRATES.

Written by Himſelf.

LONDON:

Printed for W. TAYLOR at the *Ship* in *Pater-Noſter-Row*. MDCCXIX.

Figure 0.1. Title page of first edition.

Robinson Crusoe after 300 Years

INTRODUCTION

Andreas K. E. Mueller and
Glynis Ridley

Robinson Crusoe has enjoyed, and continues to enjoy, many afterlives. As *The Strange Surprizing Adventures of Robinson Crusoe* and *The Farther Adventures of Robinson Crusoe* passed the tercentenary of their first publication in 1719, their titular character manages to sustain a popular cultural recognition that few fictional characters can boast. Appropriated by successive generations of readers as the embodiment of a range of ideological perspectives, Crusoe has proved to be an endlessly malleable figure, the inspiration for Robinsonades too numerous to mention, in formats and across media that serve only to further increase his cultural currency. In this volume, some of Crusoe's many afterlives are examined, as they intersect with the current moment both within and outside the academy.

Three essays consider some of the many generic revisions visited upon Crusoe. In "*The Martian*: Crusoe at the Final Frontier," Glynis Ridley considers Andy Weir's best-selling novel and its relationship to *Robinson Crusoe.* Originating as a personal blog in 2009, Weir's tale of an astronaut mistakenly left for dead on Mars went on to become a self-published novel on Amazon Kindle Direct, where its success led to a conventionally published hardback in 2014 with Crown Publishing. Many of those who know the novel's plot are likely familiar with the version presented by Drew Goddard's screenplay for the 2015 movie of the same name. One year after *The Martian* appeared as a movie, the original novel was reissued in a specially redacted classroom edition at the urging of America's science teachers. Across all its formats—perhaps *because* of its multiple formats—*The Martian* has been a cultural sensation. While this is a testament to Weir's conception and execution of his original idea, Ridley argues that the popularity of *The Martian* bears certain similarities to the popularity of *Robinson Crusoe* itself, and that *The Martian* should be read and viewed (in all its formats) as attesting to the enduring appeal of Defoe's original. Following the release of the first Crown issue of *The Martian*, reviewers were quick to identify similarities between Weir's creation and *Robinson Crusoe*, though Weir himself professes his greatest inspiration was from the 1995 movie *Apollo 13*. Examining claims for influence on *The Martian*, Ridley concludes that whenever and wherever fictional protagonists are portrayed in a struggle to survive against the odds, the shade of Crusoe cannot help but be present.

Whereas *The Martian* reimagines Crusoe in space, no less intriguing is his transformation into one of the most popular roles for female headliners in later nineteenth-century Anglo-American pantomime and burlesques. In "Robinson's Transgender Voyage: or, Burlesquing Crusoe," Geoffrey Sill examines this phenomenon as captured in a range of literary ephemera including newspaper advertisements, reviews, and photographs. Robinsonades built around female castaways are, of course, almost as old as Defoe's original telling of the myth, beginning with Penelope Aubin's *The Strange Adventures of Count de Vinevil* (1721). But the Robinsonades traced in Sill's paper represent voyages across gender boundaries: voyages in which the gender identity of Crusoe himself is called into question.

Sill argues that the gendering of Crusoe as female may have been implicit in some of the earliest illustrations of the book that followed the runaway success of Sheridan's Drury Lane reimagining of Defoe's text as *Robinson Crusoe; or, Harlequin Friday* (running for twenty-three months, from January 27, 1781, until December 16, 1782): Sheridan's production spawning more than a hundred subsequent pantomimes, burlesques, and extravaganzas that celebrated, caricatured, or burlesqued the myth of Crusoe. Tracing a direct line from the silent Harlequinade of Sheridan's era to the "principal boy" of pantomime, a character gendered male but played by a woman, Sill examines actress Lydia Thompson's performance as Crusoe in an 1876–1877 American tour of H. B. Farnie's *The Very Latest Edition of Robinson Crusoe*, in which Thompson appeared as Crusoe. Saving a full beard, Thompson's animal skin tunic (leaving her arms bare and legs exposed) and ostrich feather hat repeated most of the visual elements present in early representations of Crusoe, and set the stage for a host of imitators. But why should *Robinson Crusoe* have proved to be a popular subject for burlesque? Sill argues that Lydia Thompson's burlesque of Crusoe seems to represent a subtle criticism, perhaps even a repudiation of imperialism—and that the female Crusoe of burlesque theater represents the affirmation of a benevolent, feminized, and sentimental figure who was present in the eighteenth-century reception of Crusoe almost from the very beginning.

The last generic revision examined in this collection is Crusoe's transformation into a range of nonhuman animals. In "Animal Crusoes: Anthropomorphism and Identification in Children's Robinsonades," coauthors Amy Hicks and Scott Pyrz use insights and methodologies from the growing field of human-animal interaction to consider an intriguing corpus of Robinsonades featuring animal castaways as central characters—as distinct from reimaginings of Crusoe's story that include tangential animal companions. Given that such Robinsonades are invariably aimed at children, the essay brings human-animal interaction studies to bear on an exploration of children's literature. Children's Robinsonades often revise Defoe's Crusoe as an emulative figure who ensures his triumphant survival through innovation, thrift, and perseverance, and thus the tales omit the character's often inhibitory introspection and anxieties. In this way, these narratives have created their own iconic version of the castaway character—one that emphasizes identification between the child reader and Defoe's prototype, as well as his literary descendants. Yet in Robinsonades featuring anthropomorphized animal characters this identificatory impulse is often absent or inverted, despite the associations commonly made between the child and the animal. The relationship between Crusoe and animals in Defoe's novel has been explored by Defoe scholars, but the critical landscape concerning animal castaways in children's Robinsonades has gone mostly untrodden. Focusing on a small corpus of animal Crusoe stories, Hicks and Pyrz suggest that these works produce an identification between the child reader or listener and the animal castaway, in a manner that undoes the prototypical Crusoe as emulative figure and instead reintroduces the inhibitory introspection and anxieties that are often omitted in children's versions. While the presence of animal Crusoe characters in children's Robinsonades attests to the persistent appeal of Defoe's trilogy, Hicks and Pyrz explore the strange and surprising evolution of the animal Crusoe figure, as presented to young readers.

This brief survey of contrasting Generic Revisions is followed by four explorations on the theme of mind and matter. While twentieth-century criticism has drawn our attention to *Robinson Crusoe*'s generic indebtedness to the spiritual autobiography, the popular reader has perhaps been more fascinated by the book's groundedness in the direct experience of material life. Inanimate manmade objects are firmly moved center stage once Crusoe is marooned on his desert island and their use value assumes special importance: in a particularly memorable episode Crusoe famously rejects the "drug" that is money and appears ready to consign an apparently worthless collection of gold and silver coins to the bottom of the sea "as a creature whose life is not worth saying," when unspecified "second thoughts" compel him to salvage the useless objects after all. In "Defoe and Newton: Modern Matter," Laura Brown considers the seemingly inescapable attraction held by "things" in the text as they may reveal Defoe's "experiment in the representation of force." By placing Crusoe's life on the island in relation to Newtonian theories of matter, in particular Newton's favored method of developing scientific understanding through an experiential engagement with matter, Brown demonstrates that Defoe's focus on a succession of objects, including his energy-infused, detailed accounts of Crusoe's creation of useful things, "highlights these things themselves as a vital presence" in the text and generates a narrative energy that foregrounds the book's materialist premise. Reflecting a distinctly Newtonian conceptualization of matter, Defoe has Crusoe experience his island world through an "inductive, conjectural process," thereby creating a connection between eighteenth-century literary realism and experimental philosophy "at the moment when materialism finds its first modern formulation."

In a novel that frequently draws the reader's attention to material things, might they be capable of causing a transformative experience? In "Crusoe's Ecstasies: Passivity, Resignation, and Tobacco Rites," Daniel Yu provides a fresh reading of Crusoe's widely discussed religious conversion, pointing out that Crusoe's island religion rests on a material foundation: his spiritualism is induced and initially sustained by the ecstatic experiences caused by the smoking of tobacco. Alerting us to the fact that Crusoe fetishizes his earthenware pipe rather than the more frequently discussed clay pot, Yu demonstrates that Crusoe's tobacco-fueled prayers and experiences of intoxicated religious transport interrupt his productivity, which, in turn, suggests a more subversive religiosity than has hitherto been recognized. Crusoe's ecstatic moments lead to frequent periods of contemplative inactivity that distinguish him from the utilitarian Puritan and, *pace* Max Weber, distance him from the strictly ascetic Puritanism that informs the modern capitalist spirit. Instead, Crusoe's tobacco-induced religion, anchored as it is in feelings of ecstasy rather than discipline and purposeful labor, allows for significant amounts of time to be invested in unproductive activities, which suggests that the notion of Crusoe as an archetype of modern "economic man" might be a mischaracterization.

In what might be described as the flip side of Brown's notion of the generally benign vitality of objects, Jeremy Chow presents a reading of *Robinson Crusoe* that recognizes a rather more threatening, distorting presence of things. In "Taken by Storm: *Robinson Crusoe* and Aqueous Violence," Chow argues that the stormy sea, a forceful and indomitable natural object, wreaks life-consuming violence on Crusoe's shipmates and puts Defoe's protagonist through a grueling rebirth that results in long-term isolation. Conceptualizing the sea as a nonhuman environmental agent, Chow argues that the interconnection established in the text between material substances and the human is predicated on Crusoe's experiences of an "aqueous violence" that distort his relationship with self, other, and environment. The wind-whipped ocean both threatens death and imposes isolation on Crusoe but also gestates and sustains him. It is the object that unmakes him to remake him: the sea-imposed isolation drives Crusoe's radical individualism, suggests Chow, and shapes his relationship with the other. Destructive inclination flows from object to human: the sea's constant flux and periodical all-consuming violence instils in Crusoe a corresponding desire for violent action against the cannibals, who are, in a circular conceptual movement, associated with the sea. Echoing Laura Brown's and Daniel Yu's essays, Chow's argument centers on the transformative power of an experiential engagement with matter.

The traditional image of Crusoe as a busy maker, surviving at the mercy of the sea, has perhaps directed our attention away from a central aspect of Crusoe's island existence: intense boredom. In "Life Gets Tedious: Crusoe and the Threat of Boredom," Pat Rogers invites us to consider that, after an initial period of high activity during which he completes tasks that are essential for his survival, Crusoe begins to suffer the excruciating tedium of isolation and relentless daily routine. The endlessly recurring sameness of Crusoe's existence, the emptiness of many successive days, is signaled no more clearly than in the fact that several uneventful years are entirely left out of Crusoe's account of his island life. Alleviating the psychological pain of this boredom becomes, as Rogers explains, a preoccupation for Crusoe: pointless activity and a growing search for novelty (including the smoking of tobacco) assume a more central importance in his efforts to divert himself from the relentless dullness that a lonely island existence imposes on him. If, as Brown shows, objects inject force and vitality into the narrative, and if material substances allow Crusoe's spirituality to emerge, as Yu demonstrates, Rogers reminds us that we see energy equally expended on relieving the psychological pressure of an unvaryingly tedious life. In this sense, Crusoe's experiential engagement with his environment serves no higher purpose than to "create a 'diversion' in the absence of escape routes," to allow Crusoe to cope with mind-numbing boredom.

The final section of this collection focuses on Character and Form and opens with a reminder that the Crusoe of *The Life and Surprizing Adventures* is not the same as the Crusoe of *The Farther Adventures*, though both were published in the same year. In "Crusoe's Rambling," Ben Pauley asks what we have lost by separating the two works, and what we might gain in reading them together again. Pauley suggests that, to read *The Life and Strange Surprizing Adventures* in isolation, as we have done for some hundred years now, is, as Melissa Free has argued, to read only half of Defoe's story. And yet, the two parts of Crusoe's story make odd companions: they are not simply different, they are *systematically* different. Where, in the first novel, Crusoe comes to a truer possession of himself as he cultivates his dominion over the island, he spends the second pointedly lamenting his lack of fixity and his inability to master his "native Propensity to rambling."

Viewing these two quite different books as halves of a larger whole unsettles the critical commonplace (following Watt) that Defoe's fiction represents a brief for modern individualism. Taking the *Farther Adventures* into account tempers our sense of Crusoe as heroic individual because the second novel argues so strenuously for the claims of national interest. These are claims that Crusoe himself, in large measure, fails to recognize. In the *Farther Adventures*, Crusoe's individualism comes under close scrutiny, first as he fails to convert his island possession into a colony yoked to the interest of England, and second as he pursues a lucrative circuit of trading around the ports of Asia. In both cases, it is precisely Crusoe's individualism—his abstraction from English national identity, his tendency toward the deracinated pursuit of individual commercial gain—that comes in for judgment. In its condemnation of Crusoe's "rambling," *The Farther Adventures* highlights a strand that is present in the first novel, but whose significance is easy to overlook in light of Crusoe's seeming reward. It is only in the continuation that some of the first book's latent concerns come fully into view. Reading the two novels together allows us to place Defoe's most famous fiction into clearer dialogue with his broader economic and commercial thought. In this light, the novels provide a fictional meditation on a question that exercised Defoe repeatedly in his other works: how—or, indeed, whether—the restless acquisitiveness of private interests might be harmonized in service of a larger national interest.

In "Crusoe's Encounters with the World and the Problem of Justice in *The Farther Adventures*," Maximillian Novak reflects on the fact that Crusoe is no less enamored of travel than is his creator. Extrapolating Crusoe's character only from his experiences on the island risks failing to see how much his is a tale of travel and encountering other peoples—not merely Friday and his fellow cannibals, but the inhabitants of northern Africa, Brazil, Portugal, and Spain. And these experiences appear merely in the first volume of the trilogy. In the second volume, usually read along with the first until the middle of the twentieth century, Crusoe travels away from his farm in England through the world—back to his island and to Brazil, and then to Madagascar, Bengal, through the West Indies to China, and then across Siberia and back to England. Novak's essay considers aspects of Crusoe's encounters with other peoples, especially those encounters involving matters of justice and ethics. For a concern with justice is a major theme throughout *The Farther Adventures*, and it is worth asking whether Crusoe's experiences add up to any consistent vision of what makes for a just society. Exploring the meaning and understanding of "justice" in *The Farther Adventures*, Novak concludes that Crusoe's empathy for the "murther" of 150 Madagascan natives reveals that his experience with Friday has shaped his sense of justice and has led him to question relative standards of justice, not only from country to country but as implemented by any self-selected coterie against all others.

The fascination that readers have experienced with *Robinson Crusoe* over the last three centuries has undoubtedly been anchored in the multiple layers of human experience and the variety of psychological states the book vividly depicts. As a thought experiment that typically triggers imagined scenes of isolation and survival in the reader, the book has given us an archetypal character whose iconicity in Western culture is assured. The ongoing presence of the Crusoe myth in contemporary cultural productions, even when the producer is unaware of the myth's influence, speaks to the continued relevance of its thematic core of adventure and self-sufficiency in our own day. In "'To Us the Mere Name Is Enough': Robinson Crusoe, Myth, and Iconicity," Andreas Mueller encounters "Crusoe" in readily predictable as well as in rather surprising contexts: Defoe's protagonist serves to give cultural weight to a blissful vacation experience in a tropical island setting as well as a computer game that centers on a space-traveling boy shipwrecked on a distant planet. But, far more unusually, the name "Robinson Crusoe" has also been appropriated to advertise upmarket garden buildings or a smartphone application that assists its users with the cognitive structuring of research projects. While it would be stretching matters too far to suggest that the name "Robinson Crusoe" has become detached from its original signification of adventure and survival, the unbroken iconic status of the name is now characterized by a flexibility that embraces areas of experience not previously associated with Defoe's book in a direct fashion. Thus, in Mueller's reading, the powerful linguistic sign "Robinson Crusoe" is a cultural signifier that floats relatively freely without ever entirely losing the traces of its origins in Defoe's story. Since Crusoe seems unlikely to fade from the collective cultural imagination anytime soon, the appropriation of his name explored by Mueller would seem to be the beginning of a process rather than its end. Crusoe, surely, has many afterlives yet, and further adventures—and milestones—to come.

Part One

GENERIC REVISIONS

1

THE MARTIAN

Crusoe at the Final Frontier

Glynis Ridley

IN 2009, SELF-DESCRIBED "SPACE NERD" Andy Weir started self-publishing chapters of a novel on his personal blog. Centered upon the struggles of a wise-cracking astronaut, Mark Watney, whose mission commander mistakenly leaves him for dead on Mars, Weir's blog soon amassed thousands of regular readers. Among Weir's early followers, some of those with relevant scientific expertise proved willing to provide feedback on technical aspects of the story, and so the self-published chapters grew into a fully fledged work: *The Martian*. When Weir's fan base requested an e-reader version of the finished text, Weir loaded his novel to Amazon Kindle Direct and quickly became an internet publishing sensation. In a cascading series of events that could be possible only in the digital publishing age, Weir's blog led him to self-publish with Amazon, where his success caused Crown Publishing to negotiate for the rights to bring out a conventionally published novel in 2014.[1] In 2015, a movie version of the novel was released and garnered seven Oscar nominations, including one for Best Picture.[2] So successful was the movie at bringing the novel to the attention of an ever-widening audience that a specially adapted (that is, redacted) version of the text was produced for use in American grade school science classes: space exploration minus the casual swearing of a variety of characters.[3] Across all its formats—perhaps because of its multiple formats—*The Martian* has been a cultural sensation.

Following the release of the first Crown issue, which debuted at twelfth on the *New York Times* hardback fiction best-seller list, reviewers were quick to identify similarities between Weir's creation and *Robinson Crusoe*, with some linking the two via Byron Haskin's 1964 movie, *Robinson Crusoe on Mars*.[4] Weir has been asked about links between *Robinson Crusoe* and *The Martian* repeatedly. A Q&A with Weir on Crown's own website includes a direct question as to whether Defoe's text inspired him, to which Weir responds, "Not really, no. I was more inspired by Apollo 13." Aficionados of director Ron Howard's 1995 movie *Apollo 13* (based upon Commander Jim Lovell's 1994 memoir, *Lost Moon*) will certainly recognize its influence on *The Martian*.[5] But in additional to crediting *Apollo 13* as an inspiration for *The Martian*, Weir has also said "I do love a good survival story."[6] And so Crown Publishing's press release for the paperback of *The Martian* seems at pains to avoid direct mention of *Robinson Crusoe*, while at the same time acknowledging its status as the ultimate survival story, pitching Weir's novel as "*Apollo 13* meets *Castaway* in this grippingly detailed, brilliantly ingenious man-versus-nature survival thriller—set on the surface of Mars." Here, Robert Zemeckis's 2000 retelling of Crusoe's story (with Tom Hanks cast as a FedEx executive stranded on a desert island) is credited as the archetypal survival narrative, and the press release cites only movie inspirations for *The Martian* rather than *Castaway*'s own indebtedness to Crusoe's tale.

There is no reason not to take Weir at his word that his interest is in "a good survival story" rather than Defoe's text per se. But if the longevity of *Robinson Crusoe* in the popular imagination is, in large part, because it is the preeminent example of a survival story, then its influence on any "good survival story" proves impossible to escape, no matter how hard any writer or filmmaker of a survival story might try. Wherever and whenever an individual or group of fictional protagonists is up against the odds and struggling to survive in an inhospitable landscape, the shade of Crusoe will surely always be present. As for the popularity of *The Martian*, the rapid adaptation of the novel for the American high school market may be seen as replicating the popularity of *Robinson Crusoe* itself. *The Martian* should therefore be read or viewed (in all its formats) as attesting to the enduring appeal of Defoe's original.

On April 12, 1961, Soviet astronaut Yuri Gagarin became the first man successfully to complete a space flight. On May 5, 1961, U.S. astronaut Alan Shepard followed in Gagarin's footsteps, and "the space race" had begun. The decade that would culminate in Neil Armstrong's walk on the Moon on July 20, 1969 also made space exploration a significant fictional trope. In 1966, the television show *Star Trek* imagined a future in which Earth's then-rival superpowers were no longer competitors, but all their peoples (not to mention some friendly alien races) had become partners in the exploration of space, famously introduced in each episode's opening credits as "the final frontier."[7] Across the history of the space exploration genre, fiction authors have—understandably—preferred to foreground the stresses that such exploration would place on interpersonal and interspecies relationships, rather than paying sustained attention to the science that could make such exploration possible. Secure in its science, *The Martian* deliberately upends that convention, as Andy Weir explained in an interview with astrophysicist Neil deGrasse Tyson:

TYSON: In *The Martian* all we care about is whether the main character survives on his scientific wit. I don't care about interpersonal relationships. I don't care if his parents are alive or dead, if he's married, has kids. I just care if the stuff he's figuring out is going to work. And he's tapping science, technology, engineering, and math: all the STEM fields. That may be without precedent.

WEIR: Well, see, no one would accuse *The Martian* of being literature, right? The main character, Mark Watney, is exactly the same at the end of the story as he is at the beginning. He doesn't undergo any change—no personality crisis, no nothing. And I don't feel bad about that. I'm completely unrepentant.[8]

The exchange is intriguing: as an astrophysicist, Tyson admits to the novelty of a reading—and viewing—experience in which the attempted resolution of a series of scientific problems is the page turner. For his part, Weir asks us to consider *The Martian* as something other than "literature," and when subsequently asked by Tyson, "Could you have invented a new genre here?" Weir responds, "I've heard people describe it as competence porn."[9] Certainly by the time of *The Martian*'s release in conventional novel printed form in 2014, the term "competence porn" had already acquired enough currency to be deemed worth an explanation in one of Britain's most conservative broadsheets; an article headline in the *Telegraph* asking readers, "Are you hooked on competence porn?"[10] The phenomenon is described as "entertainment—novels, films or television shows—where enjoyment is garnered form witnessing impressive feats of human capability. . . . But—and this is important—competence porn doesn't make you feel inadequate or incompetent. It makes you feel empowered." Having assured readers of the confidence imparted from reading or watching human wit and ingenuity succeed against all odds, the article proceeds to ground the genre in familiar literary history, and in doing so, it traces a direct line from *Robinson Crusoe* to *The Martian*: "There's nothing new about [competence porn]. One of the first examples of the genre was Daniel Defoe's 1719 novel, in which the shipwrecked Robinson Crusoe must start from scratch to build a comfortable and civilized life for himself . . . this year, perhaps the best shipwreck scenario for MacGyvering your way to survival is explored by Andy Weir's novel *The Martian*, about an astronaut marooned on Mars whose resourcefulness is stretched to the very limits to stay alive in the brutally unforgiving extraterrestrial environment."[11] Crusoe's life on the island is, of course, far from the entirety of the first part of his story, and as Benjamin Pauley reminds us (chapter 8), the first part of *Robinson Crusoe* has a long history of appearing together with *The Farther Adventures*: the assertion that *Robinson Crusoe* is one of the first examples of competence porn is therefore true only if one accepts Crusoe's shipwrecked island experience as synecdochical—the part that has come to represent the whole. But in the global cultural imagination, this conflation of *Robinson Crusoe* (and its continuations) with the idea (if not the specifics) of a man learning to survive on an island has long since occurred. As Andreas Mueller shows (chapter 10) the name "Crusoe" may only now be in the process of becoming unmoored from the specifics of a survival story. Yet a familiarity with the first-person narratives of any of Defoe's fictional protagonists from the 1720s shows "competence porn" to be a fitting, albeit anachronistic characterization of the most memorable parts of all these texts. To a greater or lesser degree, all of Defoe's titular narrators share the common trait of being serial problem solvers, and through solving problems, they survive. (Moll Flanders may even surpass Crusoe in this regard.) One of the closing scenes of the film version of *The Martian* (a scene that has no basis in Weir's novel) shows Watney back on Earth and working as an instructor in NASA's astronaut training program, assuring a roomful of astronaut candidates that staying alive in space is sometimes a matter of solving problems and, "if you solve enough problems, you get to come home." As a sentiment, this was perhaps never truer of any fictional protagonist than Crusoe himself.

The idea of Crusoe's life as a castaway has so permeated popular culture that the image of a single footprint on a sandy shore is instantly recognized as an allusion to Defoe's text, even by those who have never read it. Beyond its iconic status, the moment of Crusoe's discovery of the footprint proves to be a useful way of dividing his experience on the island into two: before seeing the footprint, Crusoe believes himself to be alone and unlikely ever to see another human being; after discovering the footprint, Crusoe does not necessarily envisage a solitary death on the island. Even so, Crusoe's discovery of a footprint at first produces terror rather than joy: "I stood like one Thunder-struck, or as if I had seen an Apparition. . . . I came Home to my Fortification, not feeling . . . the Ground I went on, but terrify'd to the last Degree. . . . When I came to my Castle, for so I think I call'd it ever after this, I fled into it like one pursued" (130–131). Despite's Crusoe's "terror" and "fright," and the temporary relief he experiences when "I began to perswade my self it was all a Delusion" (134), a second look at the enigmatic footprint and measurement of it against his own foot proves to Crusoe that he is not alone. In *The Martian*, a comparable assurance that he is no longer alone is given to Mark Watney when, on Sol 97, he realizes that an exploratory Mars rover he dug up from a previous mission has made contact with Earth, as he hoped that it would. Whereas Crusoe initially recoils from the footprint's mute signification of other human life, Watney is ecstatic that the movement of an antenna may be a prelude to interaction with another human being:

> I just suited up and checked the lander. The high-gain antenna is angled *directly* at Earth! *Pathfinder* has no way of knowing where it is, so it has no way of knowing where Earth is. The *only* way for it to find out is getting a signal.
>
> They know I'm alive!
>
> I don't even know what to say . . . I'm going to be talking to someone again. I spent three months as the loneliest man in history and it's finally over.
>
> Sure. I might not get rescued. But I won't be alone.[12]

While the reactions of Crusoe and Watney could not be more different, each is reacting to fundamentally the same experience as the certainty of being alone is "finally over." But even before this pivotal point in Defoe's and Weir's texts, Watney arguably has more in common with Crusoe than with any astronaut, since both Crusoe and Watney are both forced to consider how to provide for that most basic of human needs: food.

Crusoe admittedly has several advantages over Watney when it comes to providing himself with sustenance, not least breathable air, fresh water, and fertile soil. Additionally, Crusoe's island yields fruits (including grapes that Crusoe dries to make raisins, and limes), roots (including cassava), and meat (both goat and tortoise). But Crusoe finds himself an accidental cultivator of grains, when some "stuff" that he had discarded before heavy rains sprouts: "And not so much as remembering that I had thrown any Thing there, when about a Month after, or thereabout, I saw some few Stalks of something green, shooting out of the Ground, which I fancy'd might be some Plant I had not seen, but I was surpriz'd and perfectly astonish'd, when, after a little longer Time, I saw about ten or twelve Ears come out, which were perfect green Barley of the same Kind as our *European*, nay, as our *English* Barley" (67).

Within a relatively short space of narrative time, Crusoe is transformed from a hunter-gatherer into a farmer, penning livestock in a stockade and laying aside corn in expectation of future harvests. Fashioning himself a pestle and mortar, Crusoe teaches himself to make bread and so adds a familiar staple to his diet, to complement what the island naturally yields. But what comes relatively easily to Crusoe must be hard won by Watney who, after only three sols alone on Mars, articulates the brutal truth that "there's enough multivitamins . . . to last years. So I won't have any nutritional problems (though I'll still starve to death when I'm out of food, no matter how many vitamins I take)."[13] Watney needs calories. A search through food supplies in the Hab yields "all sorts of things that I can plant. Peas . . . plenty of beans . . . several potatoes" though, unlike Crusoe, Watney lacks any obvious growing medium and the ability to water crops.[14] Explaining that each of the six astronauts on the Ares 3 mission had two specialties, Watney identifies himself as the mission's "botanist and mechanical engineer," and he sets to work to put both areas of expertise to good use by transforming all usable floor (and bunk) space in the Hab and two adjacent pop tents into a potato farm, with human excrement for fertilizer, and water produced by "liberating" hydrogen from hydrazine left over from the Ares 3 fuel supply.[15] (The movie neatly confines Watney's potato-growing activities to a giant plastic tent rigged up within the Hab, rather than realizing the novel's messier vision.) As a botanist, Watney might be expected to be more sanguine than Crusoe about his ability to grow food crops, but the hostile Martian environment in which Watney is forced to work makes his wonder at the generation of new plant life every bit as profound as Crusoe's. True to *The Martian*'s foregrounding of science, Watney receives his first inkling that his potato crop will be viable not by observing sprouted stalks, but by analyzing soil samples under a microscope:

> Then came the critical part . . . checking the dirt. I took a few samples from all over the Hab (remember, it's all dirt flooring now) and made slides.
>
> With shaking hands, I put a slide into the microscope and brought the image up on-screen. There they were! Healthy, active bacteria doing their thing! Looks like I won't be starving to death on Sol 400 after all. I . . . let my breathing return to normal.[16]

Crusoe and Watney may be separated by over three centuries, but each momentarily catches his breath as he marvels at evidence of new, green life. Despite the fact that Crusoe is, initially, an accidental farmer, in contrast to Watney, whose life depends upon his ability to grow a calorie-laden and carbohydrate-rich staple, both men work through essentially the same mental and physical processes in relation to their crop. Where Crusoe finds wonder and hope in "*European*, nay . . . *English* Barley," Watney counts his good fortune that NASA provided him with "twelve whole potatoes, refrigerated but not frozen. . . . Because Thanksgiving was going to happen while we were doing surface operations."[17] Crusoe cannot resist seeing his sprouting grain as *English* and Watney knows his potatoes are viable only because provided for that most *American* of holidays: Thanksgiving.[18] While Crusoe sets aside seed from his crop to sow for the following season, Watney must override seasonal cycles and condense the natural growing cycle of his potatoes in hopes of ensuring a constant supply: "Normally, it takes at least 90 days to yield full-sized potatoes. But I can't wait that long. I'll need to cut up all the potatoes from this crop to seed the rest of the field."[19] Whereas Crusoe learns to protect his sprouting grains against goats and birds, Watney's enemies are not animals but rather atmospheric conditions that he must compensate for by making the entire Hab environment serve the needs of his potatoes: "By setting the Hab temperature to a balmy 25.5°C, I can make the plants grow faster. Also, the internal lights will provide plenty of 'sunlight,' and I'll make sure they get lots of water. . . . There will be no foul weather, or any parasites to hassle them. . . . With all this going for them, they should yield healthy, sproutable tubers within forty days."[20] Crusoe's life does not depend upon his ability to grow grains, but Watney's life does depend upon his ability to grow potatoes, as *The Martian* raises the stakes of the well-worn fictional trope of 'civilized' man learning to live off the land.

In his *Second Treatise of Government* (1690), John Locke famously argues that the cultivation of land provides the cultivator with a claim to ownership, for "as much land as a man tills, plants, improves, cultivates, and can use the product of, so much is his property." Unsurprisingly, Defoe's engagement with Locke's ideas has spawned multiple readings of Crusoe's imperialism as Lockean ideology made manifest: Crusoe seeing his success in growing food on the island as giving him a superior claim to its ownership than any claims from those who merely take their (cannibal) food there.[21] Wholly unexpectedly, this facet of Locke's *Second Treatise* appears in *The Martian* as Watney establishes communication with NASA and is flooded with emails from well-wishers:

> One of them was from my alma mater, the University of Chicago. They say once you grow crops somewhere, you have officially "colonized" it. So technically, I colonized Mars.
>
> In your *face*, Neil Armstrong![22]

When the *South China Morning Post* announced in January 2019 that China had landed a spacecraft on the far side of the Moon and that its cargo included a biosphere in which potato seeds and rapeseed had begun to sprout, life seemed to be imitating art and recalling Watney's Lockean insistence that growing crops somewhere equates to official colonization.[23] But Weir does not dwell on the implications of imperial claims to extraterrestrial lands and Watney's reference to Armstrong's Moon landing is immediately followed by his consideration of an email from his parents. When the issue of colonization is next discussed in the text, the reader is more familiar with the *international* Ares 3 mission crew aboard the Hermes spacecraft that is returning to Mars to attempt Watney's rescue, and all characters are acutely aware that their rescue efforts are only possible thanks to the China National Space Administration's sacrifice of its previously secret Taiyang Shen probe to re-provision Hermes. In the spirit of internationalism, *The Martian* backtracks on any suggestion that Watney has officially colonized Mars, and it casts him instead as forced to operate outside any legal framework: "I've been thinking about laws on Mars. . . . There's an international treaty saying no country can lay claim to anything that's not on Earth. And by another treaty, if you're not in any country's territory, maritime law applies. So Mars is 'international waters.' . . . After I board Ares 4, before talking to NASA, I will take control of a craft in international waters without permission. That makes me a pirate! A space pirate!"[24] Pivetti argues that this is disingenuous since pirates historically had a complex relationship with the laws of nation-states and often operated with unofficial state sanction: Watney's self-proclaimed status as a pirate therefore "accomplishes what neither NASA nor the United States can do . . . [pirates] are liminal . . . crossing borders and violating law, but with the contradictory effect of establishing new borders."[25] Critical commentary on *The Martian* (which relates overwhelmingly to its 2015 film adaptation) has been quick to seize upon Watney's assertion that he is the "King of Mars" and his decision to name features of the Martian landscape as further evidence that this is "a celebration of neo-colonial enterprise."[26] It is perhaps an indication of how pervasive the image of Crusoe and Watney as agricultural colonizers have become in the popular cultural imagination and critical literature that more than one legal collective has committed itself to educating the public as to where current international law stands on the equation of cultivation of land with implied ownership of that land. Law students at the University of Toronto challenged the notion of Watney as a space pirate, while law and science professors at the University of Nebraska weighed in on Watney's understanding of agrarian activity as colonization and on the idea of maritime law applying to an otherwise lawless Mars.[27] Contrary to Watney's confident assertions, a rudimentary legal framework already exists governing the colonization of space and any nation's attempted appropriation of another nation's nonterrestrial hardware, the so-called Outer Space Treaty, agreed in United Nations Committee in 1966.[28] Article 3 of the treaty states that "outer space is not subject to national appropriation by claim of sovereignty, by means of use or occupation, or by any other means." While nation-states may, of course, choose to disregard United Nations' resolutions, lawyerly engagement with *The Martian* (clearly as a lighthearted public relations' exercise for the institutions concerned) reminds us that, despite critical readings of Watney as the promoter of a U.S. imperial space agenda, he exists in a post-Crusoe world of scientific cooperation rather than colonial separatism. Watney may combatively assert that planting—and growing—potatoes on Mars is an activity of greater colonial import than Armstrong's symbolic planting of an American flag on the Moon, but in reality neither action has the colonial repercussions of Crusoe solidifying his hold on what becomes his island home.

While Watney shares many traits with Crusoe, and Watney's circumstances take the archetypal struggle to survive in an unfamiliar environment to a new level, Watney's proprietary claims differ from those of Crusoe in an important respect: Watney, unlike Crusoe, evinces a well-developed sense of humor and demonstrates that he does not take himself too seriously. Those who see serious intent in Watney's claims to be both king and pirate are surely mistaking his self-deprecating video logs for Crusoe's unwaveringly humorless narrative: science is the one thing Watney does not joke about but Crusoe evinces no sense of humor at all. In a Q&A about his work, Drew Goddard, screenwriter for *The Martian*, frames its difference from other survival stories in Watney's humor and perpetual optimism, and in doing so, he genuinely seems to believe that *The Martian* is unlike other survival stories:

> CHRISTOPHER MCKITTRICK: What sets *The Martian* apart from similar "survival" stories is Watney's confident attitude. Although there are scenes where he doubts his ability to survive, his "I'm gonna have to science the shit out of this" attitude carries the film. How important was this attitude in making the audience connect with Watney?
>
> DREW GODDARD: It was certainly one of the things that attracted me to the book right way. The optimism in the face of despair felt special, like something I hadn't quite seen before. The despair is there, but we're just not overtly talking about it . . . optimism is what's keeping him alive . . . and he's using humor to save himself. . . . The optimism in the face of despair is such a key part of the soul of the movie, not just for Watney but for everyone. Refusing to give in to despair becomes bigger than Matt Damon making jokes. It becomes the point of why we're here.[29]

For Goddard, "optimism in the face of despair" is not simply the defining characteristic of Weir's protagonist and the reason that we find Watney to be a sympathetic figure, but "the point of why we're here." Tellingly, Goddard uses the word "soul" only in relation to "the soul of the movie," and Weir's novel has Watney reflect only for a moment on eschatological questions, as Watney reduces Martinez's wooden crucifix into the combustible splinters he needs to make fire: "I chipped his sacred religious item into long splinters using a pair of pliers and a screwdriver. I figure if there's a God, He won't mind, considering the situation I'm in."[30] Watney is not an overtly religious man, though he describes fellow astronaut Martinez as "a devout Catholic," and it would be possible to argue that it is both Martinez's faith *and* Watney's optimism that ultimately keep Watney alive.[31]

Returning to Goddard's insistence that Watney uses "humor to save himself," this is hardly true of Crusoe, who cannot be said to form a single humorous thought in his solitude, but Goddard is in error if he believes that Watney has a monopoly on optimism in the face of seemingly insurmountable odds. Even at one of his lowest points, Crusoe insists that "my Reason began now to master my Despondency" (57), and he draws up a list of what he finds to be "evil" about his situation with a "good" rejoinder immediately following each negative statement, for example: "Evil: I am divided from Mankind, a Solitaire; one banish'd from humane Society. . . . Good: But I am not starv'd and perishing on a barren Place, affording no Sustenance" (57). Watney, of course, cannot say as much. After listing six negatives about his situation and imagining ways in which all might have been even worse, Crusoe concludes: "Let this stand as a Direction from the Experience of the most miserable of all Conditions in this World, that we may always find in it something to comfort ourselves from, and to set in the Description of Good and Evil, on the Credit Side of the Accompt" (58).

In Crusoe's insistence that comfort may be found in the most seemingly miserable of conditions, we surely see Goddard's definition of "optimism in the face of despair": a refusal to given in to seemingly impossible odds. It is the character trait that, perhaps more than any other, unites Crusoe's heirs across the Robinsonades and makes Crusoe Watney's literary progenitor.

Yet there is a further trait that both characters share and that, on reflection, is implicit in all Robinsonades, for Crusoe's and Watney's experiences of isolation seem to act on both in the same unexpected way as they evince boredom with their solitary routines. Pat Rogers provocatively suggests that, once Crusoe is assured of the basic needs of food and shelter, he is bored by the unwavering circumstances of his island life (chapter 7). Certainly, Weir does not hesitate to make boredom one of Watney's experiences, and "boring" and its synonyms are particularly noticeable when Watney's efforts to retrieve Pathfinder require him to undertake "a long, boring drive" from the relative safety of the Hab to Pathfinder's ancient Martian delta landing side.[32] Because he must charge the solar panels that power his vehicle during the Martian day, he can drive only at night, and manages to make one of the expedition's two rovers his self-contained life-support system for the sixteen-day round trip. Describing his daily routine away from the Hab, Watney complains of the sheer tedium he experiences after laying out the solar panels to charge: "Then comes the incredibly dull part of my day. I sit around for twelve hours with nothing to do. And I'm getting sick of this rover . . . I have shitty seventies TV to watch, and a bunch of Poirot novels to read. But mostly I spend my time thinking about getting to Ares 4. . . . These thoughts pester me throughout the long, boring days."[33] The idea of Watney reading the Poirot collection of fellow astronaut Beth Johannsen appears to have been thought too dull even to warrant screen time, and in Goddard's screenplay of *The Martian*, Watney's boredom is courtesy of Commander Melissa Lewis's extensive collection of disco music, which provides an ironic accompaniment to Watney's activities. Most notably, having dug up a previously buried radioisotope thermoelectric generator (or "big box of plutonium"), Watney drives it back to the Hab to the accompaniment of the "least disco" song among Lewis's electronic files: Donna Summer's 1979 hit "Hot Stuff." It seems counterintuitive to attribute boredom to a fictional protagonist such as Crusoe or Watney for whom daily survival is hard won, but Defoe and Weir both highlight the fact that routines, once established, can be stultifying. If the essence of competence porn is serial problem solving, then it is an essence distilled from long stretches of inactivity and maintenance of the status quo.

Like Crusoe before him, Watney has to learn to reinvent himself as a type of agrarian man, learning to grow his own food. (Watney's reinvention is, of necessity, more urgent.) Also like Crusoe, Watney must learn to make fire, but as regards this skill, Weir surely enjoys the irony of forcing his protagonist into a high-tech solution to make something known to prehistoric man, as Watney declares of his environment where nothing can burn, "I had to invent fire."[34] In a seeming nod to the archetypal desert island survival story, Watney jokes, "I collected ribbons of bark from local palm trees, then got a couple of sticks and rubbed them together to create enough friction to. . . . No not really."[35] That Watney needs to make fire in order to manufacture water (from the mission's excess hydrazine supply) only adds to the text's seriocomic juxtapositions of providing for basic human needs (air, fire, food, water) with complex technological solutions. And the more problems Watney solves—making fire, firing up an antiquated Mars explorer, giving life to Martian soil, watering his crop—the more he replicates Crusoe's making and accumulation of things: to paraphrase Laura Brown, "things acquire their force, exhibit their vitality, and make the world of the *planet* manifest through this discursive enactment of energy" (chapter 4).

The potency of the survival story at the heart of *Robinson Crusoe* is such that it has never been out of print since its first publication, while a whole genre of Robinsonade is indebted to Defoe's original, to greater or lesser degrees. Among the Robinsonade one must count the 1719 text's translation into over one hundred languages and its many film and television adaptations. Nineteenth- and early twentieth-century incarnations include numerous abridged editions especially designed for children, many of which are heavily illustrated, some of which present Crusoe's island life in humorous verse, including at least one version written in rhyming couplets.[36] One constant that would appear to unite many abridged children's versions of *Robinson Crusoe* from this period of British imperialism is that Crusoe's survival skills on the island are foregrounded as emulatory even as Crusoe's island experience is shown to be the direct result of disregarding his father's counsel. As Jackie Horne says, "Almost from the time of its first printing, writers and critics pointed to the pedagogical merit of Defoe's text: Rousseau's praise of the book in *Émile* (1762), as well as its congruence with Lockean pedagogical theory, suggested its suitability for younger readers."[37] If the term "competence porn" can be applied to Defoe's text, then the competences it showcases were thought to be a valuable lesson for generations of boys destined for careers managing Britain's empire at home and abroad. Like *Robinson Crusoe*, *The Martian* has been adapted for a nonadult audience, and while the ostensible purpose of this recent adaptation is in service of science rather than empire, it is hard to imagine that any empires we could conceive of in Earth's future would not be based on technological and scientific supremacy.

Weir notes that, shortly after *The Martian* appeared in conventional book form, "I got a lot of emails from science teachers who said, 'Man I'd love to use your book as a teaching aid, but there's so much profanity in it that we can't really do that.'"[38] The profanity in question has been estimated at "more than 160 swear words . . . including two memorably deployed F-words in the novel's first three sentences."[39] Cooperative rather than combative in response to the science teachers' problem, Weir approached his publisher, Crown, to inquire about production of a profanity-free version of his text. In a testament to the popularity of Weir's creation, *The Martian: Classroom Edition* appeared in 2016, one year after the release of the movie, which itself came out one year after the appearance of the hardback. By any standards, this is a remarkably condensed time frame for a book to become a movie and to spawn its own author-approved classroom version. (Remarkably, the classroom edition would have appeared even sooner had authorities at Crown not been worried about confusing moviegoers wishing to buy the novel by having two versions of the novel available at the time of the movie's release.) Just as *Robinson Crusoe*'s abridgement as a children's book throughout the nineteenth century may have helped cement its iconic status, so *The Martian*'s adaptation for the American classroom will likely be a boon for more than the nation's science teachers: "For Mr. Weir and his publisher, getting the book into schools opens up a lucrative new market that could turn 'The Martian,' which was already a blockbuster that sold several million copies, into a perennial best seller that guarantees a built-in audience every year."[40] With at least thirty thousand copies of *The Martian: Classroom Edition* in circulation, Weir was asked to address the National Science Teachers Association's annual conference in 2017. Science curricula have been built around study of *The Martian*, which has been described as "a science teacher's dream text."[41] The *Washington Post* went even further in characterizing the importance of *The Martian*, seeing it as "an advertisement for the importance of STEM education."[42] Crusoe's discovery that he possesses the ability to feed, clothe, house, and defend himself has allowed generations of readers to experience the vicarious certainty that they could do the same under like conditions. Watney's ability to keep himself alive and make contact with Earth offers a different moral: the certainty that survival depends upon an understanding of the fundamentals of science, and an ability to harness that understanding. Those who see a sly colonial agenda in Watney's cultivation of potatoes on Mars and in his alternate claims to be both king and pirate have surely overlooked Weir's implicit moral that the future belongs not to those who claim ownership of land, but rather to those whose mastery is of science and technology.

In April 1970, as the fate of the Apollo 13 astronauts dominated the media, CBS news anchor Walter Cronkite declared "perhaps never in human history has the entire world been so united by such a global drama." Cronkite's original commentary is used in Howard's *Apollo 13*, and the end game of this "global drama" is mirrored in the conclusion to *The Martian*, where worldwide concern for the fictional Mark Watney's fate appears entirely credible thanks to the knowledge that such concern was formerly evinced for the fates of Apollo 13 astronauts Fred Haise, Jim Lovell, and Jack Swigert. Dramas that truly command the global stage are, of course, extremely rare, and while this has always been true, global dramas are surely set to become rarer still at a time when increasing numbers of people report getting the news via their social media newsfeed, and few stories break through the bubbles of political partisanship. It is all the more remarkable, then, that features of a fiction written in 1719 (specifically Crusoe's shipwreck, life on a desert island, and discovery of a single footprint on the shore) should have become lodged in the global imagination as a shorthand for man's ability to survive—and thrive—against the odds. And because Crusoe himself is a very ordinary man, thrust into an extraordinary situation, and who must learn how to provide himself with the most basic necessities, his story has become the urtext to which all similar fictions are inevitably compared. There is no reason to disbelieve Andy Weir when he insists that *Robinson Crusoe* was not his immediate inspiration for *The Martian*. The figure of Crusoe is so pervasive a feature of global culture that it is impossible not to see him as the original of any survival story or "competence porn" narrative, but that does not mean that he is always uppermost in the mind of such fiction's writers: rather, that Crusoe's influence is as an idea, allowing the vicarious thrill of believing that if Crusoe could survive, then anyone might in theory survive under similar circumstances. Crusoe's story has become, in Cronkite's words, "a global drama." With a dedicated classroom edition and a fictional premise that gains new interest every time a manned mission to Mars is proposed, *The Martian* does not seem likely to disappear from bookshelves or screens anytime soon. Indeed, when American public broadcaster PBS worked with professional pollsters in 2018 to establish America's hundred favorite novels, *The Martian*, then not even one decade old, polled at sixty-first (immediately behind Toni Morrison's *Beloved*).[43] *Robinson Crusoe* does not appear among the nation's favorite hundred reads, though Crusoe, like Mark Watney, seems assured of his place in the global imagination.

NOTES

1. Andy Weir, *The Martian* (New York: Broadway Books, 2014).
2. *The Martian*, dir. Ridley Scott (Twentieth-Century Fox, 2015).
3. Andy Weir, *The Martian: Classroom Edition* (New York: Broadway Books, 2016).
4. *Robinson Crusoe on Mars*, dir. Byron Haskin (Paramount Pictures, 1964).
5. *Apollo 13*, dir. Ron Howard (Universal Pictures, 1995). Fans of *Apollo 13* will be aware of many echoes of the movie in *The Martian*, including parallels between the rupture of the Apollo service module's oxygen tank number 2 and the breach of panel AL102 of the Hab on Sol 119; the construction of an ad hoc filtration system by Fred Haise, Jim Lovell, and Jack Swigert to deal with rising carbon dioxide levels and Watney's construction of a hydrazine burner to make water. Weir also clearly intends to recall *Apollo 13* when the crew of Hermes execute a change of course independent of Mission Control at the Johnson Space Center and begin the long journey back to Mars in hopes of rescuing Watney, sending NASA the message, "Houston, be advised: Rich Purnell is a steely-eyed missile man." In *Apollo 13*, Lovell's report that dangerous carbon dioxide levels are falling is followed by Howard cutting to the floor of Mission Control where the leader of the team that built the impromptu filter receives a handshake and the compliment that "You, Sir, are a steely-eyed missile man." Within NASA, the phrase is held to originate in the Apollo 12 mission and designates a technician or group who improvise an ad hoc solution to an otherwise intractable, potentially fatal problem. Of course, both Crusoe and Watney could also be said to improvise solutions to otherwise fatal problems.
6. http://andyweirauthor.com/books/the-martian-tr/the-martian-hc.
7. *Star Trek*, producer Gene Roddenberry (Desilu Productions, 1966–1968; Paramount Television, 1969–1970).
8. Neil deGrasse Tyson, "Geek in Space," *National Geographic*, December 2016, 26–29, 27.
9. Tyson, "Geek in Space," 27.
10. Lewis Dartnell, "Are You Hooked on Competence Porn?," *Telegraph*, April 9, 2014, https://www.telegraph.co.uk/men/thinking-man/10744879/Are-you-hooked-on-competence-porn.html.
11. Lewis, "Are You Hooked on Competence Porn?"
12. Weir, *The Martian*, 115–116.
13. Weir, *The Martian*, 10.
14. Weir, *The Martian*, 14.
15. Weir, *The Martian*, 10, 26.
16. Weir, *The Martian*, 45–46.
17. Weir, *The Martian*, 21.
18. As an instance of life imitating art, scientists have attempted growing a hundred different potato varieties in the Atacama Desert, Peru, to see if they can indeed be grown on Mars: https://www.techtimes.com/articles/181686/20161010/artificial-martian-garden-to-determine-which-vegetables-grow-best-in-mars.htm.

19. Weir, *The Martian*, 21.
20. Weir, *The Martian*, 21.
21. For discussion of Defoe's engagement with Locke, see, for example, Maximillian E. Novak, *Defoe and the Nature of Man* (London: Oxford University Press, 1963), 22–64 and Wolfram Schmidgen, *Eighteenth-Century Fiction and the Law of Property* (Cambridge: Cambridge University Press, 2002), 41–49.
22. Weir, *The Martian*, 147.
23. For the implications of China's moon landings, please see https://www.nytimes.com/2019/01/02/world/asia/china-change-4-moon.html and https://www.latimes.com/world/la-fg-china-moonlanding-20190102-story.html.
24. Weir, *The Martian*, 259–260.
25. Kyle Pivetti, "The King of Mars: *The Martian*'s Scientific Empire and *Robinson Crusoe*," in *The Cinematic Eighteenth Century: History, Culture, and Adaptation*, ed. Srividhya Swaminathan and Steven W. Thomas (New York: Routledge, 2018), 118–138.
26. Even before publication of *The Martian*, America's Pathfinder mission to Mars was criticized by some as being part of a colonial agenda. See, for example, Jason Dittmer, "Colonialism and Place Creation in Mars Pathfinder Media Coverage," *Geographical Review* 97, no. 1 (2007): 112–130.
27. For Toronto law students' views on Watney's claims to be a space pirate, please see http://ultravires.ca/2015/10/matt-damon-space-pirate/; and for an explanation of why Watney's actions cannot be considered as conveying colonial intent, please see University of Nebraska faculty opinion: https://news.unl.edu/newsrooms/unltoday/article/how-realistic-is-the-martian-unl-experts-weigh-in/.
28. The Treaty on Principles Governing the Activities of States in the Exploration and Use of Outer Space, including the Moon and Other Celestial Bodies, more conveniently known as the Outer Space Treaty, was agreed to by the United Nations General Assembly in 1966 (resolution 2222 [XXI]): http://www.unoosa.org/oosa/en/ourwork/spacelaw/treaties/introouterspacetreaty.html.
29. https://creativescreenwriting.com/life-goes-on-drew-goddard-on-the-martian/.
30. Weir, *The Martian*, 33.
31. Weir, *The Martian*, 33.
32. Weir, *The Martian*, 97.
33. Weir, *The Martian*, 96.
34. Weir, *The Martian*, 32.
35. Weir, *The Martian*, 33.
36. The anonymous rendition of Crusoe's story into rhyming couplets is *The Life of Robinson Crusoe* (Edinburgh: Thomas Nelson, before 1835).
37. Jackie C. Horne, "Review of *Children's Literature, Popular Culture, and 'Robinson Crusoe,'* by Andrew O'Malley," *Digital Defoe: Studies in Defoe & His Contemporaries* 5, no. 1 (Fall 2013): 162.
38. Alexander Alter, "Science, Minus the Swearing," *New York Times*, February 25, 2017, B1–B2, B1.
39. Alter, "Science," B1.
40. Alter, "Science," B2.
41. Alter, "Science," B2.
42. Brian Fung, "'The Martian,' NASA and the Rise of a Science-Entertainment Complex," *Washington Post*, October 6, 2015, https://www.washingtonpost.com/news/the-switch/wp/2015/10/06/the-martian-nasa-and-the-rise-of-a-science-entertainment-complex/?noredirect=on&utm_term=.285b4e031556.
43. https://www.pbs.org/the-great-american-read/books/#/.

2
ROBINSON'S TRANSGENDER VOYAGE
or, Burlesquing Crusoe

GEOFFREY SILL

IN THE THREE HUNDRED YEARS since his story was first published, Robinson Crusoe and his companion Friday have had stranger and even more surprising afterlives than their creator could have imagined for them. Among these afterlives were pantomimes, burlesques, and melodramas that were frequently performed in British and American theaters between 1781 and the final years of the nineteenth century. These performances were based on the theme of a mariner who was cast away on a deserted island for many years, until with the help of a harlequin-like sidekick he was able to defeat the evil spirits who had banished him and to return to his love interest, Polly. The pantomimes and burlesques bore little resemblance to Daniel Defoe's original novel, but they brought action, music, drama, and spectacle to a story that had been confined between the covers of a book. They connected *Robinson Crusoe* with a performative tradition much older than the book itself, one in which the subversion of dramatic conventions and the parody of revered literary characters were standard practices. Crusoe's afterlife in pantomime and burlesque was particularly surprising in that Crusoe was often portrayed by female actors who dressed and acted not as men, but as themselves—women who transgressed gender boundaries to present a Crusoe never seen before. For a brief moment, it was possible for theater critics to describe Robinson Crusoe as "pretty," a term that challenged not only the gender of this cultural hero, but the notion of gender itself.

From the publication of Defoe's *Robinson Crusoe* in 1719 to Robert Zemeckis's film *Castaway* in 2000, tales of the survivors of shipwrecks who lived out their days on islands were collectively known as "Robinsonades," a genre traditionally considered by critics to be a "masculinist imaginative form."[1] In addition to these male versions of Crusoe, however, there was an alternative genre, the "female Crusoes." According to recent research, over one hundred Robinsonades that included female Crusoes were written between 1720 and 1900.[2] One of the most popular female Robinsonades, *Emma, ou le Robinson des demoiselles* (1834), a book for children by Catherine Woillez (1781–1859), was published in nine French editions and translated into German, Dutch, and Italian.

In the title page illustration for *Emma* seen in figure 2.1, the heroine wears a fashionable gown, if a bit *sauvage* by Parisian standards; she has a sun hat, parasol, implements at her waist, and a very large dog. This female Crusoe displays pictorial elements that mimic the image of the male Crusoe, but she is clearly Emma, not Robinson. She is not cross-dressed as a man; she does not carry a musket, pistol, sword, hatchet, or any other masculine implement; and in her story she does not challenge any male prerogatives. She is defined not by her similarity to or difference from the male Crusoe, but by her independence. The early female Crusoe, in the words of critic Jeannine Blackwell, "marks the development of self-reliance and self-knowledge for the heroine" of modern fiction.[3] More recently, C. M. Owen goes a step further in her study of *The Female Crusoe* by arguing that Defoe's original Robinson is himself a "problematic feminized figure," a hybrid whose pursuit of trade, luxury, and desire led to his shipwreck and the subsequent "re-inscription of the feminine" as an essential element of his individualism.[4] Having, by the late 1830s, demonstrated her viability as a female heroine, and having inscribed her domesticity into Robinson's masculine individualism, the female Crusoe in print had prepared audiences for the female Robinsonade in theater.

In these burlesque performances, Crusoe was transformed into a sexually ambivalent figure whose role was nominally male, but whose gender was female. The part of Crusoe was played by the "principal boy," a female actor who performed the male lead role. Unlike the "cross-dressing" or "breeches" part that was common in Restoration and Eighteenth-century drama, the principal boy in burlesque retained and emphasized her sexuality through her singing, dancing, and apparel, thus inverting and parodying the male subject of the play.[5] In a breeches play, a female character disguises herself as a man in order to deceive other persons in the drama about her identity; at the end of the play, there is a general unmasking through which the original gender identities of any cross-dressed actors are restored. In burlesque, however, there is no unmasking to be done, because there has been no deception: the "she" who is the principal boy and the "he" who is the subject of the drama are, from beginning to end, the same person. The Robinson Crusoe of burlesque is neither a male Robinson in drag, nor a female Crusoe in breeches, but a person who has crossed and transformed the boundaries of gender. The nineteenth century lacked a term of critical discourse to describe this sexual transformation, but we may now say, forgiving the anachronism, that the Robinson Crusoe of burlesque has been transgendered.

EMMA

OU

Le Robinson des Demoiselles

par Mme Woillez

2me EDITION.

Telle était Emma à quinze ans.

PARIS

Langlumé et Peltier Libraires

Rue du Foin St Jacques No 11.

Figure 2.1. *Emma, ou le Robinson des Demoiselles*. Paris, 1834.

Of the many "principal boys" who performed Robinson Crusoe in burlesque, the epitome was Eliza Hodges Thompson (1838–1908), whose stage name was Lydia Thompson. As the leader of her own burlesque company, known in the American press as the "British Blondes," Thompson played Crusoe in H. B. Farnie's *The Very Latest Edition of Robinson Crusoe*, which opened in London in November 1876 and ran for six months, followed by an American tour in 1877 that included New York, Boston, Philadelphia, Washington, and Baltimore.[6] According to her biographer, Kurt Gänzl, when Thompson made her first entrance as Robinson Crusoe, "firelock over her shoulder and smoking a cigar, the house went wild" (Gänzl, 180). Her spectacular costume made several parodic allusions to the frontispiece of Defoe's 1719 novel, such as Robinson's goatskin tunic, his peaked goatskin cap, his gun (though Robinson had two), and his umbrella, while feminizing the image with white kid gloves, tights, high-laced boots, and a silver powder flask at her waist (figure 2.2).

The costume designed by Thompson was used by a succession of principal boys in British pantomimes and burlesques from the 1870s to the first decades of the twentieth century. One of the first of her imitators was a former member of the "British Blondes," Alice Atherton (1854–1899), who stepped into the role of Crusoe (in a new company organized by Samuel Colville) when Thompson returned to England in 1877 (figure 2.3).[7] Atherton, born in Cincinnati, was noted for her "remarkable versatility" and for her "accustomed sprightliness and vivacity" as a comedienne.[8] Her "laughing song" became her signature piece. She married Willie Edouin, the lead male comic of the Thompson troupe, in 1873, and (like Lydia Thompson's Zeffie) brought her daughter May up to be an actress.[9]

Ada Blanche (1862–1953) was highly regarded in Britain for her performances in pantomime, burlesque, operetta, and musical comedy when she was chosen by Sir Augustus Harris to play Robinson Crusoe in the Christmas pantomime at Drury Lane in 1893, 1894, and 1895 (figure 2.4). The pantomime included a "Fish Ballet," which took place under the sea, and "a procession of savages, elephants, giraffes, etc.," followed by "a procession of Kings and Queens of England from William the First down to the present days of grace of Her Gracious Majesty, Queen Victoria. The procession is alone worth a visit."[10] The critic for *The Times* wrote of her performance, "Miss Ada Blanche as Robinson Crusoe would probably have astonished Daniel Defoe; but her liveliness and amusing impertinence atoned for lack of fidelity to the original character."[11]

Another well-known British singer and dancer, Alice Brookes, played Crusoe in the Christmas pantomime by Oscar Barrett at the Lyceum in 1896. Although some reviewers thought her slight stature was more suited to the role of principal girl than principal boy, her dancing overcame any reservations about her imper-

Figure 2.2. Lydia Thompson as Robinson Crusoe, photographed by Jose Maria Mora, 1876.

Figure 2.3. Alice Atherton as Robinson Crusoe, 1878.

Figure 2.4. Ada Blanche as Robinson Crusoe, photographed by Albert Ellis, 1894.

sonation of Robinson: "By her pleasing singing and dainty dancing, Miss Alice Brookes, as Robinson, won the hearts of all."[12] Brookes's tailored angora dress, her elbow-length gloves, and the parrot in her cap brought the transgendered Crusoe to a new level of fashionable elegance (figure 2.5).

Georgina Delmar trained for the opera in Paris (ca. 1896–1899) and sang at Covent Garden Opera for three years (figure 2.6). At Covent Garden, she was listed among the contraltos and mezzo-sopranos. She left grand opera (ca. 1904) for a career in musical dramas and pantomimes, "in which capacity," according to the *Tatler and the Bystander*, "she has gained golden opinions all over England," apparently a reference to her financial success.[13] She appeared in the role of Robinson Crusoe at the Theatre Royal, Manchester, on December 30, 1905.

The love of the principal boy for the principal girl establishes the sexual orthodoxy of the pantomime as a form of family entertainment, while the feminine appearance of Crusoe reverses his claim to masculinity and projects the play beyond pantomime into burlesque. Blanche Marion played Polly Hopkins, Robinson's love interest, in the performance of *Robinson Crusoe* at the Theatre Royal in Bristol on Christmas Eve, 1909, while Kitty Upton played the part of Robinson (figures 2.7 and 2.8).[14]

H. B. Farnie's book for *The Very Latest Edition of Robinson Crusoe* was not held in high regard by the "Captious Critic" for the *Illustrated Sporting and Dramatic News*, who recalled the first performances at the Folly Theatre as "dreary and tame and tedious."[15] The script was "hopelessly incoherent as to plot," but since the plot in a burlesque "is more an encumbrance than otherwise," the show remained open on the strength of "a sufficiently lively alternation of ludicrous 'business,' comic songs, pretty choruses, and fascinating dances." After three months of performances, the leading actors—Lydia Thompson, Willie Edouin, and Lionel Brough—had reworked it until "it is beyond doubt that *Robinson Crusoe* has ceased to be depressingly stupid, and has become quite exhilarating and amusing." Lydia Thompson, the reviewer concedes, "never fails of being bright, lively, refined, and charming in any burlesque part she undertakes to play." The story shared nothing with Defoe's novel except the names of Crusoe, Friday, and Will Atkins, and it created new ones—Polly Hopkins, Crusoe's love interest, and Jim Cocks, Crusoe's friend, an impecunious traveling actor "pursued by duns and process servers." Jilted by their lovers, Crusoe and Cocks set out from Hull in quest of adventure, pursued by the "commercial pirate," Will Atkins. After a shipwreck, they encounter "Indians," among them Friday, who converts his fellow natives to temperance through his drunkenness. The fourth scene (of five) includes a panoramic set design of a labyrinthine jungle in which Crusoe discovers a footprint. Jim Cocks, who carries a bag throughout the play in which he collects anything

Figure 2.5. Alice Brookes as Robinson Crusoe, from *The Sketch*, February 2, 1896.

Figure 2.6. Georgina Delmar as Robinson Crusoe, 1905.

Figure 2.7. Blanche Marion as Polly Hopkins, 1909.

Figure 2.8. Blanche Marion and Kitty Upton as Polly and Robinson, 1909.

Figure 2.9. "Poot et in tha bawg!" *Robinson Crusoe* at the Folly Theatre, London (1876).

of value, tells Crusoe (in his Scottish accent) to "Poot et in tha bawg!," a line repeated so often that it was shouted out by the audience (figure 2.9).[16] In scene 5, Crusoe, Friday, and the Indians capture Will Atkins, who is tried and convicted by the judge, Jim Cocks; in the finale, Crusoe and Cocks are reunited with their lovers, Polly and Angelica. The story may have had little to do with Defoe's novel, but according to the reviewer, it was "brimful of fun."

Despite the enthusiastic popular reception of the British Blondes in America, or perhaps because of it, some critics raised objections to burlesque. The objections were not primarily to the display of female sexuality on stage, and indeed the dancers and singers remained modestly clothed throughout the performances. The objections were to the cultural effects of burlesque when it began to play in theaters reserved for "legitimate" drama, such as Wallack's Theatre and Niblio's Garden in New York. Critics lamented the degradation of popular "taste," the loss of employment for "serious" actors, and the supposed adverse effect on public morals. The most stinging criticism, however, concerned the transgression of conventional sexual boundaries. According to New York theater critic and Shakespeare scholar Richard Grant White, the "peculiar trait" of burlesque was its intent to make a "monstrosity" of the "natural and conventional" and to "cast down all the gods from their pedestals."[17] It is unclear what White meant by "monstrosity," but the term was sometimes used in the nineteenth century to refer to "an ambiguous condition of the body in which the secondary sexual characters approach those of the other sex."[18] White's critique of burlesque as a celebration of "monstrosity" followed closely upon an essay by William Dean Howells in the May 1869 issue of the *Atlantic Monthly*, in which Howells pointed out the disturbingly ambiguous treatment of gender in British burlesque. "It was . . . an indispensable condition of the burlesque's success," writes Howells, "that the characters should be reversed in their representation,—that the men's *rôles* should be played by women, and that at least one female part should be done by a man. It must be owned that the fun all came from this character, the ladies being too much occupied with the more serious business of bewitching us with their pretty figures to be very amusing" (640). In a passage that reveals Howell's underlying misogyny, he praises the male transgender actor, "with his blond wig, his *panier*, his dainty feminine simpering and languishing, his falsetto tones, and his general air of extreme fashion," which Howells found "exceedingly droll," while the women playing men were "lewd traversties."[19] Speaking of the "principal boys," Howells noted that "though they were not like men, [they] were in most things as unlike women, and seemed creatures of a kind of alien sex, parodying both. It was certainly a shocking thing to look at them with their horrible prettiness, their archness in which was no charm, their grace which put to shame."[20] Howell's oxymoron, "horrible prettiness," describes the contradictory impulses of aversion and attraction commonly felt by members of a dominant social order who encounter the "low other" of popular culture, which, in the words of Robert C. Allen, threatens to "call into question the right of higher discourses to determine the vertical order of culture to begin with" (Allen, 26). While burlesque challenged the culture of the "dominant social order" on many levels—aesthetic, political, economic—its greatest offense was the transgendering of male roles by casting them with female actors who did not conceal their sexuality by cross-dressing, but rather embraced the "monstrosity" that was the "peculiar trait of burlesque."

One such critic, a contemporary of White and Howells, was Olive Logan, a former actress become lecturer and moralist who severely attacked Lydia Thompson in print when the "British Blondes" first brought burlesque to America (figure 2.10). In her book *Before the Footlights and Behind the Scenes*, Logan complained that in 1868 "[an] army of burlesque women took ship for America, and presently the New York stage presented one disgraceful spectacle of padded legs jigging and wriggling in the insensate follies and indecencies of the hour. . . . Rivalry grew so sharp that it seemed to be a scrub race with these women as to who should sing the vilest songs, dress with the greatest immodesty, dance the most indecent dances,

Figure 2.10. Olive Logan, 1870. Public domain image.

and indulge in the supremest vulgarity and license of gesture."[21] Because these "burlesque women" degraded the public taste for theater, it was difficult for honest women with "stage training and histrionic talent" to get parts; all that mattered to theater managers was "whether [actresses] were pretty and were willing to exhibit their persons, and do as the burlesque women did" (587). In making these attacks on women who acted in burlesques, it was necessary for Olive Logan to overlook her family connections to the "leg business" that she decried.[22]

In view of Olive Logan's vociferous attacks on burlesque in general, and on Lydia Thompson in particular, it comes as a surprise to read her description of Thompson's appearance in the role of Robinson Crusoe in 1876 at the Folly Theatre in London, before the British Blondes' second American tour. Lydia Thompson, Logan wrote, was "positively bewitching": "Her wonderful white dress was composed of layer upon layer of fringe of the angora goat, sewn upon a body and short skirt of white silk. A high-peaked cap of the same material enlivened by a stiff feather of the brightest scarlet of the flamingo's wing, white satin boots and long gloves, belt and chatelaine of burnished silver, white Chinese parasol, a tame parrot perched on the forefinger of her left hand. Thus attired she made quite a striking appearance of prettiness."[23] Despite her earlier condemnation of the British Blondes, Logan clearly approves of Thompson's angora goat-skin dress, the flamingo's wing in her cap, and her tame parrot (figure 2.11). Whatever horror she had felt before at the "prettiness" of burlesque, she is prepared to accept Thompson as Robinson Crusoe.[24] We might well ask what it was that persuaded Olive Logan, who had spoken in the 1860s on behalf of the conservative Cult of True Womanhood, to approve in the 1870s of a monstrous Crusoe in skirts. One likely reason is the theatrical pedigree that stood behind the stage version of *Robinson Crusoe.* By the mid-1870s, Robinson Crusoe had become the central figure of pantomimes, melodramas, and harlequinades by such authors or "arrangers" as Isaac Pocock, William Ware, W. S. Gilbert, Henry James Byron, H. B. Farnie, E. L. Blanchard, and Augustus Harris.[25] Virtually all of these entertainments owed their generation to Richard Brinsley Sheridan's 1781 pantomime *Robinson Crusoe; or, Harlequin Friday.* Sheridan's pantomime, and the burlesques (and book illustrations) that derived from it, were instrumental in creating a popular audience for Defoe's most famous novel, an audience that not even Olive Logan could ignore.

Robinson Crusoe made his debut as a dramatic character in *Robinson Crusoe; or, Harlequin Friday* by R. B. Sheridan on January 27, 1781, at the Theatre Royal in Drury Lane. The three-act pantomime, reduced to two acts on the third and all subsequent nights, followed the main piece of the evening, *The Winter's Tale.*[26] No scenario for the play has survived, but a summary of the sixty-one scenes of the pantomime was reconstructed by John McVeagh, based on several con-

Figure 2.11. Lydia Thompson in the *Illustrated Sporting and Dramatic News*, May 6, 1899.

temporary reviews and the musical score composed by Thomas Linley.[27] The score consists of an overture, several songs, and some fifty-nine comic tunes. Each tune, or *melos*, signified a dramatic action, a sudden passion, or a change of scene. Each scene, in turn, was played before a design painted by Philip James de Loutherbourg, formerly the set designer for David Garrick.

As the first act of the pantomime begins, Crusoe is discovered in his cave, enclosed by a fence, from which he descends. After surveying the weather, Crusoe notches his post for the new day, begins working on his boat, and greets his parrot, who flies to perch on his shoulder. In a rapid series of scene changes, he is surprised by a footprint, discovers a canoe of invading cannibals, rescues Friday, arms him, defeats the invaders, and feeds his goats. As the first act concludes, Crusoe and Friday rescue the Portuguese merchant Pantaloon and his servant Pero, who had been taken captive by the cannibals, and the little army of four men attack a crew of mutineers who have come ashore. In victory, they turn the ship over to its captain, receive the surrender of the mutineers, and celebrate with a "Song of Robinson Crusoe," which was duly published in several newspapers.[28]

In the second act of the pantomime, Crusoe, the captain, and his loyal crew sail the ship to Spain, where Pantaloon has a house in Cadiz. His daughter Columbine asks Crusoe to give her Friday as her servant. Crusoe takes an affectionate leave of Friday and sails out of the pantomime. Columbine and Friday, as one reviewer put it, "grow enamored of each other in the usual style" (McVeagh, 143). Banned from the house by Pantaloon, Friday meets a magician who converts him into Harlequin. As Harlequin, Friday acquires new multicolored clothing and a magic bat, which allows him to regain access to Pantaloon's house. Harlequin and Columbine escape to a monastery, where they join the friars in an interlude of drunken comedy that includes the song "This Bottle's the Sun of our Table," borrowed from Sheridan's comic opera *The Duenna*. After a chase scene, Harlequin is captured and sentenced to death by the Inquisition. As he is tied to the stake and the fire is lit, the magician reappears and, speaking the only lines in the play, transforms the prison into a "most magnificent Temple, dedicated to Venus," in which Pantaloon and his wife consent to the marriage of Columbine to Harlequin, and the pantomime closes with a general dance.[29]

Robinson Crusoe; or, Harlequin Friday ran for twenty-three months at Drury Lane, from January 27, 1781, to December 16, 1782.[30] Without the profits from the pantomime, the Sheridans would probably have had to close or sell the theater, which had lost seven thousand pounds in the two preceding seasons.[31] In the next three decades, *Robinson Crusoe* was revived eight times at Drury Lane, in whole or in part, for runs ranging from one to twenty-three performances.[32] The popularity of the pantomime is suggested in figure 2.12, an advertisement for the

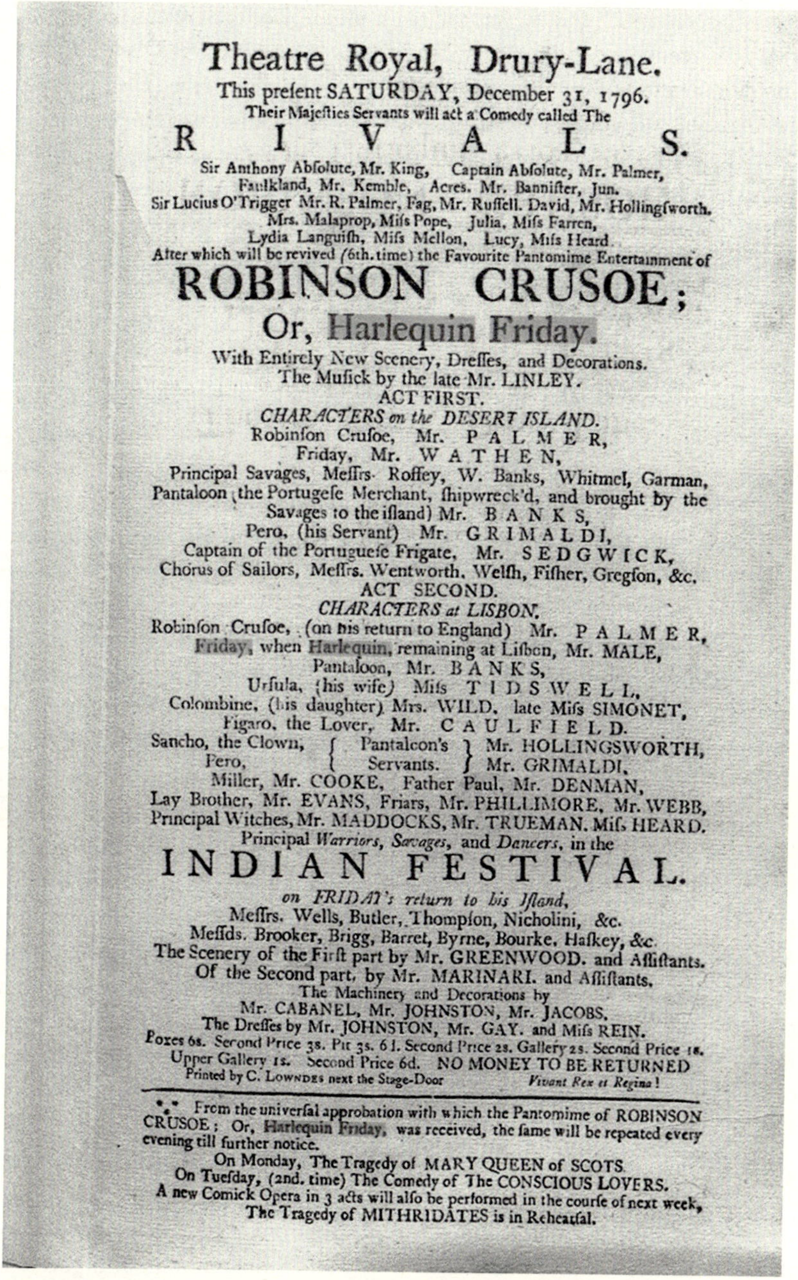
Theatre Royal, Drury-Lane.
This preſent SATURDAY, December 31, 1796.
Their Majeſties Servants will act a Comedy called The
R I V A L S.
Sir Anthony Abſolute, Mr. King, Captain Abſolute, Mr. Palmer,
Faulkland, Mr. Kemble, Acres. Mr. Banniſter, Jun.
Sir Lucius O'Trigger Mr. R. Palmer, Fag, Mr. Ruſſell. David, Mr. Hollingſworth.
Mrs. Malaprop, Miſs Pope, Julia, Miſs Farren,
Lydia Languiſh, Miſs Mellon, Lucy, Miſs Heard
After which will be revived (6th. time) the Favourite Pantomime Entertainment of
ROBINSON CRUSOE;
Or, Harlequin Friday.
With Entirely New Scenery, Dreſſes, and Decorations.
The Muſick by the late Mr. LINLEY.
ACT FIRST.
CHARACTERS on the DESERT ISLAND.
Robinſon Cruſoe, Mr. P A L M E R,
Friday, Mr. W A T H E N,
Principal Savages, Meſſrs. Roffey, W. Banks, Whitmel, Garman,
Pantaloon (the Portugeſe Merchant, ſhipwreck'd, and brought by the Savages to the iſland) Mr. B A N K S,
Pero, (his Servant) Mr. G R I M A L D I,
Captain of the Portugueſe Frigate, Mr. S E D G W I C K,
Chorus of Sailors, Meſſrs. Wentworth. Welſh, Fiſher, Gregſon, &c.
ACT SECOND.
CHARACTERS at LISBON.
Robinſon Cruſoe, (on his return to England) Mr. P A L M E R,
Friday, when Harlequin, remaining at Liſbon, Mr. MALE,
Pantaloon, Mr. B A N K S,
Urſula, (his wife) Miſs T I D S W E L L,
Colombine, (his daughter) Mrs. WILD. late Miſs SIMONET,
Figaro, the Lover, Mr. C A U L F I E L D.
Sancho, the Clown, Pero, { Pantaloon's Servants. } Mr. HOLLINGSWORTH, Mr. GRIMALDI,
Miller, Mr. COOKE, Father Paul, Mr. DENMAN,
Lay Brother, Mr. EVANS, Friars, Mr. PHILLIMORE, Mr. WEBB,
Principal Witches, Mr. MADDOCKS, Mr. TRUEMAN. Miſs HEARD.
Principal *Warriors*, *Savages*, and *Dancers*, in the
INDIAN FESTIVAL.
on FRIDAY's return to his Iſland,
Meſſrs. Wells, Butler, Thompſon, Nicholini, &c.
Meſds. Brooker, Brigg, Barret, Byrne, Bourke, Haſkey, &c.
The Scenery of the Firſt part by Mr. GREENWOOD. and Aſſiſtants.
Of the Second part, by Mr. MARINARI. and Aſſiſtants.
The Machinery and Decorations by
Mr. CABANEL, Mr. JOHNSTON, Mr. JACOBS.
The Dreſſes by Mr. JOHNSTON, Mr. GAY. and Miſs REIN.
Boxes 6s. Second Price 3s. Pit 3s. 6d. Second Price 2s. Gallery 2s. Second Price 1s.
Upper Gallery 1s. Second Price 6d. NO MONEY TO BE RETURNED
Printed by C. LOWNDES next the Stage-Door *Vivant Rex et Regina!*

⁂ From the univerſal approbation with which the Pantomime of ROBINSON CRUSOE; Or, Harlequin Friday, was received, the ſame will be repeated every evening till further notice.
On Monday, The Tragedy of MARY QUEEN of SCOTS.
On Tueſday, (2nd. time) The Comedy of The CONSCIOUS LOVERS.
A new Comick Opera in 3 acts will alſo be performed in the courſe of next week,
The Tragedy of MITHRIDATES is in Rehearſal.

Figure 2.12. Advertisement for *Robinson Crusoe; or, Harlequin Friday* at the Theatre Royal in Drury Lane, December 31, 1796.

entertainment in 1796 in which the main piece, also by Sheridan, occupies less than 20 percent of the print area, while *Robinson Crusoe* receives a detailed description of its two acts, its personnel, and its transformation scene. The managers of the Theatre Royal at Covent Garden, noticing the popularity of the pantomime at Drury Lane, developed an entirely new production, *Robinson Crusoe; or, The Bold Buccaneers*, which they advertised as "a new Grand Romantick Melo-drama." The Covent Garden melodrama, written by Isaac Pocock, opened on April 7, 1817, and ran for nineteen performances. For the next twenty years, these two versions of *Robinson Crusoe—Harlequin Friday* and *The Bold Buccaneers*—were frequently revived in London, in provincial English towns, and in New York, Philadelphia, Boston, and Washington (figure 2.13).[33]

The success of *Robinson Crusoe* as pantomime, harlequinade, and melodrama prepared the way for its transformation into burlesque, particularly because that transformation was mediated by the book illustrations of such artists as Thomas Stothard, George Cruikshank, and Ernest Griset, each of whom had an interest in theater. With the exception of the 1719 frontispiece, illustrations of Crusoe in British books in the eighteenth century depicted, as David Blewett put it, "clusters of near stick-figures engag[ing] in activities not always immediately discernible."[34] The first British artist who opened a window into Crusoe's emotional life was Thomas Stothard. In 1781, the same year as Sheridan's pantomime, Stothard created a series of seven illustrations for an edition of *Robinson Crusoe* that composed volume 6 of James Harrison's *The Novelist's Magazine*.[35] These early illustrations were "essentially random, providing rhetorical emphasis for some of the more poignant or pathetic scenes in Crusoe's story" (Blewett, 48). During the 1780s, Stothard observed the narrative method of Sheridan's pantomime, which was frequently performed in that decade, and the scenic designs painted by Philip James de Loutherbourg. In 1781, de Loutherbourg introduced his designs for the *Robinson Crusoe* pantomime to the Royal Academy, to which he was duly elected as a member. Stothard was at that time enrolled in the academy, so it is likely that they knew of each other's work.[36] In 1790, Stothard contributed fourteen illustrations and two frontispieces to John Stockdale's sumptuous edition of *Robinson Crusoe*, which helped to establish Defoe as a major novelist (Lovett #89). Unlike his 1781 illustrations, the designs for this new edition provide a "visual summary of the main lines of the story" and are thus "an instance of eighteenth-century narrative painting" (Blewett, 49). The influence of de Loutherbourg on Stothard may be inferred from plate 8, "Robinson Crusoe discovers the Print of a Man's Foot," in Stockdale's 1790 edition of *Robinson Crusoe*. In this illustration (figure 2.14), we see what the audience of Sheridan's pantomime might have witnessed in scene 7 of Sheridan's pantomime, "Robinson Crusoe sees the mark of a Foot" (McVeagh,

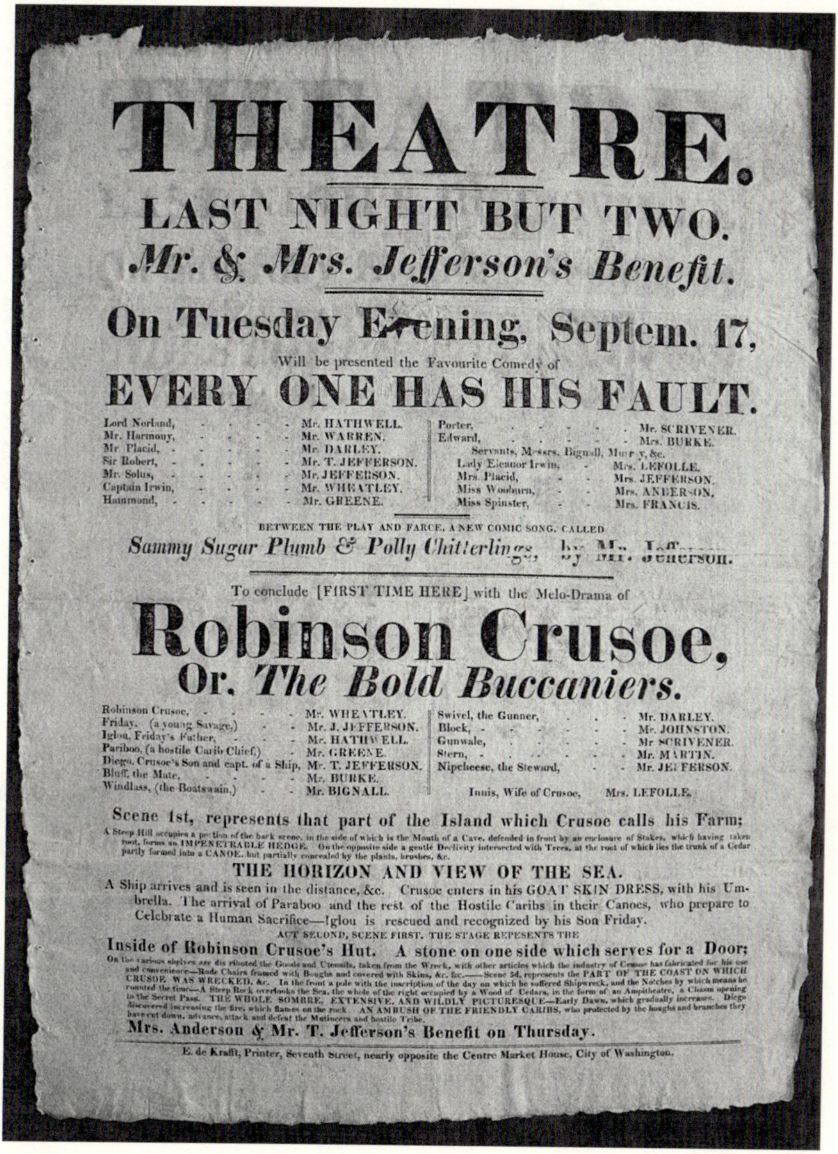
THEATRE.

LAST NIGHT BUT TWO.

Mr. & Mrs. Jefferson's Benefit.

On Tuesday Evening, Septem. 17,

Will be presented the Favourite Comedy of

EVERY ONE HAS HIS FAULT.

Lord Norland,	Mr. HATHWELL.
Mr. Harmony,	Mr. WARREN.
Mr. Placid,	Mr. DARLEY.
Sir Robert,	Mr. T. JEFFERSON.
Mr. Solus,	Mr. JEFFERSON.
Captain Irwin,	Mr. WHEATLEY.
Hammond,	Mr. GREENE.
Porter,	Mr. SCRIVENER.
Edward,	Mrs. BURKE.
Servants, Messrs. Bignall, Murry, &c.	
Lady Eleanor Irwin,	Mrs. LEFOLLE.
Mrs. Placid,	Mrs. JEFFERSON.
Miss Wooburn,	Mrs. ANDERSON.
Miss Spinster,	Mrs. FRANCIS.

BETWEEN THE PLAY AND FARCE, A NEW COMIC SONG, CALLED

Sammy Sugar Plumb & Polly Chitterlings, by Mr. Jefferson.

To conclude [FIRST TIME HERE] with the Melo-Drama of

Robinson Crusoe,

Or, *The Bold Buccaniers.*

Robinson Crusoe,	Mr. WHEATLEY.
Friday, (a young Savage,)	Mr. J. JEFFERSON.
Iglou, Friday's Father,	Mr. HATHWELL.
Pariboo, (a hostile Carib Chief,)	Mr. GREENE.
Diego, Crusoe's Son and capt. of a Ship,	Mr. T. JEFFERSON.
Bluff, the Mate,	Mr. BURKE.
Windlass, (the Boatswain,)	Mr. BIGNALL.
Swivel, the Gunner,	Mr. DARLEY.
Block,	Mr. JOHNSTON.
Gunwale,	Mr SCRIVENER.
Stern,	Mr. MARTIN.
Nipcheese, the Steward,	Mr. JEFFERSON.
Innis, Wife of Crusoe,	Mrs. LEFOLLE.

Scene 1st, represents that part of the Island which Crusoe calls his Farm;

A Steep Hill occupies a portion of the back scene, in the side of which is the Mouth of a Cave, defended in front by an enclosure of Stakes, which having taken root, forms an IMPENETRABLE HEDGE. On the opposite side a gentle Declivity intersected with Trees, at the root of which lies the trunk of a Cedar partly formed into a CANOE, but partially concealed by the plants, brushes, &c.

THE HORIZON AND VIEW OF THE SEA.

A Ship arrives and is seen in the distance, &c. Crusoe enters in his GOAT SKIN DRESS, with his Umbrella. The arrival of Paraboo and the rest of the Hostile Caribs in their Canoes, who prepare to Celebrate a Human Sacrifice—Iglou is rescued and recognized by his Son Friday.

ACT SECOND, SCENE FIRST. THE STAGE REPESENTS THE

Inside of Robinson Crusoe's Hut. A stone on one side which serves for a Door;

On the various shelves are distributed the Goods and Utensils, taken from the Wreck, with other articles which the industry of Crusoe has fabricated for his use and convenience—Rude Chairs framed with Boughs and covered with Skins, &c. &c.——Scene 3d, represents the PART OF THE COAST ON WHICH CRUSOE WAS WRECKED, &c. In the front a pole with the inscription of the day on which he suffered Shipwreck, and the Notches by which means he counted the time—A Steep Rock overlooks the Sea, the whole of the right occupied by a Wood of Cedars, in the form of an Ampitheatre, a Chasm opening to the Secret Pass. THE WHOLE SOMBRE, EXTENSIVE, AND WILDLY PICTURESQUE—Early Dawn, which gradually increases. Diego discovered increasing the fire, which flames on the rock. AN AMBUSH OF THE FRIENDLY CARIBS, who protected by the boughs and branches they have cut down, advance, attack and defeat the Mutineers and hostile Tribe.

Mrs. Anderson & Mr. T. Jefferson's Benefit on Thursday.

E. de Krafft, Printer, Seventh Street, nearly opposite the Centre Market House, City of Washington.

Figure 2.13. Playbill for the melodrama *Robinson Crusoe; or, The Bold Buccaneers.* Washington, DC, September 17, 1822.

Figure 2.14. Thomas Stothard, illustrator. *The Life and Strange Surprising Adventures of Robinson Crusoe*, 1790.

149). Set against the natural phenomena of high surf, a rainstorm, and screaming birds in flight, Crusoe stops midstride, his left hand extended in a gesture of alarm, his eyes on the sand before him, his posture a mimesis of puzzlement, apprehension, and surprise. The representation of moments of emotional intensity through natural phenomena, silent gestures, and expressive action became the new standard in both set design and book illustration after de Loutherbourg and Stothard.

Another illustrator whose drawings prepared the reading and theatergoing public for the burlesque of Crusoe was George Cruikshank, who was "fond of attending" pantomimes, particularly *Robinson Crusoe* (Blewett, 73). Cruikshank is thought to have illustrated the story several times, the most important being the edition published by John Major in 1831 (Lovett #301). Unlike the full-page copper plates used by Stothard, Cruikshank interspersed numerous half-page vignettes throughout the book, as if in imitation of the sixty-one brief scenes that made up Sheridan's pantomime. Instead of Stothard's depiction of Crusoe's complex and deeply felt emotions, Cruikshank sought to capture, through exaggeration, caricature, and the grotesque, the humor of Crusoe's situation. Cruikshank was, in Blewett's words, the first illustrator who seems to have been "truly aware of the comic element in Defoe" (Blewett, 72). After Cruikshank, it was possible to think of Crusoe not as the hero of a Christian parable, but as the heroine of a sentimental story whose virtue was always, or always about to be, in distress.

In Cruikshank's drawing of Crusoe discovering the footprint, the setting—a rolling surf and cloudy sky accented with birds and a nervous dog—strongly recalls Stothard's design, and presumably also de Loutherbourg's painted sets for Sheridan's pantomime. Cruikshank's Robinson, however, is more grotesque than Stothard's, closer to the "stock figures, exaggerated gestures, and dumb shows" of popular theater. His oversized parasol and posture of horror look forward to Lydia Thompson's burlesque of the same moment, which she appears to perform with Cruikshank's image in mind (figures 2.15 and 2.16). Although the set design for Thompson's burlesque lacks (at least in this publicity photograph, probably taken in a studio) the rolling surf, the screaming birds, and the worried dog of Stothard's and Cruikshank's illustrations, it does mimic the central elements of their designs: the parasol, the gun, and the expression of surprise, wonder, and alarm that is struck by the goatskin-clothed and capped figure of Crusoe. The comic effect of the scene depends upon the audience having previously seen, and now recalling, previous depictions of the same moment in pantomimes, melodramas, and book illustrations, which this scene burlesques.

A third illustrator who facilitated the reception of Crusoe in burlesque is Ernest Griset, who contributed nearly one hundred illustrations to the hundred fiftieth anniversary edition of *Robinson Crusoe* published in 1869 by John Camden

Figure 2.15. George Cruikshank, "Robinson Crusoe Discovers a Footprint." *The Life and Surprising Adventures of Robinson Crusoe*, 1831.

Hotten, with an introduction by William Lee (Lovett #525). In the colored frontispiece, Crusoe and Friday set out on a hunting expedition. Crusoe appears as something of a buffoon, a character from *opéra bouffe*, jolly but self-important in his mock-majestic outfit. His axe and bags of powder and shot hang down before him in parodic allusion to his masculinity. Friday is dressed in European fashion, his multicolored shirt and vest reminiscent of Sheridan's Harlequin. He carries not the traditional armaments of the hunt, as Crusoe does, but two paddles and a harpoon (figure 2.17). Griset's readers might see in them the magic bat and the sharp stick (or red-hot poker) that Harlequin used to prick his enemies and work his transformations.[37] Seven years later, a reviewer of the first performance of *The Very Latest Edition of Robinson Crusoe* at the Folly Theatre would write of Willie Edouin,

Figure 2.16. Lydia Thompson as Crusoe discovering the footprint, photographed by Jose Maria Mora, 1877.

Figure 2.17. Ernest Griset, "Crusoe and Friday on an Expedition." *The Life and Strange Surprising Adventures of Robinson Crusoe*, 1869.

who played Friday, that "his make-up as Friday is capital—like a realized sketch by Griset," a confirmation that playgoers in the 1870s interpreted theatrical performances in visual terms derived from book illustrations, rather than from the text of the novel itself.[38]

Several explanations have recently been offered for the emergence of burlesque in nineteenth-century British theater, and for the public's fascination with *Robinson Crusoe* in particular. Kirsten Pullen sees parallels between the British Blondes and the efforts of "nineteenth-century feminists who also struggled to underscore feminine agency and equality."[39] At the same time, burlesque "seemed to echo nineteenth-century prostitutes' transgressive desire" (Pullen, 116). For Pullen, feminism, prostitution, and burlesque were all discourses in which women "struggled to attain what had previously been only masculine privilege through their clothing, their economic independence, and their discursive agency" (98).

Andrew O'Malley attributes the popularity of pantomimes such as *Robinson Crusoe* to their ability to present a story dramatically in a form accessible to children and "plebian audiences."[40] The value of pantomimes to adults and authorities was pedagogical: pantomimes taught children (and the lower orders) to value domesticity, to obey their parents (and other authorities), to forego individualism, and (paradoxically) to become independent and self-sufficient. This useful if uninspiring pedagogy was caricatured in songs and nursery rhymes, in which Robinson became "Poor Old Robinson Crusoe," who was "victimized by some unseen authority," such as parents.[41] Instead of the masculine hero of the Robinsonade, Crusoe was the passive, feminized recipient of favors from a supernatural fairy and a harlequin Friday armed with slapsticks and magic bats (108). From this point, says O'Malley, it was a small step for Crusoe to be played "by a cross-dressed woman, which came to be known as the 'breeches role'" (108)—though Lydia Thompson and her imitators did not wear breeches.

A final theory for the rise of burlesque representations of *Robinson Crusoe* is offered by Marty Gould, who argues that the sharp rise in the number of new plays after 1860 with "Robinson Crusoe" as the first words of the title was due to a "shift" in British colonial policy after about 1860.[42] According to Gould, the early eighteenth-century colonialist mission to civilize the unknown parts of the world was replaced in the Victorian era by an ideology of imperialism, the objective of which was to seize power and land from irrepressibly savage populations (66). The increased interest in Crusoe, says Gould, may be the result of this new enthusiasm for world dominance. Many historians agree that such a shift did occur, but would place it a century earlier.[43] Even if Gould's timeline were correct, an enthusiasm for imperialist ideology would seem inconsistent with burlesque, in which the female "principal boy" appears to undercut Crusoe's masculinist adventures.

Nor would it explain the popularity of Robinson Crusoe in America, which had rejected British imperialism a century earlier. Gould's theory, however, works well if the burlesque of Crusoe is read as *anti*-imperialist, a covert form of resistance to elite culture on the part of the middle and laboring classes.

All three of these interpretive theories offer partial explanations for the popularity of Crusoe in burlesque, but none of them is entirely convincing. It has been the purpose of this chapter to remind readers that pantomime and burlesque, which belong to an earlier tradition than the novel, entertain and divert their audiences by disrupting the conventions of the dominant social order of the time. By casting "pretty" female actors in roles that were nominally male, burlesque troupes like Lydia Thompson's British Blondes created imaginary characters who were not cross-dressers, monsters, prostitutes, feminists, children, or imperialists, but free beings who challenged such normative categories as gender and race. The burlesquing of the masculinist hero Crusoe and his otherworldly sidekick Friday appealed to audiences of the 1870s because such parodies followed naturally from a hundred fifty years of female Crusoes, book illustrations, caricatures, pantomimes, and melodramas that presented alternative or transgressive versions of Robinson Crusoe.

The argument may be summed up with a single image, a publicity still of Lydia Thompson as Crusoe and Willie Edouin as Friday (figure 2.18). At first we may be shocked and embarrassed by the apparent racism of this photograph from the Blondes' American tour in 1877. But we must remember that the image we are considering is from a *burlesque*, in which all of the leading characters are meant to be transgressive in one way or another. If Thompson's Crusoe confuses and makes nonsense of gender roles, then Edouin's Friday is a caricature of racial otherness rather than a representation of it. Friday appears in blackface, with wild hair and a costume that exaggerates the racial differences between himself and Crusoe. He kneels before Crusoe in a posture that both justifies and ridicules his colonization. He holds in his hands a book, which in some reviews of the play is identified as a dictionary, a sign of his difficulties with the English language (Gänzl, 182). His unkempt hair, his elongated feet, and the ill-fitting animal skins he wears present him, unlike Stothard's Friday, as a highly racialized figure, or rather as a caricature of one. Edouin's Friday may have amused some members of the audience (as the reviewers tell us) by his drunkenness and his inept use of words, but other persons in the audience appear to have been made uneasy by the racial stereotypes his performance evoked—which after all is the point of satire.[44]

Thompson's Crusoe in this image is equally problematic. She points toward heaven with her left hand, while holding in her right what appears to be a switch.

Figure 2.18. Lydia Thompson and Willie Edouin as Crusoe and Friday, photographed by Jose Maria Mora, 1877.

Her gesture heavenward may indicate that the book in Friday's hands is a Bible, not a dictionary. Whether the book is a Bible or dictionary, the relationship between Crusoe and Friday is paternalistic, pedagogical, and imperial—or a satire on all of those forms of power. The switch is an instrument of discipline that enforces her imperial (or paternal) authority over Friday (or perhaps inspires, at least among children, apprentices, and adults who have seen Sheridan's pantomime, some sympathy for harlequin Friday). Thompson's Crusoe is a figure of authority mixed with domesticity, a man/woman who belongs neither to Olive Logan's Cult of True Womanhood nor to the ideology of masculine individualism. She represents a woman freed from the defining constraints of her sex, but she also depicts the end point of a process of feminization of Robinson Crusoe that began soon after Defoe's invention of the famous mariner. Defoe would indeed have been astonished at the afterlife of Robinson Crusoe, who completed his travels far beyond the known boundaries of place, time, and gender.

NOTES

1. Martin Green, *The Robinson Crusoe Story* (University Park: Pennsylvania State University Press, 1990), 6.
2. Anne Birgitte Rønning, "Female Robinsonades—A Bibliography," https://www2.hf.uio.no/tjenester/bibliographfi/Robinsonades. Rønning wrote in 2014 that "so far I have documented ninety-two robinsonades with female authors and/or female protagonists from the period 1719 to 1900." See also Anne Birgitte Rønning, "With Mother on a Desert Island: Gender and Genre at Stake in Madame de Montolieu's *Le Robinson Suisse*," *Knjizenstvo* (2014), www.knjizenstvo.rs.
3. Jeannine Blackwell, "An Island of Her Own: Heroines of the German Robinsonades from 1720 to 1800," *German Quarterly* 58, no. 1 (Winter 1985): 5–26.
4. C. M. Owen, *The Female Crusoe: Hybridity, Trade and The Eighteenth-century Individual* (Amsterdam: Rodopi, 2010), 4. See also Nancy Armstrong's observation that "it was no doubt because Crusoe was more female, according to the nineteenth century understanding of gender, than either Roxana or Moll that educators found his story more suitable reading for girls than for boys of an impressionable age." *Desire and Domestic Fiction* (New York: Oxford University Press, 1987), 16.
5. Jeffrey Richards, *The Golden Age of Pantomime: Slapstick, Spectacle and Subversion in Victorian England* (London: Tauris, 2015), 29–30.
6. The Blondes made three tours of America, the first in two parts: August 1868–May 1873 and August 1873–May 1874, a total of sixty-eight months. The second tour, which featured *Robinson Crusoe*, covered five months, August–December 1877. A third tour lasted nine months, February–August 1886. Kurt Gänzl, *Lydia Thompson, Queen of Burlesque* (New York and London: Routledge, 2002), 84–165, 185–188, 202–211.
7. For Alice Atherton, see *National Police Gazette*, October 4, 1879, 1–2; Gänzl, *Lydia Thompson*, 188. Figure 2.3 is from the author's collection.
8. *The Era*, January 1886, 114; *The Theatre*, October 1, 1888, 220. See also David S. Shields, *Still: American Silent Motion Picture Photography* (Chicago: University of Chicago Press, 2013). For Willie and May Edouin, see G. Spencer Edwards, "Concerning Willie Edouin," *Illustrated Sporting and Dramatic News*, October 12, 1901, 200–201.

9. Lydia Thompson's daughter was Zeffie Agnes Lydia Tilbury (1863–1950), who debuted on stage with her mother in *Nine Points of the Law* (Theatre Royal, Brighton, 1881). She appeared in more than seventy films, usually as a wise old woman or grandmother, such as Grandma Joad in *Grapes of Wrath* (1940) and Grandma Lester in *Tobacco Road* (1941) (Gänzl, *Lydia Thompson*, 197).
10. *The Ludgate Illustrated Magazine*, November 6, 1893, 442–447.
11. For Ada Blanche, see *Art and Drama*, October 13, 1893, 380; *The Sketch*, December 27, 1893, 468; *The Sketch*, January 2, 1895, 449; *The Times* [London], March 12, 1896, 6; and the *Oxford Dictionary of National Biography*, s.v. "Lydia Thompson," accessed October 12, 2020, http://www.oxforddnb.com. Eight photographs of Ada Blanche as Crusoe were taken by Alfred Ellis on January 29, 1894, at 20 Upper Baker Street, London. They are available online at the National Archives in Kew, 261–268.15385. This photo first appeared in *The Sketch*, January 31, 1894, 7.
12. For Alice Brookes, see *The Theatre*, February 1, 1896, 104–105; *The Sketch*, February 12, 1896, 108–111; *The Sketch*, January 2, 1895; *The Sketch*, January 20, 1897.
13. For Georgina Delmar, see *The Sphere* 5 (1901), which lists her among contraltos and mezzo-sopranos at Covent Garden; *Musical News*, March 22, 1902, 22:288; *Tatler and Bystander*, October 28, 1903, 152; *Tatler and Bystander*, November 17, 1909. This photo is from the author's collection; another is in the National Archives UK, 1/492/278, not digitized.
14. For this photograph I am indebted to Nigel Ellacott, www.its-behind-you.com. For the probable date of the performance, see *Western Daily Press* [Bristol], December 24, 1909.
15. This quotation and those immediately following are from *Illustrated Sporting and Dramatic News*, February 24, 1877, 537, which illustrates the principal actors in costume. See also "Robinson Crusoe at the Folly Theatre," *Illustrated Sporting and Dramatic News*, November 18, 1876, 178, which has a detailed summary of the plot.
16. *Illustrated Sporting and Dramatic News*, November 25, 1876, 197.
17. Richard Grant White, "The Age of Burlesque." *Galaxy*, August 1869, 256–266, quoted in Robert C. Allen, *Horrible Prettiness: Burlesque and American Culture* (Chapel Hill: University of North Carolina Press, 1991), 25.
18. *The Encyclopedia Britannica*, 11th ed. (New York: Encyclopedia Britannica, 1910–1911), 17–18:742, s.v. Monster.
19. The word "traversties" in this passage may be a neologism derived from *traverser*, "a person who crosses over or passes through" (*OED*). Alternatively, it may be an error for "travesties." In either case, the modifier "lewd" makes its misogynistic intention clear.
20. William Dean Howells, "The New Taste in Theatricals," *Atlantic Monthly*, May 1869, 635–644, quoted in Allen, *Horrible Prettiness*, 25.
21. Olive Logan, *Before the Footlights and Behind the Scenes: A Book about "The Show Business" in All Its Branches* (Philadelphia: Parmelee, 1870), 586. Virtually the same text was published as *The Mimic World and Public Exhibitions* (Philadelphia: New World, 1871). Logan also attacked "burlesque women" in *Apropos of Women and Theatres* (New York: Carleton, 1869), "The Leg Business," *Galaxy*, August 1867, 40–44, and "The Nude Woman Question," *Packard's Monthly*, July 1869, 193–198. The engraving of Olive Logan is from T. Allston Brown, *The History of the American Stage, from 1733 to 1870* (New York: Dick and Fitzgerald, 1870), 223.
22. Three of Olive Logan's sisters, Alice, Kate, and Grace Logan, were amateur members of the British Blondes. Alice and Grace Logan had parts in *Ixion*, Thompson's first American burlesque—Alice was cast as Juno, and Grace as Cupid—while Kate took the role of Juana in *Ernani*. The owner of the theater where *Ixion* was staged—Wood's Museum and Metropolitan Theatre—was George Wood, the husband of another of Olive's sisters, Eliza, who

had herself begun her acting career in London as a burlesque dancer (Gänzl, *Lydia Thompson*, 124; T. Allston Brown, *A History of the New York Stage*, 3 vols. [New York: Benjamin Blom, 1903], 1:384–385, 2:524–525, 527, 529).

23. Logan's description of Thompson's dress was widely reprinted in British and American newspapers, such as the *St. Louis Globe-Democrat*, February 18, 1877, 3.
24. It was common for critics to praise and fault burlesque actresses at the same time for being "pretty." A generally supportive review by "Our Captious Critic" in the *Illustrated Sporting and Dramatic News*, for February 24, 1877, 537, says that "when such artists as Miss Lydia Thompson and Willie Edouin have the chief share of the singing and dancing, when the pretty choruses are sung by the prettiest of pretty girls, attired in the brightest and most ravishing of burlesque costumes, the gratification of one's theatrical senses is a foregone conclusion."
25. Michael R. Booth, *English Plays of the Nineteenth Century* (Oxford: Clarendon, 1976), 5:50–51, 249–253. Authors of pantomimes and harlequinades were called "arrangers" because they had little control over the material; their task was to construct a framework upon which the comics and ballet masters could devise extravagant effects.
26. The pantomime was performed in three parts (including a bullfight) on Saturday, January 27, and Tuesday, January 30, but a review in the *Gazetteer and New Daily Advertiser* on January 30 found that the play "wants compression." The reviewer suggested that "perhaps if the two latter acts were thrown into one, and the redundancies removed, the whole would have a better effect," which was accordingly done. On Wednesday, January 31, the *Gazetteer* advertised that *Robinson Crusoe* would be performed "in two Acts" on that evening.
27. John McVeagh, "*Robinson Crusoe*'s Stage Début: The Sheridan Pantomime of 1781," *Journal of Popular Culture* 24, no. 2 (Fall 1990): 137–152. McVeagh's "surmises" about the action of the play are drawn from the reviews noted above, from an account in *Lady's Magazine* for February 1781, and from a pamphlet, *A Short Account of the Situations and Incidents exhibited in the Pantomime of Robinson Crusoe at the Theatre-Royal, Drury-Lane* (London, 1781), which consists largely of extracts from the novel. Linley's score for the overture, the songs, and the melodies was edited by Robert Hoskins as *The Pantomime of Robinson Crusoe* (Artaria Editions, 2005). Hoskins's contribution to the understanding of *Robinson Crusoe* as a "melodrama" is discussed by Michael V. Pisani in *Music for the Melodramatic Theatre in Nineteenth-Century London & New York* (Iowa City: University of Iowa Press, 2014), 22–24.
28. See, among others, the *Whitehall Evening Post* for February 3, 1781, and the *Gazetteer and New Daily Advertiser* for February 5, 1781.
29. This description of the action and the quotation are based on McVeagh's summary and on a twenty-seven-page pamphlet, *Robinson Crusoe; or, Harlequin Friday. A Grand Pantomime, in Two Acts, as Performed at the Theatre Royal, Newcastle upon Tyne, in 1791*, printed by Hall and Elliot (ca. 1791).
30. The closing of the pantomime was advertised in the *Gazetteer and Public Advertiser*, December 16, 1782, and its reopening in Bristol was advertised in *Felix Farley's Bristol Journal*, December 28, 1782.
31. Fintan O'Toole, *A Traitor's Kiss: The life of Richard Brinsley Sheridan* (New York: Farrar, Straus and Giroux, 1997), 156.
32. *Nineteenth-Century Collections Online/Archive: British Theatre/Playbills* (Gale), https://www.gale.com/primary-sources/nineteenth-century-collections-online. Information about *Robinson Crusoe; or, The Bold Buccaneers* at Covent Garden (below) is also from this website.
33. The playbill in figure 2.13 is for the melodrama of *Robinson Crusoe; or, The Bold Buccaneers* by R. Pocock (perhaps an error for Isaac Pocock) at the Washington Theatre on September 17, 1822, as advertised in the Washington, DC, *Daily National Intelligencer* for that date. The playbill was reproduced with the kind assistance of Eric Frazier, Rare Books and Special Collections Division, Library of Congress.

34. David Blewett, *The Illustration of* Robinson Crusoe, *1719–1920* (Gerrards Cross: Colin Smythe, 1995), 46.
35. Robert W. Lovett, *Robinson Crusoe: A Bibliographical Checklist of English Language Editions (1719–1979)* (New York: Greenwood Press, 1991), #63.
36. *Encyclopedia Britannica*, 7–8:973, s.v. De Loutherbourg, and 25–26:971, s.v. Stothard.
37. According to an essay by George Augustus Sala, "Getting Up a Pantomime," in *Household Words* (1855), a red-hot poker was essential to the success of a pantomime. Sala's essay is reprinted as "Appendix C. Pantomime Production, Rehearsal, and Performance" in Booth, *English Plays of the Nineteenth Century*, 5:485–518; the reference to "red-hot pokers" is on 497. The ways in which Harlequin's escapades constituted a threat to social order are considered in the first chapter of John O'Brien, *Harlequin Britain: Pantomime and Entertainment, 1690–1760* (Baltimore: Johns Hopkins University Press, 2004), 1–29.
38. *Illustrated Sporting and Dramatic News*, November 18, 1876, 178.
39. Kirsten Pullen, *Actresses and Whores: On Stage and in Society* (Cambridge: Cambridge University Press, 2005), 116.
40. Andrew O'Malley, *Children's Literature, Popular Culture, and* Robinson Crusoe (Basingstoke: Palgrave Macmillan, 2012), 107.
41. O'Malley cites and discusses (96–101) the song "Poor Old Robinson Crusoe," which is reprinted and annotated in Iona and Peter Opie, eds., *Oxford Dictionary of Nursery Rhymes* (Oxford: Clarendon, 1955). The song was printed under the title "Robinson Crusoe" in *A Garland of New Songs, Containing 1. Robinson Crusoe 2. Jack at the Windlass 3. The Sons of Brittannia* (Newcastle Upon Tyne: Angus Printer, ca. 1800).
42. Marty Gould, *Nineteenth-Century Theatre and the Imperial Encounter* (New York: Routledge, 2011), 31. Gould breaks this number down by decade: 1860–1869, 4 plays; 1870–1879, 27; 1880–1889, 36; 1890–1899, 49; and 3 undated (220).
43. T. O. Lloyd argues in *The British Empire, 1558–1983* (New York: Oxford University Press, 1984) that "the changes of 1757–63 mark the point at which the British moved on an appreciable scale into the imperial activity of gaining new subjects in the process of expansion" (84). See also Roxann Wheeler, "The Complexion of Desire: Racial Ideology and Mid-Eighteenth-Century British Novels," *Eighteenth-Century Studies* 32, no. 3 (1999): 309–332 (n. 25).
44. Reviewers commonly remarked on the "extravagancies" or the "bad taste" of Edouin's performances, which appears to mean that his satire of Friday made audiences uncomfortable. A typical notice ran in the *London Reader* for December 2, 1876: "Mr. Edouin has a drunken scene in which he makes poor Friday commit the wildest extravagancies. Yet the audience once or twice signified that the fun of the piece was carried too far, and disapprobation was expressed" (100).

3

ANIMAL CRUSOES

Anthropomorphism and Identification in Children's Robinsonades

AMY HICKS AND SCOTT PYRZ

CHILDREN'S ROBINSONADES OFTEN revise Daniel Defoe's Crusoe to be an emulative figure who ensures his triumphant survival through innovation, thrift, and perseverance, and thus the tales omit or downplay the character's often inhibitory introspection and anxieties. In this way, these narratives for young people have created their own iconic version of the castaway character—one that emphasizes emulation and identification between the child reader and Defoe's prototype, as well as his literary descendants. Yet in Robinsonades featuring anthropomorphized animal characters the identification impulse is often weakened, absent, or inverted, despite the common assumption that "pets and zoos and animal stories are 'natural' steps on the child's way up to adult."[1] Crusoe as an anthropomorphized animal complicates the presumed natural affinity between children and animals and the child reader's purported need to find kinship with animal characters.

This chapter explores the various ways implied child readers identify with or are distanced from animal Crusoes in children's texts by using what Maria Nikolajeva calls the "identification fallacy" between the reader and the animal castaway in Robinsonades as a starting point for our analysis. We focus on a small corpus of animal Crusoe stories, including Clifton Bingham's *The Strange and Surprising Adventures of Jumbo Crusoe: As Related by Himself* (ca. 1905), Beatrix Potter's *The Tale of Little Pig Robinson* (1930), Ivy L. Wallace's *Getup Crusoe* (1948), William Steig's *Abel's Island* (1976), Mark Burgess's *C.A.T. Crusoe* (1993), and James Stevenson's *The Castaway* (2002), to examine this transformation. These texts represent varied examples of the changes common to children's Robinsonades featuring animals that occupy the Crusoe role as the primary castaway character and exhibit behaviors commonly associated with humans (e.g., talking and wearing clothes). Animal Crusoes are often not emulative figures when their narratives introduce stronger and more capable Friday-like companions, place emphasis on the Crusoe figure's animality, and position the animal Crusoe as irrational or inept. These depictions contrast with the traditional representation of a human Crusoe as capable, rational, autonomous, Western, liberal humanist subject. This chapter examines the evolution of the Crusoe figure to anthropomorphized animal form, the issues surrounding emulation that this evolution creates, and how these issues reflect adults' shifting ideologies about children and childhood in the twentieth and twenty-first centuries.

Soon after the initial publication of Defoe's *Robinson Crusoe*, abridgements and adaptations were created specifically for child readers. The changes made to these *Crusoe* adaptations reflect adults' ideologies concerning what types of stories children presumably enjoy, but also how children should learn and behave. Andrew O'Malley has written extensively about how eighteenth- and nineteenth-century children's remediations of *Robinson Crusoe* create both an emulatory figure (signifying a source of inspiration) and a commiseratory figure (signifying a target of sympathy) through redefining the prototypical castaway character. In late eighteenth- and early nineteenth-century abridgements and adaptations, for instance, certain aspects of Defoe's novel are excised, emphasized, or moderated to align with contemporary pedagogical theories and reflect divine, social, and familial hierarchies. To do this work, authors "stretched the pre-island episodes, specifically Crusoe's father's injunctions against the sea-faring life, and repeatedly linked the agonies Crusoe suffers back to his initial act of filial disobedience."[2] These revisions ensure that, "in order for children (particularly boys) to become the independent, self-sufficient individuals prized by middle-class ideology and epitomized in the figure of *Robinson Crusoe*, their inherent dependence and subordination within both familial and social orders had constantly to be asserted."[3] The reassertion of familial orders is solidified, as O'Malley claims, in later Robinsonades and children's editions of *Robinson Crusoe* by emphasizing "domestic features of Crusoe's story" through including illustrations of the castaway in his island home and casting Friday in a pseudo-son role.[4]

Through these remediations, Crusoe becomes a character to inspire children to ascribe to contemporary ideologies perpetuated and upheld by adults. Still other abridgements of Defoe's novel fashion Crusoe as both an emulatory and identificatory figure by positioning the castaway characters as a folk hero in inexpensive chapbook editions. The original details that support Crusoe's initial middle-class status are removed, and instead readers see Crusoe "[enjoy] the type of miraculous rise up the social hierarchy about which many readers, especially those at the bottom of the social order, would naturally fantasize."[5] As such, the lower classes that could afford inexpensive chapbooks would be able to not only identify with

Crusoe's initial class standing, but also envision a hopeful future for themselves because of Crusoe's inspiring climb up the social ladder.

Children's editions of *Robinson Crusoe* and Robinsonades published in the eighteenth, nineteenth, and twentieth centuries highlight the pervasive appeal of Defoe's narrative for young readers. Since these early remediations, castaway texts have populated their islands with not just boys, but also girls, dolls, robots, and animals to refashion the Crusoe figure to mirror and reiterate contemporary ideologies and communicate ideals about children. (A selection of each type of children's Robinsonade may be found in the appendix.) Though animal castaway characters inhabit islands in numerous twentieth- and twenty-first-century children's Robinsonades, surprisingly few critics have paid heed to the evolution of the Crusoe figure and story to include anthropomorphized characters.

This dearth of scholarship is perhaps a result of the assumed natural association between children and animals. As Ursula Le Guin argues in *Cheek by Jowl*, "It appears that we give animal stories to children and encourage them to be interested in animals because we see children as inferior, mentally 'primitive,' not yet full human."[6] Similarly, C. S. Lewis argues that the connection between children and fantasy (a genre to which anthropomorphic animal stories belong), though accepted as natural, is actually "accidental," since animal stories "gravitated to the nursery when [they] became unfashionable in literary circles, just as unfashionable furniture gravitated to the nursery in Victorian houses."[7] Children are given anthropomorphic animal stories not only because adults often see them as "inferior" and thus aligned with the animal, but also because (until relatively recently) adults have dismissed the genre of fantasy as childish.

Assuming that the child is naturally aligned with animals leads to a number of problematic conclusions. For instance, Karen Coats has argued that "if it is true that the child will 'recognize himself in the other,' then what the child subject will recognize . . . is his smallness and his isolation."[8] In other words, the adult often assumes that the small and powerless child identifies with the animal character, because the child sees an analogous diminutive stature and powerlessness and is comforted or more interested because of this apparent connection. Nikolajeva's ideas about what she calls the "identification fallacy" highlight the issue with using anthropomorphized animals as a vehicle to promote identification between child readers and animals in books for young people. The "identification fallacy" is the ungrounded notion that "readers must adopt the subject position of a literary character."[9] Nikolajeva discusses the issue with anthropomorphic animals in children's books by first pointing out the "contemptuous attitude of bundling children and animals together" (as similarly discussed by Le Guin and Lewis) and then claiming that "[anthropomorphic] animals in the vast majority of stories are used to empower the readers who do not identify with the characters but rather feel superior to them."[10]

Children's literature scholars have recently renewed interest in children's animal stories, with some, like Amy Ratelle, acknowledging that "the reliance on animals in children's literature over the past two centuries has become a key means by which the civilizing process that children go through has been mediated by the animal body. Children are asked both implicitly and explicitly to identify with animals, *but then to position themselves as distinctly human* through the mode of their interactions with both lived animals and those depicted in literature and film."[11] Thus, as Ratelle argues, children are socialized through their interactions with both fictional and real animals. While children are tasked to first identify with animals, they are then tasked to eventually distance themselves from animals by recognizing their differences from them. The distancing of the child from the animal through interactions that position the child as "distinctly human," however, is what ultimately positions the child in opposition to the animal and as its superior, since children are also socialized to abandon their impulse to identify with the animal as part of growing up. Ratelle also, however, points out a seemingly contradictory notion that anthropomorphic animal characters in children's texts blur the human/animal distinction and that "Western philosophy's objective to establish a notion of an exclusively human subjectivity is continually countered in the very texts that ostensibly work to configure human identity."[12] So while Ratelle acknowledges that children are socialized through real and fictional animals, this socialization works to collapse the idea of "an exclusively human subjectivity" by creating (or acknowledging) animal subjectivities and by collapsing the distance between the animal and the child to instill kinship.

Animal Crusoe stories provide much to explore in terms of the child reader's presumed affinity with its characters, particularly in light of critics' claims about the identification impulse fostered by not only the Crusoe figure, but also the Robinsonade more broadly. Diane Loxley claims, "Much of the attraction of the desert island genre is said to be derived precisely from the fact that the reader (particularly child readers) is, in a classic case of under-distanciation, 'drawn into' the fabric of the fiction, made to 'identify' personally with the predicament of the major character(s)."[13] Much of this identification that implied child readers feel for castaway characters is driven by a common question that Robinsonades elicit: "how would *we* keep alive?"[14] This question invites readers to not only find ways to identify with fictional castaways, but also access their rationality to determine solutions to the problems inherent in being cast away. In animal Robinsonades, however, significant distance between the characters and the implied child reader is created when animal Crusoes embrace their animality to survive and when they reveal their powerlessness through frequent struggles caused by their limitations, fears, and need to be rescued by another more experienced, more resourceful, or otherwise more "adult" companion.

Bingham's *Jumbo Crusoe,* which features a bipedal elephant castaway, includes these patterns that create distance between the animal Crusoe and child readers, most notably the inverted Crusoe/Friday relationship that highlights Jumbo's limitations. A marked departure from Thompson's frontispiece image that features a prostrate Friday with Crusoe's foot on his head, Bingham's Bear Friday is, by turns, Jumbo Crusoe's friend, protector, and savior. In this way, Bear Friday deviates from the conventional depiction of Friday as a servant or pseudo-son figure for Crusoe in children's adaptations of Defoe's novel but demonstrates how this traditionally "savage" and ignorant character becomes more capable and adventurous than his castaway counterpart. Though Jumbo Crusoe ensures Bear Friday's survival from a "savage band" of wolves, it is Friday who saves Crusoe when the wolves return to the island for a second time. Jumbo Crusoe recounts the scene: "Bear Friday, with his gun, was brave, / And banged quite madly; / He hit no foe, but made great noise, / Which frightened them as badly."[15] The accompanying image of Friday shooting at the "savage" wolves while Crusoe watches with a lowered gun from a safe distance serves to highlight Friday's capabilities in a time of danger.

The inhibitory anxieties experienced by Defoe's Crusoe that are often downplayed in children's editions of the novel are reintroduced in *Jumbo Crusoe* when Bingham's castaway frets that the "savages" may return to the island. Jumbo Crusoe implores Friday,

They're enraged
Because I rescued you,
So now put on your thinking cap
And think what we can do.
We must do something very soon,
Because these constant fights
Are making me quite thin and pale,
I cannot sleep o' nights.[16]

Jumbo Crusoe reveals not only his pervasive fear, but also his inability to devise a rational plan to ensure their safety by capitulating to the character who successfully defended him from harm moments prior. Bear Friday's idea to build a home effectively "protected [them] from the foe," and yet, "Friday grew ambitious" and decides to "build a boat, / and so escape!"[17] Though the boat they craft is not seaworthy, Friday and Crusoe are rescued by "Lion Tars" soon after. This conclusion reiterates that Bear Friday is essential to Jumbo Crusoe's ability to not only survive, but also thrive while cast away, since he is the one to comfort his companion and shield him from harm.

While implied child readers may find Jumbo Crusoe a sympathetic character because they, too, experience fear and are dependent on others, he is not an emulative figure because of his unwillingness or inability to innovate or be resourceful once another character appears on the desert island. Indeed, Jumbo Crusoe's behavior once he saves Bear Friday shifts considerably. Prior to this, he experienced hardships while cast away but nevertheless managed with his available resources or cultivated nascent skills, such as using his trunk to fish. After the arrival of Friday, however, Crusoe regularly defers to his seemingly braver, more capable companion. In this way, Bingham's Crusoe does not exemplify the stalwart individualism intrinsic to Defoe's Crusoe depicted in other children's adaptations but does reveal some adults' ideologies about children. The relationship between Jumbo Crusoe and Bear Friday shows adults' belief that children should work collaboratively with others, and when necessary, defer to those who are more experienced than them.

Like *Jumbo Crusoe*, the stalwart individualism and rationality of Defoe's Crusoe are lacking in Potter's *The Tale of Little Pig Robinson*, which places emphasis on the protagonist's animality throughout. Potter's titular character is sent to market by his two aunts, who are both too large to make the four-mile trip to town. After his basket is filled with tea, wool, and yeast, it becomes too heavy for the little pig to carry as he searches for the final item requested by his aunts. Here, readers become aware of Robinson's weakness as an animal, since he cannot carry what is an ostensibly a light, albeit full, basket. Yet it is when he is accosted by a sailor that "complimented him, and said he had five chins" that his animality is clearly emphasized.[18] In the accompanying illustration, Robinson's frame is much smaller than the sailor's. Because of Robinson's small stature, the predatory sailor perceives the naive little pig as easy prey. Because of this, Robinson is not an emulatory figure for children who are often told that their small size puts them in danger of being harmed by adult strangers. For Little Pig Robinson, his diminutive size that may endear him to child readers serves to remind child readers of the constant danger inherent to their existence. This becomes even more central to Little Pig Robinson's story as it becomes apparent that his ultimate foible is that he allows the sailor to lead him to the ominously named ship, the *Pound of Candles*. Readers gain insight into Robinson's thoughts and are reminded of the danger he is in, namely because he is an animal: "Robinson did not very much like the name [of the ship]. It reminded him of tallow, of lard, of crackle and trimmings of bacon. But he allowed himself to be led away, smiling shyly, and walking on his toes. If Robinson had only known . . . that man was a ship's cook!"[19] While Pig Robinson is initially none the wiser, readers are told explicitly that he is at risk of being eaten. While readers might sympathize with Little Pig Robinson's predicament, they are also reminded of his ignorance as he is "smiling" while on his way to his presumed death.

One of the primary anxieties of Defoe's Crusoe that children's animal Crusoes reintroduce is the fear of being consumed, which is also seen in *Jumbo Crusoe*, *Abel's Island*, and *C.A.T. Crusoe*. Because Robinson is a pig, the distance between the implied child reader and animal Crusoe is foregrounded due to his status as a food animal, whereas other animal Crusoes are small creatures that are often childhood pets and are potentially easier for children to identify with. The narrator states, "It must not be supposed for one moment that Robinson was ill-treated on board ship. Quite the contrary. He was even better fed and more petted on the [ship] than he had been at [home]. . . . The only persons who refused to treat him as a joke were the yellow tom-cat and Captain Barnabus Butcher, who was of a sour disposition."[20] Here, readers may also see Robinson "as a joke" or as a creature too naive to recognize the perilous nature of being on a ship with a crew of hungry men who are patient and wise enough to fatten him up, so much so that he overlooks the fact that the captain of the ship is quite literally a butcher. Rather than Robinson becoming suspicious of this seemingly benevolent behavior, he instead "eats as much as he pleased" and "got lazier and lazier as the ship sailed south into warmer weather."[21] Thus, this animal Crusoe is not only a recognizable source of food for child readers, but also a source of potential disdain because of his naivety and subsequent descent into indolence.

Little Pig Robinson's naivety illustrates adult anxieties about the susceptibility of children to danger and serves as a lesson for readers to be wary of strangers—especially ones who are bigger and stronger than them. Moreover, *Little Pig Robinson* also reiterates the ideology communicated in *Jumbo Crusoe* concerning the value of community and working collaboratively when a cat on board the *Pound of Candles* helps to ensure Robinson's safety and survival. In both these animal Robinsonades, primacy is given to an exploration of the value of cooperation and community before self-reliance. This contrasts with Robinsonades that foreground self-reliance, but arguably stays true to the resolution of Defoe's original, in which Crusoe achieves his aim of escape through the intervention of others.

Unlike Little Pig Robinson whose castaway experience is a result of his naivety, the anthropomorphized toy animals in Wallace's *Getup Crusoe* "play Robinson Crusoe and get shipwrecked and live on a Desert Island" after reading Defoe's story with their human owner, Timothy.[22] Timothy's toy animals intentionally set out to reenact the story for their own amusement. The fact that the toys yearn to "play Robinson Crusoe" demonstrates the emulatory nature of the character himself, particularly when Woeful the monkey and Gumpa the bear argue over who will be Crusoe during their castaway game. As the title suggests, however, it is Getup the giraffe who ultimately assumes this role after the animals' raft crashes, water washes away his spots, and he runs away to "hide his spotlessness for ever."[23]

Getup's "spotlessness" is the impetus for him to cast himself away, and perhaps more significantly, his resulting humiliation reminds readers that he is a material object constructed for a child's amusement. A stuffed toy is arguably one meant to be a comfort object for a child, since it is soft and can be pressed against a child's body; however, a stuffed toy can also be used in rough play because it can be easily manipulated, thrown about without significant damage, and washed if soiled. For example, in *Getup Crusoe*, "Gumpa can swim quite well" after "Timothy taught him in the bathtub."[24] When Getup is damaged, readers are reminded that he is not only a toy, but also a substandard one when the other animals respond to his "spotlessness." Woeful notes, "Humph! *All* the best woollen Animals are *fast-coloured*. Only cheap flannel coats run!"[25] Getup's shame and Woeful's judgment of the giraffe's purported cheapness position him as a character to be commiserated with, but not necessarily one to be inspired by. Readers are then reminded that Getup's appearance is of great importance to ensure his existence as a child's treasured toy. Getup bemoans, "I do not think Timothy *could* love an ugly woolly Animal like me!"[26] Getup's concern implies that, without Timothy's love, he may be relegated to a less prominent position in his owner's bedroom or even be deemed as expendable. His concern also suggests that Timothy's love and care is dependent on Getup's materiality. The implied child reader is surely here in receipt of a didactic lesson: sympathetic to Getup's spotlessness and his sadness, a child might feel secure in the difference that separates child and toy, for no child wishes to believe their love and care depend upon their appearance, but the realization that appearance may determine the responses of others is surely the beginning of empathy.

Getup's spots are restored before he returns to Timothy, but it is not through his own resourcefulness. Just as Jumbo Crusoe relies on Bear Friday to solve problems and ensure his well-being, Little Mut, the smallest and seemingly least capable toy of all the stuffed animals, provides Getup with a way to return home. After finding Getup in a house he built among the foxgloves, Little Mut devises a plan: "'Mr. Trig's lost Parrot is sitting on our roof!' he squeaked, 'and there is a big Reward offered for him! You can take him back and be a hero, Getup! If you are a famous hero nobody will mind about your lost spots!'"[27] Getup capitalizes on the plan, and for his reward, Mr. Trig restores the giraffe to his former "splendid spotted" self.[28] Mr. Trig, the other animal toys, and Timothy assume that Getup is the hero that Little Mut designated him to be. At the book's conclusion, "there was no argument who should be Mr. Crusoe," but the story makes clear that Getup is able to assume this desired role primarily through the help of a capable companion.[29] Like *Jumbo Crusoe* and *Little Pig Robinson*, *Getup Crusoe* communicates the ideology that children should work collaboratively, receive help from others, and learn that self-reliance develops over time. Wallace's book also reiterates the belief that intelligence and creativity are desirable qualities that children should aspire to, since it is the smallest toy of the bunch who engineers the plan to redeem Getup.

Steig's *Abel's Island* introduces young readers to an altogether different kind of Crusoe figure, with the titular castaway of this Newbery Honor book being a foppish mouse. While having a picnic, Abel is swept away during a sudden rainstorm and is left without his wife on a deserted island. Steig's animal Crusoe struggles to shrug off his privileged ways and must learn to fend for himself while cast away. Indeed, a significant portion of the novel details the many struggles Abel encounters as he attempts to find food, shelter, and a way back to his wife and comfortable home.

Consistently reinforced through numerous illustrations, Abel's nonhuman form is an aspect of the narrative that is difficult to ignore, particularly when his small size and lack of strength contribute to many of his struggles. Whether it is when he devises ways to escape the island, when he discovers his talent for gnawing, or his ability to avoid being eaten, Abel's animality is consistently reinforced and reminds readers of their distinctly human position. Abel's attempts to escape the island serve to reinforce not only his incompetence, but also his lack of power due to his small stature. Abel attempts to escape the island multiple times and in various ways. The most significant of these attempts are the ones that highlight Abel's physical limitations. For instance, when he attempts to build a walkway through a river with stones, his mouse's body proves too small and weak to carry stones that are large enough to keep him above the water. In other attempts to escape, his physicality limits his ability to throw a rope to the other side of the river or to bend the tree enough (it only bends "two and a half tails . . . to his strength") to provide the force necessary to catapult him to the other side.[30] Abel also barely considers that catapulting himself across the river is dangerous and could result in serious harm or injury. While it could be argued that each of these instances serves to connect Abel to the implied child reader—they too are naive and physically limited—Abel's initial inability to escape the island surely provides an implicit contrast with popular (mis)conceptions of Crusoe's experience. The reader of Defoe's text knows that Crusoe's is ultimately saved through the arrival of others, but in the popular imagination Crusoe is arguably his own savior, resourceful and strong.

Abel further reminds child readers of their difference from him when his experiences highlight his animality. When building his boat, he finds a piece of driftwood that is "somewhat disgusting since it had been gnawed and bored and channeled by lower forms of life."[31] Abel's vague reference to "lower forms of life" begs the question as to what forms of life are lower than him. A description of the driftwood as "gnawed" evokes images of rodent teeth—like Abel's own—albeit that "channeled" then suggests shipworms or other marine borers. Abel's reference to lower forms of life and gnawing therefore momentarily suggests his perception of his own worth relative to lowly marine organisms, while readers may pause at their realization that they simply see all "gnawers" in a single, troublesome, category.

Abel's animality consistently provides him with unique capabilities and opportunities that help him survive his time on the island. In one such instance, readers are presented with a scene where Abel accepts that being one of those lower forms not only is more efficient for him but also is a position in which he finds enjoyment and pleasure. The scene is worth quoting in its entirety: "It was slow work with the small penknife. Not thinking, he fell to using his teeth. What? He drew back for a moment, in revulsion. Then he continued to gnaw away. He had never before gnawed on anything but food. But the grooves were done in no time, and he didn't honestly mind the taste of the somewhat decayed wood."[32] This passage reveals several key elements about Abel's animality: First, he falls to using his teeth "without thinking"; second, he is initially repulsed when he realizes what he is doing; third, the grooves were done in "no time"; and finally, he liked the taste of "somewhat decayed wood." Abel's animality is highlighted in this scene, since it includes using his teeth for gnawing materials other than food and is an activity many human children are taught not to do early in their lives. His initial revulsion at using his teeth for this purpose shows how removed he has become from his own animal nature. The fact that the grooves are finished in no time once he starts using his teeth reinforces their fitness for purpose, and proves to be the most efficient, ideal way for Abel to construct his boat—in a sense, he is naturally equipped with the "tools" upon which Crusoe has to depend. That Abel also comes to *like* the taste of decayed wood emphasizes his animality, since it reminds readers that he, unlike us, can consume decayed and rotten things without adverse effects. While these reminders of Abel's animality distance him from child readers, they also serve to illustrate a lesson about finding solutions through "working the problem" and that trying new things can be productive, even enjoyable, leading to the discovery of previously unknown skills and capabilities.

The specter of cannibalism and the fate of being eaten that is given center stage in *The Tale of Little Pig Robinson* also becomes a theme in *Abel's Island* when Abel encounters and escapes from an owl and a cat. The description of each escape emphasizes Abel's animality, since he eludes his predators by "diving into a crevice between two rocks,"[33] by running circles around the base of the tree until the "mad carousel . . . offended the owl's ancient sense of decorum,"[34] and by "playing dead out of long-forgotten instinct."[35] By escaping consumption through instinct, agility, and his diminutive size, Abel reminds children that they have capabilities that adults do not have, such as the ability to hide in small spaces—and seemingly boundless energy. But, like Little Pig Robinson, Abel's escapes also remind child readers of their powerlessness in the world and the inherent danger of their existence. While Abel does eventually recognize the benefit of his animal instinct (by playing dead), he is slow to realize that he is at risk from others until faced directly with a predatory attack. Indeed, neither Little Pig Robinson nor Abel exhibits any of Crusoe's natural caution in his dealings with unfamiliar others and environments. This revision of the Crusoe mythos is also present in Burgess's *C.A.T. Crusoe.*

Burgess's *C.A.T. Crusoe* focuses solely on the protagonist's castaway adventure and has numerous similarities to *Abel's Island,* most notably in the ways the protagonists are depicted. Like Abel, Caractacus Algernon Tobias (C.A.T.) is a foppish dandy, as evidenced by his name and the three-piece suit and tie readers see the character wearing in Burgess's illustrations. Because the narrative is compressed into a short picture book format, the same thematic elements that may cause the implied child readers to place distance between themselves and the animal Crusoe are amplified through direct phrasing and evocative images. Perhaps the most compelling thematic tie between *Abel's Island* and *C.A.T. Crusoe* that inverts or erases the identification impulse between reader and castaway character are the shortcomings of the books' protagonists. Caractacus assumes not only that his rescue is inevitable, but that his absence must already be noted, and his rescue will be under way moments after he is cast away on the island. Caractacus's initial reaction to being marooned is to believe that his situation is "quite inconvenient . . . but no doubt the ship will turn back to look for [him]."[36] Caractacus is self-important and distances himself from readers through his arrogance. The narrative emphasizes its protagonist's conceit: "Now Caractacus was a rather spoiled cat. Usually all he had to do was ask and his meals would be brought to him. Caractacus couldn't see anyone to ask. He shouted and shouted but nobody answered. He began to realize that he would have to find some food for himself."[37] Here, child readers are invited to see Caractacus not as an inspirational character but rather as a comical one, because of his spoiled nature. (There is of course a possibility for sympathy and identification with Caractacus's spoiled nature as *C.A.T. Crusoe*'s target age-range readers may never have considered finding food for themselves.) Caractacus's unrequited and repeated shouting may also be familiar to many adults and children alike, but here familiarity does not equate with desirability. Immediately upon being stranded on an island, Caractacus assumes that the privileges afforded to him on the mainland will continue by food being brought to him. Once he recognizes his perilous state, this animal Crusoe's survival is ensured by luck, rather than something akin to Crusoe's system of trial and error in Defoe's novel. Caractacus fails at catching fish and cracking a coconut with his umbrella, and his hunger is satiated only after he throws the umbrella in frustration and it gets stuck in a banana tree. Caractacus admits, "What luck . . . he loved bananas."[38] Caractacus survives and eats, then, not because he exhibits rational behavior worth emulating, but because his anger and impetuousness cause him to cast away his umbrella—part of his connection to humanity—and be rewarded for doing so.

Caractacus's shortcomings are showcased in a scene reminiscent of Crusoe's repeated observation of cannibalistic behavior on the island. Caractacus sees large mice gathering around a cooking pot and allows his arrogance to lead him into trouble. As a cat, Caractacus "is never afraid of mice, even *big* mice, and Caractacus decided to be friendly to them in case they could help him."[39] In this moment, readers see Caractacus assume both that a predator should never fear his natural prey, and that the animals he naturally preys upon will assist him in a time of need. Only luck saves him from his erroneous assumptions—and the cooking pot—as Caractacus "tripped over a stone and fell headlong into his umbrella. The umbrella wrapped itself around him and he rolled down the slope towards the giant mice. He looked exactly like a red-hot cannonball hurtling towards them."[40] Caractacus evades his potential captors not through his intelligence or any rational course of action but through chance, as the umbrella that previously secured him bananas once again saves the day. These moments of arrogance arguably distance Caractacus from his child readers, because they set him up for failures and dangers that he only narrowly and luckily escapes.

Caractacus's luck and flawed behaviors continue throughout the story, and when he saves another cat named Friday from the giant mice's cooking pot, the feline Friday is distinguished from Defoe's original by quickly and efficiently exercising power over his rescuer. Though Caractacus suggests they fashion the cooking pot into a boat for their escape from the island, "Friday did all the working-out bits and told Caractacus what to do."[41] Their inverted Crusoe/Friday relationship continues to the book's conclusion with Friday ordering his companion to sail westward and Caractacus dutifully responding "aye, aye Cap'n."[42] Similar to Jumbo Crusoe, Little Pig Robinson, and Getup Crusoe, Caractacus relinquishes leadership and responsibility to a Friday character to ensure his survival. While *C.A.T. Crusoe* highlights the importance of relying on another with more knowledge, it also demonstrates the necessity of shrugging off one's hubris in order to do so. If there is a concluding moral to Burgess's book, it is that one's own ideas are not necessarily the best and the (child) reader may benefit from the superior skills of others: as an animal castaway, Caractacus is very different to Crusoe in this regard.

Revising Defoe's novel to feature anthropomorphized animal characters has continued on into the twenty-first century, with Stevenson's *The Castaway* as an example of a more recent publication from those discussed earlier in this essay. Like *Robinson Crusoe*, *The Castaway* details its protagonist's experiences before, during, and after island isolation. What is notable about Stevenson's picture book is its focus on a young mouse, Hubie, who is portrayed as an animal child. With the exception of *The Tale of Little Pig Robinson*, the other animal Crusoe stories discussed in this essay render their adult castaways childlike because of their dependence on others for their personal survival, naivety, or susceptibility to danger. Because Hubie is a child, albeit a mouse child, Stevenson arguably invites even greater identification between reader and subject than in other anthropomorphized Crusoe stories.

The Castaway begins with a conversation between Hubie's father and older brother that serves to establish their views on Hubie's character and also to reflect common tropes about children and their emotional capabilities: Hubie's father states, "I hope this movie isn't too grown-up for Hubie . . . ," and Hubie's brother replies, "Hubie always gets scared!"[43] Here, readers learn that Hubie is often fearful, his father wants to protect him from situations that could induce his fear, and Hubie's brother views his sibling's fearfulness derisively. Readers may find Hubie a sympathetic character because they too may have fears, experience the injustice of not being "grown-up" enough in certain situations, and encounter judgment from older siblings; however, the protagonist in *The Castaway* does seem afraid of many things. After watching a film about explorers on a dangerous island, Hubie has a newfound fear of not only islands, but "ships and planes and cannibals and volcanos."[44] Despite his anxieties and protestations, his parents decide to spend a family vacation on Barabooda Island. As they travel there by dirigible, Hubie unluckily tumbles out of an escape hatch and finds himself cast away. Perhaps surprisingly, this animal Crusoe finds enjoyment on the island where he lands, particularly after encountering Leo, another castaway. Leo encourages Hubie to stave off loneliness and fear by engaging in potentially dangerous, but adventurous, activities. Once Hubie reunites with his family, enjoys his island vacation with them, and returns home, the story concludes with his telling proclamation as the family ponders the location for their next vacation: "How about we climb Mt. Everest?"[45] Ending the book in this way emphasizes the growth Hubie has experienced after learning to be more courageous and positions him as laudable—a bolder Crusoe figure than the animal castaways who do not seem as transformed by their island adventures.

The Castaway is somewhat of an outlier among the selection of animal Crusoe stories examined in this essay because Stevenson is at pains to make Hubie a child (albeit an animal child) castaway and to allow him a classic narrative arc of facing his fears and ultimately "outgrowing" them. His fears, which were the source of his parent's concern and his older sibling's derision, emphasize his childlike nature, but with Leo's encouragement Hubie learns a newfound sense of independence and self-reliance. These are precisely the qualities that nineteenth- and early twentieth-century adult readers valued in *Robinson Crusoe* when viewing it as a tutelary text for generations of children.

The authors of animal Robinsonades often revise relationships and tropes from Defoe's work and do so in a way that makes these fictions distinct from children's remediations of *Robinson Crusoe*. And since animal Crusoes may create empathy but also generate distance between themselves and their implied readers, they offer new ways to consider how anthropomorphic characters function in children's texts. Tracing the development of the animal Crusoe character over time may also offer a window onto changing ideologies about children—who they are and how they should behave—that have changed considerably since the publication of early *Robinson Crusoe* children's adaptations. If there is a feature that is shared by most animal Robinsonades, it is surely the disappearance of the self-reliance and rationality of the Crusoe character that is foregrounded in early children's adaptations of Defoe's work. Yet as *The Castaway* shows, a twenty-first-century animal Robinsonade may choose to embrace traditional values. Animal Crusoes are a distinct group within the Robinsonades, and their potential as vehicles for exploring changing ideas about child psychology and animal representation has not been exhausted yet.

APPENDIX: CHILDREN'S ROBINSONADES

The following books are a selected collection of children's picture books and novels featuring characters that are cast away on islands or other isolated places.

Animals

R. M. Ballantyne's *The Dog Crusoe* (1860)
Racey Helps's *Littlemouse Crusoe* (1948)

Russell E. Erickson's *Warton and the Castaways* (1980)
John Patience's *Castaways on Heron Island* (1980)
Andrea Beck's *Elliot's Shipwreck* (2000)
Lisa Wheeler's *Castaway Cats* (2006)
Laurent de Brunhoff's *Babar on Paradise Island* (2014)

Boys

Barbara Hofland's *The Young Crusoe, or the Shipwrecked Boy* (1830)
R. M. Ballantyne's *The Coral Island* (1858)
Armstrong Sperry's *Call It Courage* (1940)
Jean Craighead George's *My Side of the Mountain* (1959)
Theodore Taylor's *The Cay* (1969)
Mark Taylor's *Henry the Castaway* (1972)
Ann McGovern's *Nicholas Bentley Stoningpot III* (1982)
Gary Paulsen's *Hatchet* (1987)
Michael Morpugo's *Kensuke's Kingdom* (1999)
Will Hobbs's *Wild Man Island* (2002)
Lisa Doan's *Jack the Castaway* (2014)

Girls

Mrs. George Corbett's *Little Miss Robinson Crusoe* (1898)
Mrs. Herbert Strang's *The Girl Crusoes: A Story of the South Seas* (1912)
Carol Ryrie Brink's *Baby Island* (1937)
Winifred Scott's *Girl Castaways* (1954)
Scott O'Dell's *Island of the Blue Dolphins* (1960)
Jean Craighead George's *Julie of the Wolves* (1972)
Harry Mazer's *The Island Keeper* (1981)
James Mayhew's *Miranda the Castaway* (1996)
Mary Casanova's *When Eagles Fall* (2002)
Terry Pratchett's *Nation* (2008)
Eddie Pittman's *Red's Planet* (2016)

Dolls

Miss Robinson Crusoe: The Story of a Desert Isle (190-?)
Anne Parrish's *The Floating Island* (1930)

Robots

Carol Ryrie Brink's *Andy Buckram's Tin Men* (1966)
Peter Brown's *The Wild Robot* (2016)

NOTES

1. Ursula Le Guin, *Cheek by Jowl* (Seattle: Aqueduct, 2009), 51.
2. Andrew O'Malley, *Children's Literature, Popular Culture, and* Robinson Crusoe (Basingstoke: Palgrave Macmillan, 2012), 37.
3. O'Malley, *Children's Literature*, 47.
4. Andrew O'Malley, "Crusoe's Children: Robinson Crusoe and the Culture of Childhood in the Eighteenth Century," in *The Child in British Literature: Literary Constructions of Childhood, Medieval to Contemporary*, ed. Adrienne E. Gavin (New York: Palgrave Macmillan, 2012), 95.
5. O'Malley, *Children's Literature*, 92.
6. Le Guin, *Cheek by Jowl*, 51.
7. C. S. Lewis, *On Stories: And Other Essays on Literature* (Orlando: Harcourt, 1966), 36.
8. Karen Coats, *Looking Glasses and Neverlands: Lacan, Desire, and Subjectivity in Children's Literature* (Iowa City: University of Iowa Press, 2004), 47.
9. Maria Nikolajeva, "The Identification Fallacy: Perspective and Subjectivity in Children's Literature," in *Telling Children's Stories: Narrative Theory and Children's Literature*, ed. Mike Cadden (Lincoln: University of Nebraska Press, 2010), 188.
10. Nikolajeva, "Identification Fallacy," 196.
11. Amy Ratelle, *Animality and Children's Literature and Film* (London: Palgrave Macmillan, 2015), 10, emphasis added.
12. Ratelle, *Animality and Children's Literature and Film*, 4. See also Zoe Jacques, *Children's Literature and the Posthuman: Animal, Environment, Cyborg* (New York: Routledge, 2015), 23–108.
13. Diana Loxley, *Problematic Shores: The Literature of Islands* (New York: St. Martin's, 1990), 10.
14. John Rowe Townsend, *Written for Children: An Outline of English-Language Children's Literature* (London: Lothrop, Lee, and Shepard, 1965), 64.
15. Clifton Bingham, *The Strange and Surprising Adventures of Jumbo Crusoe: As Told by Himself* (Buffalo: Berger, 1905), 14.
16. Bingham, *Jumbo Crusoe*, 16.
17. Bingham, *Jumbo Crusoe*, 18.
18. Beatrix Potter, *The Tale of Little Pig Robinson* (1930; repr., New York: Penguin, 1988), 81–83.
19. Potter, *Little Pig Robinson*, 83.
20. Potter, *Little Pig Robinson*, 96–97.
21. Potter, *Little Pig Robinson*, 97.
22. Ivy L. Wallace, *Getup Crusoe* (London: Collins, 1948), 5.
23. Wallace, *Getup Crusoe*, 29.
24. Wallace, *Getup Crusoe*, 17.
25. Wallace, *Getup Crusoe*, 27.
26. Wallace, *Getup Crusoe*, 33.
27. Wallace, *Getup Crusoe*, 51.
28. Wallace, *Getup Crusoe*, 55.
29. Wallace, *Getup Crusoe*, 57.
30. William Steig, *Abel's Island* (New York: Square Fish, 1976), 43.
31. Steig, *Abel's Island*, 22.
32. Steig, *Abel's Island*, 22.
33. Steig, *Abel's Island*, 61.
34. Steig, *Abel's Island*, 73.

35. Steig, *Abel's Island*, 110.
36. Mark Burgess, *C.A.T. Crusoe* (London: Orion, 1993), 3.
37. Burgess, *C.A.T. Crusoe*, 3.
38. Burgess, *C.A.T. Crusoe*, 5.
39. Burgess, *C.A.T. Crusoe*, 7.
40. Burgess, *C.A.T. Crusoe*, 10.
41. Burgess, *C.A.T. Crusoe*, 16.
42. Burgess, *C.A.T. Crusoe*, 23.
43. James Stevenson, *The Castaway* (Hong Kong: Greenwillow Books, 2002), 1.
44. Stevenson, *Castaway*, 9.
45. Stevenson, *Castaway*, 30.

Part Two

MIND AND MATTER

4

DEFOE AND NEWTON

Modern Matter

LAURA BROWN

FOR LITERARY CRITICS TODAY, defining and engaging with matter, objects, and "things" and with the extended notion of "new materialism" can be a challenging undertaking in a diffuse context. *Robinson Crusoe* offers a response to this challenge, as well as a concrete model for the form of imagination that new materialism seeks to identify. Distinct and even incompatible accounts of the nature of the "thing" mark recent critical studies. In Jonathan Lamb's understanding, the thing is entirely removed from the human—to be understood as "things purely as they are"; these "pure" things "disturb" literary texts because they are "obstinately solitary, superficial, and self-evident, sometimes in flight but not in our direction; they communicate only with themselves and have no value in the market that they reckon."[1] For Jane Bennett though, far from being removed or "solitary," the thing is "vitally" engaged and efficacious. Bennett's enabling quality is "thing-power" and its impact is transferrable, in that "attentiveness to (nonhuman) things and their powers can have a laudable effect on humans."[2] For Diana Coole and Samantha Frost, the emphasis is specifically ontological—extending beyond "vitality" to the actual agency of matter: "material forces themselves manifest . . . agentic capacities" that are "active, self-creative, productive" and that require the "rethinking of the whole edifice of modern ontology . . . regarding change, causality, agency."[3] And distinctively, for Ileana Baird and Christina Ionescu the challenge presented by the eighteenth-century thing resides in its "multifarious array of functions"—exemplified by the range of thing-protagonists in the "so-called 'it narrative'" that arises in midcentury (Baird, 12, 14). The singular defining quality of all these things then becomes movement; things may be extraordinarily diverse, but their common denominator is exchangeability or circulation. Thus their impact is generated through their "global peregrinations": things create "relational maps" and "more expansive geographies."[4]

We now have in our critical discourse an informed conceptual overview of new materialism, which offers us accounts of the context, the developing tradition, and the core parameters of the "thing."[5] But as the diverse explanations of the nature and role of things that is reflected in the selective list above suggests, new materialism's impact on literary study is muted by the range of routes that a critic might take—moving from the "thing" itself to texts, imaginative experience, literary culture, or literary history—which have been offered as ways to enact a transformative materialist literary study for our time. Matter, objects, or "things" might indicate obstinate solitude, a vital efficacy, an "agentic' force, or expansive global movement. These things might disrupt or undermine human structures of communication or expression; they might efficaciously merge their powers with the forces of human activity; they might act on their own with a force equivalent to or expansive of the category of being; or they might level and renegotiate global structures and processes by crossing geographical and temporal boundaries. This profusion of meanings complicates the vital next step for literary critique: a conceptually coherent—though not a singular—project and methodology. Our next task is to develop a methodology by activating these meanings in relation both to the material world or worlds of the "thing," on the one hand, and the imaginative realms of representation, texts, and literary traditions, on the other.

Given the concrete, local nature of the thing itself, the challenges that it presents to a coherent literary critique might best be addressed concretely or inductively: from the core moment of the portrayal of matter, objects, and "things" onward toward the recognition of materialism's status in the literary history of modernity and the broader conceptualization of materialism's impact as a method of literary critique. As a concrete test case, this essay juxtaposes two distinctive, contemporary, corollary portrayals of matter, objects, or "things": Daniel Defoe's *Robinson Crusoe* (1719) and Isaac Newton's "Queries" to the *Optics* (1704, 1717–1718, 1730). It uses these two experiential encounters with matter, and the inductive or conjectural methods they employ, to characterize a key moment in the modern redefinition of things, and to suggest the relevance of that moment and of these two texts to a materialist literary critique.

The iconic portrayals of matter for our time are Defoe's *Robinson Crusoe* and Newton's speculative writing on the forces of gravitation. From their own age onward, their contribution to the status of the "thing" has been widely visible: readers have understood that Newton "was trying to reshape the entire conception of matter,"[6] and that *Robinson Crusoe* represents for literary history "an expression of modern materialism."[7] These texts inspire and enact a redefinition of the material world—one for the new science, and the other for the new imaginative experience of literary realism.

In the case of *Robinson Crusoe,* we are in the presence of the most often redacted literary text of the modern period. The recent film *The Martian* (2015) demonstrates the currency of Defoe's representation of the "castaway" (Matt Damon), the "desert island" (Mars), and the compelling assemblage of things that come to populate an "empty" landscape. The label "Robinsonade" was coined in 1731 by Johann Gottfried Schnabel in his preface to *Die Insel Felsenburg,* but this subgenre had its inception immediately, in the year after the publication of *Robinson Crusoe,* with the publication in 1720 of the *Voyages, Dangerous Adventures, and Imminent Escapes of Captain Richard Falconer.*[8] Across a range of scenarios—from survival, labor, production, accumulation, economic agency, children's literature, and even homemaking—*Robinson Crusoe*'s immersion in the world of objects has drawn modern readers to its imaginative world. For example, even in the context of children's literature, where adventure would seem to be the source of attraction, the world of objects presides: *Robinson Crusoe* can be seen as supporting or even helping to establish an educational theory of experiential learning, which promoted "fictions *about* direct experience of the object world."[9]

In the discipline of economics, immediately emergent in the decades following the novel's publication, the engagement with *Robinson Crusoe* begins with David Hume and Adam Smith, then famously includes Karl Marx, and extends to the present day. A recent collection of essays—*Robinson Crusoe's Economic Man* (2011)—continuing the novel's visibility among economists and for the development of this field of study, "uses the device of Robinson Crusoe to contribute to a genealogy of economic agency and a critique of the discipline of economics."[10] *Robinson Crusoe* has been cited in conceptualizations of instrumental rationality, of labor and value and the nature of their connection, and of the *homo economicus*—for which Crusoe is the model. Marx, most significantly, uses *Robinson Crusoe* to illustrate the labor theory of value, crediting the long-standing role of the novel for theorists on this topic—"Crusoe's experiences are a favourite theme with political economists":

> [Crusoe] knows that his labour, whatever its form, is but the activity of one and the same Robinson, and consequently, that it consists of nothing but different modes of human labour. . . . This our friend Robinson soon learns by experience, and having rescued a watch, ledger, and pen and ink from the wreck, commences, like a true-born Briton, to keep a set of books. His stock-book contains a list of the objects of utility that belong to him, of the operations necessary for their production; and lastly, of the labour time that definite quantities of those objects have, on an average, cost him. All the relations between Robinson and the objects that form this wealth of his own creation, are here so simple and clear as to be intelligible without exertion. . . . And yet those relations contain all that is essential to the determination of value.[11]

Ian Watt brought the "Robinson Crusoe Economy (RCE)"[12] into the canonical literary critical conceptualization of the rise of the novel, by highlighting Crusoe's established status as an economic paradigm:

> [Defoe] takes his hero to a primitive environment, where labour can be presented as varied and inspiring, and . . . there is an absolute equivalence between individual effort and individual reward . . . [thus enabling] Defoe to give narrative expression to the ideological counterpart of the Division of Labour, the Dignity of Labour. . . . *Robinson Crusoe* is certainly the first novel in the sense that it is the first fictional narrative in which an ordinary person's daily activities are the centre of continuous literary attention . . . the dignity of labour helped to bring into being the novel's general premise that the individual's daily life is of sufficient importance and interest to be the proper subject of literature.[13]

Watt connects the novel's distinctive portrayal of labor with Calvinist individualism and introspective discipline; the eighteenth-century secularization of Puritan ideology explains *Robinson Crusoe*'s canonical role in the rise of the novel. But, Watt concedes, "Defoe departs from psychological probability" (88). For Watt's *Rise of the Novel*, significantly, *Robinson Crusoe* is both designated as "the first novel" but also strangely tangential to Watt's core thesis, which counterposes Richardson and Fielding through Watt's important analysis of the relationship between "realism of presentation" and "realism of assessment."

Virginia Woolf helps us to explain this ambiguity, and to define the tension within Watt's engagement with this novel. Her account of *Robinson Crusoe* acknowledges the striking absence that Watt identified as a lack of "psychological probability":

> It is a masterpiece, and it is a masterpiece largely because Defoe . . . thwarts us and flouts us at every turn. . . . It is, we know, the story of a man who is thrown, after many perils and adventures, alone upon a desert island. The mere suggestion—peril and solitude and a desert island—is enough to rouse in us the expectation of some far land on the limits of the world; of the sun rising and the sun setting; of man, isolated from his kind, brooding alone upon the nature of society and the strange ways of men. Before we open the book we have perhaps vaguely sketched out the kind of pleasure we expect it to give us. We read; and we are rudely contradicted on every page. There are no sunsets and no sunrises; there is no solitude and no soul.[14]

But Woolf sees what Watt neglects: there is no human soul on *Robinson Crusoe*'s island, but there is a powerful nonhuman entity:

> There is no solitude and no soul. There is, on the contrary, staring us full in the face nothing but a large earthenware pot. . . . By believing fixedly in the solidity of the pot and its earthiness, [Defoe] has subdued every other element to his design. . . . And is there any reason, we ask as we shut the book, why the perspective that a plain earthenware pot exacts should not satisfy us as completely, once we grasp it, as man himself in all his sublimity standing against a background of broken mountains and tumbling oceans with stars flaming in the sky? (285, 287)

Woolf here feels the force of the material thing in this novel so strongly that she posits a dramatic contrast with "man himself"—with human subjectivity—in which even the most "sublime" definition of human being does not eclipse the power of the pot. In fact, as Woolf expresses the efficacy of the pot here, the thing actually gathers the sublimity of the world—as seen through human being—into its own solidity and completeness.[15]

Woolf's eloquence—or her ventriloquy of *Robinson Crusoe*'s eloquence on behalf of the pot—urges us to extrapolate across the scope of the Robinsonade, from castaways to labor value, and from homemaking to children's instruction, to posit a powerful through line in the reception of *Robinson Crusoe* over the last three centuries: the "completeness" of the material thing even in the face of "man himself in all his sublimity." The pot is an intuitive icon for this completeness. In fact, this pot has become a very resonant metonymy, on its own, for the human engagement with the thing. Like Woolf, Bill Brown, in referring to Heidegger's conceptualization of the "thing" as a resource for new materialist thinking, also portrays this same powerful pot. Brown calls attention to Heidegger's notion of *das Krug*: its "independence," its "self-sameness," the "force of [its] form," its capacity to "be in its Being,"[16] and by that means ("thinging")[17] to make the world manifest—"the thing things world" (Heidegger, 178). This capacity of completeness is a kind of climax in the theorization of new materialism for Brown. He argues that it "culminates Heidegger's strategy for thinking beyond the Subject . . . for overcoming the merely ontic and the merely phenomenological: for overcoming the subject" (30).

And just as the encounter with the pot enables Woolf to assemble the scene of "man himself" and his "mountains . . . oceans . . . and sky," *das Krug* raises for Heidegger the status of the maker of the pot—or, in its originary occasion, Crusoe the potter. The potter—even or especially Crusoe—serves to establish the solidity of the pot as an object of production: the completeness of the pot. Brown develops Heidegger's account of the potter's "giving way" to the pot by emphasizing the potter's solitude and on the potter's definition as producer rather than consumer: "[Heidegger casts] the potter as the sole human actor to emphasize the production of the object rather than, say its consumption or its use. And once the potter exists, the objectness of the object (its relation to a subject) can give way to the thingness of the thing . . . thingness here . . . the (indissociable) thinging of the world, names an activity, a productive function—but an activity animated by no human aim" (31). This Heideggerian pot, Brown shows us, has a long-standing heritage. *Das Krug* comes to Heidegger by way of Georg Simmel, Ernst Bloch, and Theodore Adorno—from Simmel's engagement with the handle of *das Krug* as a mediating instrument for negotiating the subject-object relation, to Bloch's understanding of *das Krug* as "the imbrication of subject and object" (Brown, 31), to Adorno's offering that "the hollow depths of the pot express . . . not a metaphor; to be in those depths . . . would be to be in the thing-in-itself, in what it is in the nature of the human being that eludes introspection."[18] And, as Brown then argues, "in Heidegger's rewriting of the episode, such concern for the human being . . . is effectively beside the point, except insofar as they are assembled (gathered) by the thing" (31).

These anecdotes of a jar—its completeness, its power of "thinging," its "dominion everywhere"[19]—suggest that the pot is a heuristic for modernity's engagement with and theorization of materialism. In this sense, Heidegger, Bloch, and Adorno's pot enables us to see the prescience of Woolf's understanding of Defoe's pot, going forward in this history. Or, going backward, Woolf's pot marks the ongoing realization of Defoe's iconic materialist vision, now redacted as a (so-called) "new" materialism. All these portrayals of the pot implement Defoe's redefinition of matter, of the complete "thing" as possessed of a new force "standing against" the "sublimity" of the human.

Newton's understanding of gravity launched a vigorous, visible, sustained debate about whether the forces of repulsion and attraction—the motion observed in particles affected by gravitation—were an indication of powers inherent in matter itself, or were imposed by an external source. According to John W. Yolton, "The understanding of gravitation and motion centered on what matter was thought to be capable of on its own."[20] This question of matter's power or completeness "on its own" was a nexus of tension in Newtonian thought and in the scientific, philosophical, and theological debates of the eighteenth century. In this context, as Ernan McMullin asserts, "Newton was trying to reshape the entire conception of matter" for the new science and for modern ontology (1), in an effort that was an ongoing process of reflection and revision. McMullin shows that Newton's Laws of Motion and their Corollaries, examined in context, while clearly indicating "the abandonment of the principle of the strict passivity of matter which had so heavily influenced earlier mechanics . . . [reflect] obvious ambiguity [which] was to give Newtonians many a headache in the century that followed" (35). This ambiguity arose from Newton's simultaneous insistence both on the existence of "force" and on the inertness of matter, through his representation of intertia—the *vis inertiae*—as itself as a *vis insita*—a form of "force." McMullin explains that "in the story of the concept of matter, Newton plays a paradoxical role . . . he struggled with the intricacies of this concept for sixty years while building his system of the world around it. Yet . . . he provided scientists with a neat and manageable substitute for it, one which would later supplant the older concept in the explicit symbolic systems of modern science" (1).

In Newton's representations of the capacity of matter, throughout his works, the operative and challenging words were force, power, energy, pulling, attraction, and acting upon. Though Newton often sought to weaken this portrayal of active or vital forces by claiming that his language was figurative or that these notions were only mathematical, his readers interpreted these words to indicate that "gravitational force existed truly" and that they constituted, as Robert E. Schofield argues, "a new dynamic theory of matter."[21] Ernan McMullin describes the ways in which Newton in the *Principia* attempted to "restrict that work to an ontologically neutral sense of such dynamic terms . . . a sense which would be descriptive and mathematical, merely attributing certain sorts of regularity of motion to one body in proximity to another, without postulating the kind of agency responsible . . . [but] Newton's terminology was difficult to de-ontologize in this way. When he spoke . . . of bodies 'attracting,' or 'pulling,' or 'acting upon' one another, it was difficult to take these words as figures of speech. . . . Not only were his critics unpersuaded, but Newton, in his incessant drafting and redrafting, was just as prone as they to take such terms as 'attraction' to mean what they say" (70–71).

Newton's most direct and sustained claim for the intrinsic motive force of matter occurs in the second edition of the *Optics* (1713), to which he added a set of "Queries" that "gave Newton greater freedom to speak more openly" (Yolton, 93). Query 31 states, "Have not the small Particles of Bodies certain Powers, Virtues or Forces, by which they act at a distance, not only upon the Rays of Light for reflecting, refracting, and inflecting them, but also upon one another for producing a great Part of the Phænomena of nature? For it's well known that Bodies act one upon another by the Attractions of Gravity, Magnetism, and Electricity; and these Instances show the Tenor and Course of Nature, and make it not improbable but that there may be more attractive Powers than these."[22] Newton's portrayal of these "powers" may be attributable to his study of alchemy. In describing Newton's alchemical notes from the decades from 1675 to 1695, McMullin shows that he was "seeking clues to the nature of chemical and vital processes and because the mechanical philosophy could not help him, alchemy seemed a likely place to look. . . . The alchemical literature he pored over was full of references to the active principles responsible for the transformations of matter. The alchemists' belief was that the matter of all things is one and the same, and that variety and activity alike come from the animating principles they disguised under code names. . . . The gradual transition from alchemy to chemistry in no way diminished Newton's conviction that the world is permeated by active principles of all kinds" (41–45). The recent recognition of Newton's references to alchemy highlights our appreciation of the significance and scope of the redefinition of matter, in the realms of knowledge and of the imagination.

The notion of the inherent capacity or completeness of matter is a motivating component of contemporary thought, extending from Newton across philosophical and theological discourse. For Locke, the question of the power of matter "on its own" is construed in terms of the power of "thinking":

> We have the ideas of *matter* and *thinking*, but possibly shall never be able to know, whether any mere material being thinks, or no; it being impossible for us, by the contemplation of our own ideas, without revelation, to discover, whether Omnipotency has not given to some systems of matter fitly disposed, a power to perceive and think, or else joined and fixed to matter so disposed, a thinking immaterial substance. . . . For since we must allow he has annexed effects to motion, which we can no way conceive motion able to produce, what reason have we to conclude, that he could not order them as well to be produced in a subject we cannot conceive capable of them, as well as in a subject we cannot conceive the motion of matter can any way operate upon?[23]

The proposal, for Locke, is expressed as a core ontological challenge—in Yolton's words: "could thought be an intrinsic or natural property of matter?" (92). And Locke explicitly expressed the corollary assertion that the immortal spirit need not be linked exclusively to immateriality:

> The properties of a rose, a peach, or an elephant, superadded to matter, change not the properties of matter; but matter is in these things matter still. But if one venture to go on one step further, and say, God may give to matter thought, reason, and volition, as well as sense and spontaneous motion, there are men ready presently to . . . tell us that he cannot do it; because it destroys the essence . . . but whatever excellency, not contained in its essence, be superadded to matter, it does not destroy the essence of matter, if it leaves it an extended solid substance; wherever that is, there is the essence of matter.[24]

The objection that Locke cites here reflects the urgent contemporary negotiation around the capacity of bodies in themselves: whether bodies are essentially, intrinsically defined by inherent activity, or whether power, force, or "thought" is not attributable to bodies themselves but rather arises from an external source. The translation from the material to the theological debate was immediate for Locke, Newton, and their contemporaries. And the counterposition to the activity of matter—the notion that matter is "inactive, impenetrable, and resistant to change [and] has no active powers" (Yolton, 96)—is expressed as the argument that "all those effects currently ascribed to certain natural [or inherent] powers residing in matter are immediately produced by the power of an immaterial Being."[25] In his account of this debate, Yolton demonstrates the scope and impact of this issue, for Andrew Baxter, Joseph Priestley, George Berkeley, George Cheyne, Samuel Clarke, Robert Clayton, Anthony Collins, David Hartley, David Hume, Isaac Watts, and Richard Price, among others, showing that this challenge "raised a storm of protest and discussion right through to the last years of the eighteenth century" (17).

The Newtonian representation of matter is significant methodologically as well as conceptually. Throughout his lifelong engagement with the material world, Newton sought to model a form of knowledge creation and a mode of discourse that emerge directly from experience. Method, of course, is fundamental to Newton's contribution to the establishment of experimental philosophy, and Newton explicitly promoted and systematically pursued experiential reasoning in all his work. McMullin shows how, in the case of any particular physical claim or theory, Newton persistently seeks to argue from "an experienced property of experienced bodies"; for Newton, this experiential stance is a direct methodological counter to the "rational reflection so much relied on by Descartes" (McMullin, 23). Newton expresses his commitment to this method directly in query 31 (*Optics*): "to derive two or three general Principles of Motion from Phænomena, and afterwards to tell us how the Properties and Actions of all corporal Things follow from these manifest Principles, would be a very great step in Philosophy, though the Causes of those Principles were not yet discover'd" (401–402).

Query 8 (*Optics*) illustrates the experimental method, and compellingly highlights its rhetorical tenor and its distinctive discursive effect. Here Newton is describing the sources of vibrations that cause bodies to emit light:

> As for instance; Sea-Water in a raging storm; Quick-silver agitated in *vacuo*; the Back of a Cat, or Neck of a Horse, obliquely struck or rubbed in a dark place; Wood, Flesh and Fish while they putrefy; Vapours arising from putrefy'd Waters, usually call'd *Ignis Fatui*; Stacks of moist Hay or Corn growing hot by fermentation; Glow-worms and the Eyes of some Animals by vital Motions; the vulgar *Phosphorus* agitated by the attrition of any Body, or by the acid Particles of the Air; Amber and some Diamonds by striking, pressing or rubbing them; Scrapings of Steel struck

> off by a Flint; Iron hammer'd very nimbly till it become so hot as to kindle Sulphur thrown upon it; the Axletrees of Chariots taking fire by the rapid rotation of the Wheels. (340–341)[26]

Here, the Wood, the Hay or Corn, the scrapings of Steel, the Amber and Diamonds, the Axletrees of Chariots—these are Newton's "things," powerful in their efficacy, their solidity, and their completeness as "experienced bodies."

Newton's formidable contribution to the contemporary engagement with matter and experienced things matches up with *Robinson Crusoe*'s imaginative world, in a way that suggests a connection between literature and experimental philosophy at the moment when materialism finds its first modern formulation. This connection suggests, first, that natural history's theory of matter and *Robinson Crusoe*'s portrayal of things are both conceptual and methodological, in the sense that they engage the representation or experience of objects, in order to offer a new way of understanding the essence of the material world. Second, if they are placed in the Newtonian context, Defoe's things offer a distinctive perspective on the material and narrative premises, and the discursive traits, of modern realism.

Robinson Crusoe is an experiment in the representation of force. The novel is full of energy and activity: the solidity and completeness of Crusoe's pot is framed by a set of shifting, intense, and vibrant scenes of action for its own sake. These are unmoored, contingent scenarios of indiscriminate force. They express an unbounded, "rough and terrible" (10) energy, but they are conceptually rationalized by reference to contemporary religious and economic principles—from Protestantism and from financial models of risk and speculation. First, referencing a prominent strain of Protestant ethics, the novel describes Crusoe's emphatic rejection of his father's counsel to "settle" for the "easy circumstances" of the "middle Station of Life" (6). The subsequent scenes of action and adventure enable Crusoe, in embracing contingency, to demonstrate the Protestant principle of submission to divine providence: Martin Luther describes the true Christian as "not presuming upon the future, and not trusting in any man or in oneself but clinging to God alone."[27] Thus Crusoe—and the text itself—pursues activity, "adventures," and "undertakings out of the common road" (6). In this context, uncertainty in regard to the engagement in the turbulent affairs of that world becomes an end in itself, and the allusion to doctrinal principle is matched by an immediate release of narrative energy.

Second, the context of unpredictable economic activity and risk, which is reflected in Crusoe's choice of "enterprize" over "the middle State" (6), evokes the core tenet of venture capitalism, with its direct activation of contingency and indeterminacy as sine qua non. The vital economic engagement with risk—the accelerating speculation of the stock exchange; the institutionalization of risk in the rise of international capital markets, loans and mortgages, credit and debt, discounts, shares, futures, and securities; the attempts to manage risk in the establishment of actuarial science and in the development of joint stock charters and insurance—all attest to the centrality of contingent activity to the so-called financial revolution of the eighteenth century. Here, indeterminacy underwrites "a highly speculative and volatile economy, full of enterprise and initiative, open to an extraordinary degree to the vagaries of fashion and fad, encouraging quick returns and setting a premium on highly flexible and imaginative business strategies"[28]—the "Ambition," "Vicissitudes," "Uneasinesses," and volatile activity that Crusoe's father describes in his warnings to his son.

In its opening scenes, *Robinson Crusoe* dramatically and repeatedly enacts these imaginative engagements with energy and force. The sequence of storm scenes that take control of the narrative upon Crusoe's leaving his father's house introduce and immediately highlight this representation of unmoored, dynamic activity. The portrayal of the ocean reflects an immense, unfocused, and shifting power:

> The Sea went Mountains high, and broke upon us every three or four Minutes: When I could look about, I could see nothing but Distress round us: Two Ships that rid near us we found had cut their Masts by the Board, being deep loaden; and our Men cry'd out, that a Ship which rid about a Mile a-Head of us was foundered. Two more Ships being driven from their Anchors, were run out of the Roads to Sea at all Adventures, and that was not a Mast standing. The light Ships fared the best, as not so much laboring in the Sea; but two or three of them drove, and came close by us, running away with only their Sprit-sail out before the Wind. (11–12)

Formally, this account is multifaceted, proliferative, and directionless: it refers to size—"Mountains high," to speed—"running away . . . before the Wind," and to dispersed action—"near us" / "a Mile a-Head of us" / "out of the Roads to Sea" / "close by us"—all at once. To "look about" in this world is to step out of an artificial assertion of "Temperance, Moderation, Quietness" (6) into the experience of unstructured power and force.

This experiment with the representation of force dominates the pre-island imaginative experience of *Robinson Crusoe*, generating a persistent sense of proximate vitality: more storms, more "Mountain-like" waves of "mighty Force," a fight with pirates, and even an encounter with a "dreadful Monster" (25). And all this energy results in more decisions "hurried on" (36) or "push'd . . . forward" (14), in a scenario characterized by ongoing "Confusion of Thought" (39).

The island systematically and suddenly redirects this vitality and resolves this confusion. Storms, waves, winds, pirates, and monsters are decisively replaced by a sequential proliferation of objects. The narrative retains the rapidity generated by the storms, as well as the attitude of experimental succession portrayed in those rapidly repeated opening scenes, but turns now to a distinctive imaginative engagement with materiality itself. The "desert island" is a singular enabling locale for this experiment with matter because it excludes the multifaceted vortices of energy that fill the world beyond its perimeter. Its isolation and barrenness offers a focal point for force, and turns that focus to the narrative engagement with objects—with "experienced bodies"—whose powerful collective efficacy, like that of Newton's list of the sources of vibrations in bodies, is revealed through the experimental method that assembles them.

This engagement with the material world is marked by an impersonal momentum, which repeatedly gathers a "strange multitude of little Things" (100) into a generative sequence of production—a sequence that impels the objects into motion and change in relation to each other. One "Thing" gives rise to another "Thing," in a series that occupies the attention of the reader and the producer (Crusoe), and that populates the island world itself—in an activity that is aligned with Heidegger's "thinging." Here is the sequence of production of the earthenware pot, beginning with "the Clay":

> [Crusoe must] dig it [the Clay], . . . temper it, . . . bring it home and work it; . . . [then he makes] two large earthen ugly things . . . Jarrs . . . [which lead next to] little round Pots, flat Dishes, Pitchers, and Pipkins, [then comes the firing of the pots] . . . I . . . plac'd three large Pipkins, and two or three Pots in a Pile one upon another, and plac'd my Fire-wood all round it with a great Heap of Embers under them, I ply'd the Fire with fresh Fuel round the out-side, and upon the top, till I saw the Pots in the inside red hot quite thro', and observ'd that they did not crack at all; when I saw them clear red, I let them stand in that Heat about 5 or 6 Hours, till I found one of them, tho'd it did not crack, did melt or run, . . . so I slack'd my Fire gradually till the Pots began to abate of the red Colour, and . . . in the Morning I had three very good, I will not say handsome Pipkins; and two other Earthen Pots, as hard burnt as cou'd be desir'd; and one of them perfectly glaz'd with the Running of the Sand. (102–103)

"Clay" brings forth "Jarrs," next come a proliferation of "little round Pots, flat Dishes, Pitchers and Pipkins" which then become the glazed "Earthen Pots." Those then lead to the generation of the "Mortar," the "Pestle," and the "Sieve":

> I had made an Earthen Pot that would bear the Fire. . . . My next Concern was, to get me a Stone Mortar, to stamp or beat some Corn in . . . after a great deal of Time lost in searching for a Stone I gave it over, and resolv'd to look out for a great Block of hard Wood, . . . and getting one as big as I had Strength to stir, I rounded it, and form'd it in the Out-side with my Axe and Hatchet, and then with the Help of Fire, and infinite Labour, made a hollow Place in it. . . . After this, I made a great heavy Pestle or Beater, of the Wood call'd the Iron-wood. . . . My next Difficulty was to make a Sieve, or Search, to dress my Meal, and to part it from the Bran . . . at last I did remember I had among the Seamens Cloaths which were sav'd out of the Ship, some Neckcloths of Callicoe, or Muslin; and with some Pieces of these, I made three small Sieves. (103–104)

Activity is incessant in these sequences. Locally, the energy is portrayed through an allusion to the local contributions of the producer—"I ply'd the fire," "as I had Strength to Stir"—but in the broader structure of these passages, energy is generated by the rapid, sequential emergence of the things, one after another. This energy is absorbed into the things that are represented as its outcome—in the sense that these things themselves, in their hurried transformation to a subsequent product, reflect a restlessness and potential for changeableness.

Again, here the following account of the progress of production of a "long Shelf" describes an irresistible trajectory marked by an engagement with "inexpressible" energy:

> A large Tree . . . was to be cut down, because my Board was to be a broad one. This Tree I was three Days a cutting down, and two more cutting off the Bows, and reducing it to a Log, or Piece of Timber. With inexpressible hacking and hewing I reduc'd both the Sides of it into Chips, till it begun to be light enough to move; then I turn'd it, and made one Side of it smooth, and flat, as a Board from End to End; then turning that Side downward, cut the other Side, till I brought the Plank to be about three Inches thick, and smooth on both Sides. (98)

In the course of the movement from a "large Tree" to a "Log, or Piece of Timber" to a "Board" to a "Plank" and to a "long Shelf," the producer's "hacking and hewing" is another local signal—pointing to the force empowering the cumulative generation of objects in the sequence.

The experiment in the representation of force, on *Robinson Crusoe*'s island, takes the form of rapid and irresistible sequence. The successive presence of these things generates a narrative energy and attaches a portrayal of vitality to matter itself. As we have seen here, Crusoe's plying, cutting, hacking, hewing, and stirring are absorbed into the activity of the things so as to augment their own material force. This force is an immediate narrative effect of these passages, and it highlights these things themselves as a vital presence—for Crusoe and for the reader. Crusoe's solitary, repetitive, incessant activity enables the irresistible trajectory of the things themselves to dominate the narrative, foregrounding the "thingness" of these things, and their consequent power of "thinging." As Heidegger argues, the potter's solitude demonstrates the thing-oriented activity of production rather than the human-oriented phenomenon of consumption, leaving the thing as "an activity animated by no human aim" (Brown, 31). In Heidegger's concept "that which in the jug's nature is its own is never brought about by its making. Now released from the making process, the self-supporting jug has to gather itself for the task of containing. In the process of its making . . . the jug must first show its outward appearance to the maker. But what shows itself here . . . characterizes the jug solely in the respect in which the vessel stands over against the maker as something to be made" (Heidegger, 166). Lynn Festa, from her focus on the discursive function of objects in relation to novelistic subjectivity, turns this "thinging" process toward the potter himself: "What we are given to see of the object—what Crusoe's narrative describes—constitutes much of what we get of Crusoe's subjectivity. . . . Character emerges through the subjective perception of objects, rather than through the transparent depiction of inwardness" (452, 453).

Through this distinctive narrative impact, then, the force of the succession of "Things" constitutes a materialist premise, a theory of "Thinging." Before the assemblage of "Things," the island is emphatically "barren" (46). Crusoe's first awareness, when he "began to look round me to see what kind of Place I was in," results in the observation that "in a Word, I had nothing" (41). And this context of "nothing" immediately sets off a frenetic sequence in the assembly of Things from the grounded ship: "Bisket," "Rum," "Cordial Waters," "two Pistols," "rusty Swords," "Barrels of Powder," "two Saws, an Axe, and a Hammer" (43–44), and then,

> I now began to consider, that I might yet get a great many Things out of the Ship. . . . I resolv'd to set all other Things apart, 'till I got every Thing out of the Ship that I could get. . . . I brought away several Things very useful to me . . . Bags full of Nails and Spikes, a great Skrew-Jack, a Dozen or two of Hatchets, and . . . that most useful Thing call'd a Grindstone. . . . Besides these Things, I took all the Mens Cloths that I could find, and a spare Fore-top-sail, a Hammock, and some bedding." (47)

As a site of isolation and barrenness the island immediately prompts the gathering of "Things": in fact, the island is entirely constituted by these incoming "Things." The "Earthen Pot" is a condensed example of this narrative's focused engagement with the vitality of matter; it stands for the array of "Things" that populate *Robinson Crusoe*'s "desert island"—"thinging" its central site of absence, making it manifest as a world.

This encounter—between the "inexpressible" energy of *Robinson Crusoe*'s things and Newton's experiments with force—reflects the scope and impact of the modern engagement with matter. It records the mutually constitutive roles of imaginative literature and the new science for modern materialism. Tita Chico makes this mutuality the premise of her study of *The Scientific Imagination*: she seeks to define "the historical moment when what we now think of as literature and science were not codified as distinct epistemologies, but were understood as deeply . . . implicated in one another . . . [to] reveal a doubled epistemological trajectory: experimental observation utilizes imaginative speculation and imaginative fancy enables new forms of understanding."[29]

The encounter between *Robinson Crusoe* and Newton, in a "doubled epistemological trajectory," brings two manifestations of materialism into view, both for the eighteenth century and for our own time. First, the perspective provided by Newton here demonstrates the particular manner by which and the particular components in terms of which modern matter is founded—in an inductive, conjectural process that records the tangible world of Newtonian physics. Today's "new materialism" emerges from that process and that world; viewing its conceptualization through the lens of Newton, then explains and specifies current claims for the vitality and power, for the agency and autonomy, and for the movement of material things. In this context, for instance, Jane Bennett's eloquent effort to "theorize a vitality intrinsic to materiality as such, and to detach materiality from the figures of passive, mechanistic, or divinely infused substance" can be understood as an acknowledgment of a powerful modern hermeneutic, rather than an "estrangement" (*Vibrant Matter*, xiii).

Second, the perspective provided by *Robinson Crusoe* suggests that that very inductive process—driven by the representation of "experienced bodies" and leading on sequentially from body to body, or from thing to thing—is activated through the literary imagination as a narrative of irresistible succession. This is the literary form of modern matter; things acquire their force, exhibit their vitality, and make the world of the island manifest through this discursive enactment of energy. *Robinson Crusoe,* then, offers a formal model for the mobilization of matter for literary critique, within a particular text and in literary history. This model brings to earth the wide range of outcomes for literary texts that have been assigned to the portrayal of "things"—from power or autonomy, to disruption or obstinate solitude, to efficacy, expansiveness, or innovation. From this perspective, power, disruption, and innovation are all heuristics for the imaginative creation of gravitational force—a common ground that offers a basis for interpretive coherence, for new materialist literary critique.

The modern engagement with matter that we are witnessing in Newton and *Robinson Crusoe* is an encompassing event, with vast consequences for modern thought and modern culture. Of course it shapes the science of physics and models empirical scientific method. It undergirds and continues to inform the modern conceptualization of economic forces. It establishes the discursive practice out of which the literary mode that we now call "realism" emerges—featuring the concrete, particular materials and experiences of a tangible, secular world. In describing the encompassing nature of this event across realms of understanding and imagination, Michael H. Turk includes the contributions of Montesquieu, Voltaire, Diderot, Smith, and d'Alembert with those of Newton and Defoe, in order to outline

> the bridging [of] the scientific with the philosophical and the literary. . . . One might take the general resemblance in . . . ideas [across these realms as] evidence of a commonality in consciousness, a mark of the intellectual currents, broadly understood, sweeping across Western Europe in the course of the eighteenth century. Those established an environment in which the conjectural, imagined as such or even cast in the form of fiction, would be perceived as leading to the construction or expansion of defined fields of knowledge.[30]

The pot is both a form of imagination and a form of knowledge—as knowledge, it records the inductive character of modern matter; as imagination, it asserts the power of the tangible world.

NOTES

1. Jonathan Lamb, *The Things Things Say* (Princeton: Princeton University Press, 2011), xii, xi.
2. Jane Bennett, "The Force of Things: Steps toward an Ecology of Matter," *Political Theory* 32, no. 3 (2004): 347–372, 348.
3. Diana Coole and Samantha Frost, "Introducing the New Materialisms," in Coole and Frost, eds., *New Materialisms: Ontology, Agency, and Politics* (Durham, NC: Duke University Press, 2010), 8, 9.
4. Ilena Baird, "Introduction: Peregrine Things: Rethinking the Global in Eighteenth-Century Studies" and Christina Ionescu, "Introduction: Through the Prism of Thing Theory: New Approaches to the Eighteenth-Century World of Objects," in Baird and Ionescu, ed., *Eighteenth-Century Thing Theory in a Global Context: From Consumerism to Celebrity Culture* (Farnham: Ashgate, 2013), 1–16 and 17–30, 2, 8, 14.
5. See, for example, Jane Bennett, *Vibrant Matter: A Political Ecology of Things* (Durham, NC: Duke University Press, 2009); Baird, "Introduction" and Ionescu, "Introduction"; Bill Brown, "Thing Theory," *Critical Inquiry* 28 (2001): 1–22; Bill Brown, ed., *Things: A Critical Inquiry Book* (Chicago: University of Chicago Press, 2004); Coole and Frost, "Introducing the New Materialisms." Meanwhile, critical analysis of description per se and of the appearance

of objects—especially in eighteenth- and nineteenth-century literature—continues to deepen our formal engagement with this topic; for example, Lynn Festa, "Crusoe's Island of Misfit Things," *Eighteenth Century* 52 (2011): 443–471; Elaine Freedgood, *The Ideas in Things: Fugitive Meaning in the Victorian Novel* (Chicago: University of Chicago Press, 2006); Cynthia Wall, *The Prose of Things: Transformations of Description in the Eighteenth Century* (Chicago: University of Chicago Press, 2006); Mark Blackwell, ed., *The Secret Life of Things: Animals, Objects, and It-Narratives in Eighteenth-Century England* (Lewisburg, PA: Bucknell University Press, 2007); Julie Park, *The Self and It: Novel Objects and Material Subjects in Eighteenth-Century England* (Stanford, CA: Stanford University Press, 2009); Bill Brown, *A Sense of Things: The Object Matter of American Literature* (Chicago: University of Chicago Press, 2004).

6. Ernan McMullin, *Newton on Matter and Energy* (Notre Dame: University of Notre Dame Press, 1979), 43.
7. Wolfram Schmidgen, "The Metaphysics of *Robinson Crusoe*," *ELH* 83 (2016): 101–126, 101.
8. Andrew O'Malley, *Children's Literature, Popular Culture, and Robinson Crusoe* (Basingstoke: Palgrave Macmillan, 2012), 48. For this context, see also Michael V. White, "The Production of an Economic *Robinson Crusoe*," in *Robinson Crusoe's Economic Man: A Construction and Deconstruction*, ed. Ulla Grapard and Gillian Hewitson (New York: Routledge, 2011) (originally published in *Southern Review* 15 [1982]: 115–142).
9. Alan Richardson, *Literature, Education, and Romanticism: Reading as Social Practice, 1780–1832* (Cambridge: Cambridge University Press, 1994), 132, cited in O'Malley, *Children's Literature*, 29.
10. Ulla Grapard and Gillian Hewitson, "Introduction: Economics and Literature," in Grapard and Hewitson, *Robinson Crusoe's Economic Man*, 1–12, 5.
11. Karl Marx, *Capital*, trans. Samuel Moore and Edward Aveling (1906; repr., Mineola, NY: Dover, 2011), 88.
12. This is Michael V. White's coinage in "Production of an Economic *Robinson Crusoe*."
13. Ian Watt, *The Rise of the Novel: Studies in Defoe, Richardson, and Fielding* (Berkeley: University of California Press, 1957), 72–74.
14. Virginia Woolf, from *The Second Common Reader* (1932; repr., San Diego: Harcourt, 1986), reprinted in Michael Schinagel, ed., *Robinson Crusoe: A Norton Critical Edition*, 2nd ed. (New York: Norton, 1975), 283–287, 285.
15. Lydia H. Liu connects materialism and colonialism through Defoe's pot. She sees this moment of efficacy in Woolf's account as a "fetishized metonomy . . . between man and the thing he makes," demonstrating that Defoe's pot is an unacknowledged product of the eighteenth-century global network of the porcelain trade and thus that Defoe's text is powerfully formative of the "colonial disavowal" that underlies eighteenth-century imaginative literature (139, 146). Lydia H. Liu, "Robinson Crusoe's Earthenware Pot: Science, Aesthetics, and the Metaphysics of True Porcelain," in *Romantic Science: The Literary Forms of Natural History*, ed. Noah Heringman (Albany: State University of New York Press, 2003), 139–171.
16. Bill Brown, *Other Things* (Chicago: University of Chicago Press, 2015), 29–30.
17. Martin Heidegger, "The Thing," trans. Martin Hofstader, in *Poetry, Language, Thought* (New York: Harper & Row, 1971), 175. Heidegger uses "thinging" here in the following context: "The jug is a thing insofar as it things. The presence of something present such as the jug comes into its own, appropriatively manifests and determines itself, only from the thinging of the thing."
18. Theodore Adorno, "The Handle, the Pot, and Early Experience," in *Notes to Literature*, vol. 2, ed. Rolf Tiedeman, trans. Shierry Weber Nicholson (New York: Columbia University Press, 1992), 218.

19. Wallace Stevens, "Anecdote of the Jar" (1919):

    I placed a jar in Tennessee,
    And round it was, upon a hill.
    It made the slovenly wilderness
    Surround that hill.
    The wilderness rose up to it,
    And sprawled around, no longer wild.
    The jar was round upon the ground
    And tall and of a port in air.
    It took dominion everywhere.
    The jar was gray and bare.
    It did not give of bird or bush,
    Like nothing else in Tennessee.

20. John W. Yolton, *Thinking Matter: Materialism in Eighteenth-Century Britain* (Minneapolis: University of Minnesota Press, 1984), 94.
21. Robert E. Schofield, *Mechanism and Materialism: British Natural Philosophy in an Age of Reason* (Princeton: Princeton University Press, 1970), 8–9. Also see McMullin, *Newton on Matter and Energy*, 144n135, for examples of Newton's attempts to "de-ontologize."
22. Isaac Newton, *Optics*, based on the 4th ed. (London, 1730; repr., Mineola, NY: Dover, 1952), queries 1–31, query 31, p. 376.
23. John Locke, *An Essay Concerning Human Understanding*, ed. Kenneth P. Winkler (Indianapolis: Hackett, 1996), 4.3.6, 236–237.
24. Locke, *Essay Concerning Human Understanding*, "Stillingfleet Correspondence," 349, cited in Yolton, *Thinking Matter*, 18.
25. Andrew Baxter, *An Enquiry into the Nature of the Human Soul*, vol. 1, 2nd ed. (London, 1737), sect. 2 heading, p. 79, cited in Yolton, *Thinking Matter*, 95.
26. Milton Wilson cites this passage in his account of "literary invention" in Newton: "Reading Locke and Newton as Literature," *University of Toronto Quarterly* 57 (1988): 471–483, 477–478.
27. Martin Luther, *Trade and Usury*, in *Luther's Works*, vol. 45, ed. Walther I. Brandt and Helmut T. Lehman (Minneapolis: Fortress Press, 1962), 245–310, 257. For this argument, see Dwight Codr, *Raving at Usurers: Anti-finance and the Ethics of Uncertainty in England, 1690–1750* (Charlottesville: University of Virginia Press, 2016).
28. John Brewer, "Commercialization and Politics," in *The Birth of a Consumer Society: The Commercialization of Eighteenth-Century England*, ed. Neil McKendrick, John Brewer, and J. H. Plumb (Bloomington: Indiana University Press, 1982), 213.
29. Tita Chico, *The Experimental Imagination: Literary Knowledge and Science in the British Enlightenment* (Stanford, CA: Stanford University Press, forthcoming).
30. Michael H. Turk, "Economics as Plausible Conjecture," *History of Political Economy* 42 (2010): 521–547, 533–534.

5

CRUSOE'S ECSTASIES

Passivity, Resignation, and Tobacco Rites

Daniel Yu

LITERARY CRITICS HAVE HAD LONG-STANDING disagreements over which traits find expression in the character of Robinson Crusoe. A dominant strand of interpretation asserts that the protagonist of Defoe's 1719 novel is best described as an individual of practicality and industry, making him the prototype of the modern capitalist. This point of view is sometimes at pains to reconcile Crusoe's supposed rationality with the irrational and unproductive activity filling the pages of his journal. Such economically inclined interpretations have tended to treat Crusoe's religion (especially in its material and ritual manifestations) as inessential accoutrements of the predominantly secular narrative.[1] Religiously inclined readings, on the other hand, can fall into the habit of expecting everything to be easily explained by religious ideas and ideal types. With this emphasis on professions of belief, Crusoe's aberrant passivity and worshipful use of tobacco go unnoticed.[2] The tendency to attribute causal efficacy either wholly to material interests or wholly to religious ideas is surprising given how prominently the sociology of Max Weber has been cited in *Robinson Crusoe* studies in the past half century and more.[3] Weber's approach to religion attends to the influence that religious ideas have on material conditions and vice versa.[4] Returning to certain of Weber's concepts regarding the Protestant ethic and its relation to capitalism may show how materialist readings of *Robinson Crusoe* can afford to be more hermeneutical and, equally, how spiritualist readings have not been sufficiently material.[5] In a material account of Crusoe's religion, I examine Crusoe's treatment of tobacco as a sacred substance, his attachment to his smoking pipe, and his propensity for engaging in long bouts of passive contemplation. Together, these traits and tendencies demonstrate that Crusoe's religious ethic is characterized less by an ascetic stance toward the world than by a pietistic withdrawal from the world.

In *Defoe and Spiritual Autobiography*, G. A. Starr argues that *Robinson Crusoe* adopts the formal conventions of late seventeenth-century Protestant self-writing. Like the Presbyterian minister James Fraser, the narrator of Defoe's novel reports his spiritual journey in a measured way, eschewing the "rhapsodic religious fervor" evident in Quaker and Baptist texts from the first half of the century.[6] According to Starr, the first-person account of Crusoe's conversion on the island shows considerable literary restraint, indicative of the embarrassment that Defoe's contemporaries felt toward the earlier, more fanatical iterations on the genre. D. Bruce Hindmarsh offers an account of the rapturous quality of these earlier conversion narratives, which were written by self-proclaimed prophets of the end times and "illustrate well the impetus given to spiritual autobiography by eschatological fervour."[7] Yet Hindmarsh notes that this same fervency can be found in narratives written in the wake of religious persecution in the 1660s. Moreover, some eighteenth-century dissenters remembered the zeal of their forbears with fondness. Hindmarsh writes, "For many later Nonconformists in the eighteenth century, this period represented the heroic age in their movement, against which they measured the 'decay of the Dissenting interest' in their own day" (50). Thus, whether Crusoe's journal represents a reaction against fanaticism or a reprisal of animated piety remains an open question.

The precise moment in the account of his conversion is presented as an ecstatic ebullience: "I threw down the Book, and with my Heart as well as my Hands lifted up to Heaven, in a Kind of Extasy of Joy, I cry'd out aloud, *Jesus*, thou *Son of David, Jesus, thou exalted Prince and Saviour, give me Repentance!*" (82–83). Nevertheless, Starr argues that this "Extasy of Joy" is not yet evidence of Crusoe's religious enthusiasm or fanaticism. Starr cites *The Family Instructor*, in which Defoe states his position on spiritual ecstasies, stipulating that conversion might be accompanied by ecstasy and "strong impressions of the Spirit of God" while still being far from "*Enthusiastick*, or affected."[8] In the record of his conversion, Crusoe primarily presents his own words and bodily movements, dwelling minimally on his emotions. Thus, Starr argues, the moderation of James Fraser's gentlemanly memoir is also exhibited in the account of Crusoe's conversion. They are both characterized by "quiet deliberateness," being "analytical, not agitated; reflective, not rapturous" (41).

The element that escapes this analysis is tobacco, which, in the events that directly precipitate the conversion, Crusoe ingests in almost every way possible: through inhaling the smoke, chewing the leaf and swallowing the liquid infusion. In the days prior to his conversion, Crusoe suffers from a debilitating illness that he is at a loss to treat. It occurs to him that native Brazilians use tobacco as a panacea of sorts. Guided by divine providence, he opens one of the chests salvaged from the shipwreck and finds in it a roll of tobacco as well as a Bible: "a Cure, both for Soul and Body" (80).[9] Ignorant of the methods that natives employ with regard to the tobacco, Crusoe experiments with various means. "I first took a Piece of a Leaf, and chew'd it in my Mouth, which indeed at first almost stupify'd my Brain, the Tobacco being green and strong" (80). Afterward, he takes some more tobacco after steeping it in rum, and then forces himself to inhale tobacco smoke for as long as he can stand it.

While under the influence of the tobacco, Crusoe picks up his Bible and attempts to read it, though he is too intoxicated to read for long. The text's repetitive insistence on Crusoe's intoxication bears mention. His brain is "stupify'd" and his head is "disturb'd" and "doz'd." The tobacco-steeped rum that he forces down is so potent he says "it flew up in my Head violently" (80–81). Certainly, Crusoe's illness may make him more susceptible to these effects, but it is clear that the tobacco and rum are altering his consciousness. In this state, he happens upon lines from the Psalms that make an impression on him: "*Call on me in the Day of Trouble, and I will deliver, and thou shalt glorify me*" (81). These words cause him to reflect deeply on the possibility of his deliverance from the island.

As he prepares to go to bed, feeling the soporific effects of the tobacco, Crusoe prays. "I did what I never had done in all my Life, I kneel'd down and pray'd to God to fulfil the Promise to me, that if I call'd upon him in the Day of Trouble, he would deliver me; after my broken and imperfect Prayer was over, I drunk the Rum in which I had steep'd the Tobacco, which was so strong and rank of the Tobacco, that indeed I could scarce get it down; immediately upon this I went to Bed" (81). For the first time, Crusoe prays in this specific manner. The specificity may reside in the kneeling posture or the particular contents of the prayer. It is not the first time that he had appealed to God's mercy.[10] Moreover, the narrator seems to be unsure of what to call it, since he describes a later prayer of repentance, the one delivered in the "Extasy of Joy," as his very first prayer "in the true Sense of the Words" (83). He deems this later prayer true because it is said in the knowledge of human sinfulness and with the hope of redemption. In contrast, the narrator probably understands the bedside prayer for deliverance, said under the influence of tobacco and fear of death, as an inchoate attempt at adequate prayer, preparing the way for the fully cognizant prayer that occurs less than a week later.

Crusoe's proto-prayer may be imperfect for another reason besides his incomplete understanding of his condition. Crusoe kneels down and prays for deliverance. After praying, he takes the rum, which is infused with tobacco. The performance of these actions in sequence mimics the Eucharist. As a principal rite of both the Protestant and Catholic traditions, the Eucharist typically involves a period of prayer during which one prepares oneself to partake in communion.

When ready, one receives the ritual elements, wine and bread, and consumes them. During the sixteenth and seventeenth centuries in England, the rite was a constant source of contention, with dissenters objecting to aspects of its performance in the conforming church, including the use of a common prayer book as opposed to extemporaneous prayer or scripted bodily movements like bowing before the altar and kneeling to receive the bread and wine.[11] The dissenters found these aspects reminiscent of medieval superstition and the doctrine of transubstantiation, according to which the body of Jesus is made present in the wine and bread. In 1623, the church courts in York excommunicated a man for refusing to kneel while receiving communion, demonstrating the seriousness of divergence from ritual prescriptions (Turrell, 286).

The debates surrounding proper performance of the rite intersected with those surrounding the use of tobacco. Almost from the moment it arrived in the Old World, tobacco was implicated in the ongoing polemic against idolatry and illegitimate religion. Marcy Norton shows how sixteenth-century writers associated tobacco with idolatry, thereby affirming the legitimacy of Christian conquest.[12] The use of tobacco in ritual to induce a trance state marked native religion as counterfeit since it relied on this indispensable external and material aid. In seventeenth-century England, Anglican authorities decried the use of tobacco as "barbarous and beastly" while also implicating their religious opponents in Europe. In his "Counterblaste to Tobacco," King James I satirizes Catholic superstition and Puritan self-righteousness in the same breath: "O omnipotent power of Tobacco! And if it could by the smoke thereof chace out devils, as the smoke of Tobias did (which I am sure could smel no stronglier) it would serve for a precious Relicke, both for the superstitious Priests, and the insolent Puritanes, to cast out devils withall."[13] In this document, the use of tobacco, particularly for religious purposes, indicates counterfeit religion both in the uncivilized world and in Christendom.

As demonstrated by the rapid rise of a global tobacco economy in the seventeenth century, not everyone viewed tobacco with the same suspicion. Those in literary circles were particularly fond of the substance, and its popularity had reached a peak by the time of James I's pronouncement. F. W. Fairholt maintains that "the commencement of the seventeenth century was the golden age of tobacco. It was favoured by all, and valued for imputed virtues more than it possessed. It received a large amount of literary notice, larger than ever after fell to its share. Poets were inspired with a desire to sign its praises, and exert their fancy in its honour."[14] The acclaim was not entirely universal, however. Fairholt cites a poem in print from 1669 to 1719 that shows the survival of a more conservative sentiment denouncing smoking as sacrilegious. One stanza reads: "The pipe, that is so foul within, / Shews how man's soul is stain'd with sin, / And then the fire it doth require: / Think of this when you smoke tobacco" (103).

Mounting a spiritual offensive against tobacco consumption was necessary in part because its homologies with communion threatened the sanctity of the rite. European ethnographies long depicted native American tobacco use as an inverted sacrament in which the barbarians communed with the devil instead of God. Norton writes, "The association of tobacco as a diabolical sacrament originated with New World chroniclers' efforts to make sense of native Americans' ritual consumption of tobacco; like the consecration of bread and wine that allowed transubstantiation, shamanic ingestion of tobacco allowed a union with the divine" (248). The anxiety surrounding this proximity between the diabolical and the divine resulted in a 1642 papal bull that prescribed excommunication for anyone taking tobacco within or near a church (232).[15]

The episode in *Robinson Crusoe* extends the parallels between tobacco consumption and Christian communion but without depicting it as an inverted sacrament. The prayer for deliverance is "broken and imperfect," yet it is never repudiated or condemned as sacrilegious. In the aftermath of the prayer and his consumption of the makeshift elements, Crusoe is delivered from his life-threatening illness, suggesting the tacit approval of Providence. In the context of Crusoe's spiritual journey, the tobacco-fueled prayer could be understood as indicating a primitive superstitious stage that the protagonist transcends after his conversion and gradual regeneration. Tracing such a trajectory through the narrative would be too simple, however. In fact, Crusoe never leaves tobacco behind, continuing to cherish his smoking pipe above almost everything else. Tobacco, the sacred substance that catalyzes Crusoe's conversion, persistently reappears in the narrative as a reminder of the material basis of his religion and its dangerous proximity to heathenism.[16]

The preoccupation with material goods and objects in *Robinson Crusoe* has been taken as a mark of the narrative's secularity rather than its potentially transgressive religiosity. Virginia Woolf describes the novel as lacking soul and sublimity where one would expect to find them: "We read, and we are rudely contradicted on every page. There are no sunsets and no sunrises; there is no solitude and no soul. There is, on the contrary, staring us full in the face nothing but a large earthenware pot."[17] Woolf concentrates on an earthen vessel that Crusoe is at pains to manufacture, demonstrating the utter mundanity of this adventure story. There is no solitude on the island in the sense of an existential dread or descent into madness—both of which are rather brought on by evidence of company, the footprint in the sand. There is no soul, Woolf says, because Crusoe considers everything from a commonsense or matter-of-fact perspective, subduing even Providence to the laws of reason. "He is incapable of enthusiasm," Woolf says in a remark that might have pleased Defoe (31). The earthenware pot, as the only marvel in all of the adventures, stands as the symbol of Crusoe's utilitarian perspective.

Against Woolf's hyperbolic assertion that there is nothing but the earthenware pot, Defoe's narrator plainly states that there is both a pot and a pipe. The subject of earthenware first comes up in a discussion of Crusoe's two great wants that he has yet to fulfill, and the context of this discussion shows Crusoe to be capable of a kind of sublimity after all (92). His first want is a pot with which to make broth and stew meat; while such a vessel is not critical to Crusoe's survival, since he has other methods to cook food and store liquids, neither is it an extravagant luxury. Lydia H. Liu explores the significance of Crusoe's experiments with earthenware, arguing that the pot alludes to Chinese porcelain, which Britain was unable to produce at the beginning of the eighteenth century. The account of Crusoe's invention poses the question: "Was porcelain not a *type of earthenware* that a British man could have invented all by himself?"[18] Manufacturing the earthenware pot fulfills a practical purpose, but it also serves a symbolic one, in demonstrating the fantastical autonomy of the English subject.

Crusoe's second want is a pipe for smoking tobacco, which is harder to justify from the point of view of practicality. Yet it is the second vessel that Crusoe dedicates the most effort to making and with which he is most enamored in the end. He remarks on his creation, the design of which he had to invent on his own: "I was never more vain of my own Performance, or more joyful for any thing I found out, than for my being able to make a Tobacco-Pipe. And tho' it was a very ugly clumsy thing, when it was done, and only burnt red like other Earthen Ware, yet as it was hard and firm, and would draw the Smoke, I was exceedingly comforted with it" (122). If the description of the pipe cannot but register as phallic to the modern reader, then the analysis of Woolf and Liu regarding the earthenware pot is even more pertinent with regard to the pipe, which neither explicitly mentions: Crusoe's "fixation on the solidity and earthiness of the pot takes on an aura of fetishism. . . . The pot can thus be read as a fetish, though not a primitive's fetish but a modern man's, because it carries the symbolic burden of human intentionality that threatens to subdue the natural elements to his design" (Liu, 729). Not the pot but the pipe is most appropriately termed a fetish because tobacco and smoke are in fact the ritual elements that accompany Crusoe's religious initiation. In another facsimile of communion, the earthen vessel that draws smoke becomes a sacred implement, destitute of practical value but nevertheless providing "exceeding" comfort. This luxuriant enjoyment of tobacco smoke bears some resemblance to the opulence of Catholic rites involving incense. Regarding this element of excess, Romano Guardini writes that "the offering of incense is a generous and beautiful rite. The bright grains of incense are laid upon the red-hot charcoal, the censer is swung, and the fragrant smoke rises in the clouds. In the rhythm and the sweetness there is a musical quality; and like music also is the entire lack of practical utility: it is a prodigal waste of precious material."[19] For Crusoe, luxuriating in smoke involves the expenditure of time and resources in an activity that does not even benefit from the sanction of institutional religion.

Apart from its earthenware construction, the aesthetic features of Crusoe's tobacco pipe also find parallels in "idolatrous" Chinese culture.[20] In the *Farther Adventures*, Crusoe expresses a general antipathy toward the Chinese, calling them "a contemptible Herd or Crowd of ignorant sordid Slaves, subjected to a Government qualified only to rule such a People" (298).[21] A polemic in the *Serious Reflections*, the final volume of the Crusoe trilogy, denounces the Chinese practice of idol worship in particular, remarking how senseless it is to bow before something "ten thousand Times more disfigured than the Devil."[22] The error consists in paying reverence "not to the Work of Mens Hands only, but the ugliest, basest, frightfullest things that Man could make; Images so far from being lovely and amiable, as in the Nature of Worship is implied, that they are the most detestable and nauseous, even to Nature" (135). The ugliness of the idol, it seems, compounds the sin of idolatry by making it not only irreligious but also unnatural. Even if Crusoe does not exactly prostrate himself before his ugly, clumsy tobacco pipe, his adoration for it is suspect. Despite its deformity, Crusoe's creation remains his most coveted, perhaps for no other reason than that it reifies the religious transports that he first experienced in the events leading up to his conversion.

While Crusoe's most distinctive religious traits persist through his conversion, it nevertheless represents a pivotal moment in his spiritual development. The narrative account provides indications that Crusoe's ecstatic experience has an appreciable impact on his way of life. Following his conversion, Crusoe begins to regulate some of his habits and behaviors in a way that suggests rationalization, thereby bringing him closer to the model of ascetic Protestantism.[23] The changes are intermittent, leading some critics to suggest that Crusoe's wavering, including his ethical failures in dealing with natives and captives, is evidence that his religiosity is shallow and his conversion less than genuine. By contrast, J. Paul Hunter maintains that the inconsistencies in Crusoe's ethical behavior and daily activity should not be received as a lack of seriousness, since his religion is that of the Everyman. Because he is not a saint, he is prone to lapses in judgment and temperament during his spiritual regeneration.[24] Hunter instead argues that the systematizing effect that Crusoe's conversion has on his life is proof enough of his sincerity. During the first year of his stay, Crusoe listlessly moves about on the island. His scavenging attempts are haphazard and mostly unfruitful. The conversion that he undergoes has the effect of imposing some order on his way of life: he consciously (and conscientiously) endeavors to make his "Way of living" as regular as possible, and to this end he divides his time into regular intervals. Hunter suggests that this transformation in Crusoe's character indicates spiritual growth, since the wayward and violent tendencies are turned into peaceful and productive ones (172–175).

The methodical and systematic manner that Crusoe *partially* adopts is indeed that which is propagated by the ascetic ethic of what Weber calls the historically decisive types of Protestantism. The religiously motivated transformation of Crusoe's way of life, if it can be said to have achieved a high level of consistency, would be the strongest argument for his adoption as the mythic progenitor of modern capitalists, since the rationalization of life is crucial to the overcoming of economic traditionalism. Yet if Crusoe rationalizes his life and work only to a limited extent, leaving much of his activity to be directed haphazardly, then the kind of religious experience that he undergoes may not necessarily be aligned with the development of utilitarian individualism or modern capitalism. His experience may very well constitute an obstacle to this development, since an emphasis on religious feeling can tend to vitiate the active asceticism that a rationalized sense of calling requires.

Unlike Weber's typical Puritan, Crusoe is not primarily motivated by an unceasing drive to work hard in his calling in order to testify to his status as one of God's elected; rather, he is motivated by intense but momentary revelations and religious feelings. This is the kind of motivation that Weber subsumes under the type of German Pietism, which, when compared to Calvinism, the type par excellence that contributes to the propagation of the ascetic work ethic, requires less of a systematic approach to daily life.[25] Weber's description of German Pietism, drawn from his reading of seventeenth- and eighteenth-century ecclesiasts Francke, Spener, and Zinzendorf, occupies a marginal position in his larger argument, serving to explain only some relatively small variations in the adoption of capitalist forms in Northern Europe. It is, however, instructive for the analysis of religion in *Robinson Crusoe*; Crusoe, after all, is the son of immigrants from Bremen, a Hanseatic city, and their German name, before it was Anglicized, potentially points to the family's journey toward redemption.[26]

In *The Protestant Ethic*, Weber notes that rationalized capitalism was not the dominant economic ethic of the early modern period. Rather, what prevailed was economic traditionalism, a very strong and rooted predilection. The representatives of this kind of traditionalism were the early modern piece-rate workers who reacted to a pay increase by working less because they would work only as much as they had to in order to maintain their usual way of life (84–85). The ardent defender of economic traditionalism in Defoe's novel is Robinson Crusoe's father, who extolls the virtues of the middle station. The stance represented by the elder Crusoe is essentially what Weber describes as a way of living and working that hews close to common sense, seeing work as the necessary means for obtaining one's wants in this life. The father's inclination toward economic traditionalism, which values abiding in one's station, along with his appeal to the comforts and pleasures of a middle-class way of life, confirms that the religious upbringing in the household was not that of the strict, ascetic Calvinism that Weber judges to be historically decisive. Crusoe's claim that, before his conversion experience, he had never prayed in such a fashion also suggests a laxity in spiritual matters during his youth. The account of Crusoe's conversion and the ecstatic address that is accompanied by emphatic gestures of the body are further indications that his religiosity resembles that of Pietism more than strict Calvinism.[27]

This assessment is consistent with Maximillian E. Novak's argument that Defoe's novel should really be understood as a conservative warning to all Englishmen who, like the young man of York, were tempted to leave their stations in life to pursue extravagant riches. Novak applies the conclusions of both Weber and R. H. Tawney concerning the Lutheran concept of calling to his understanding of Crusoe's character and fatal flaw. The "original sin" of Crusoe is specifically his refusal to stay within his calling, and the adventures amount to a cautionary tale that supplies in vivid detail all the ways in which God punishes those who are not content to make their living as they are meant to make it. This pattern of God-ordained calling and refusal to comply recapitulates Jonah's attempt to flee from God's command to go to Nineveh. Crusoe, Novak says, "is continually running from this world. He views his story as a struggle between his reason, which tells him to follow his calling, and his triumphant passions, which force him to wander."[28] Novak's description of Crusoe struggling to subdue his passions is thus able to account for those inclinations in Crusoe's persona that are opposed to the deliberate pursuit of profit as well as his tendency to engage in risky ventures.

The association of *Robinson Crusoe* with a Lutheran ethic places the novel at a significant remove from modern capitalism. Noting the *anemic* effect that Lutheranism has on the rational organization of work and life, Weber aligns it with traditionalism because the Lutheran idea of calling advocates resignation to one's present state of affairs: "Thus, Luther's conception of the calling remained tied to economic traditionalism. As a divine decree, the calling is something that must be *submitted to*: persons must 'resign' themselves to it" (*Protestant Ethic*, 104). Weber goes on to say that this emphasis on resignation overshadows the active implications of a calling in the world. One's duty is more so to passively resign oneself to a divinely ordained station than to actively perform a task or function as a tool of

God. In the end, Lutheranism "did not involve an ascetic notion of duty. Hence any possibility for a surpassing of the routine morality of daily life was eliminated" (104). Capitalism would have to wait for the arrival of Calvinism, in which could be found a truly active asceticism.[29]

While it is true that, shortly after his conversion, Crusoe makes an orderly division of his time, dedicating portions of it toward utilitarian endeavors, it is equally true that he spends a seemingly inordinate amount of time on unproductive activities. He makes use of certain imaginative reflections to help him fend off discontent (and occasional boredom) with his situation on the island. Thus, he devotes himself to a kind of meditation in which he cultivates feelings of gratitude toward God by imagining how his life could be worse. "I spent whole Hours, I may say whole Days, in representing to myself in the most lively Colours, how I must have acted, if I had got nothing out of the Ship" (111). According to Crusoe's recollection, he goes days at a time doing nothing but contemplating disasters that could have been. This inactivity is the work of imagination and fictional representation rather than work that garners a profit through toil. The liveliness of Crusoe's imagination is reprised at the beginning of *The Farther Adventures*, where he loses himself in reveries about the island from which he was rescued. Crusoe recounts, "But this I know, that my Imagination worked up to such a Height, and brought me into such Extasies of Vapours, or what else I may call it, that I actually suppos'd myself upon the Spot, at my old Castle behind the Trees" (3).

The picture of Crusoe spending entire days imaginatively ruminating on the disasters that might have befallen him is evidently a departure from Weber's description of the anxious Calvinist tirelessly applying himself to a worldly calling in order to secure the certainty of his salvation. Moreover, it differs from the attitude of watchful suspicion over one's naturally wayward thoughts that the Puritan divine Richard Baxter imparts to his flock. Weber, well versed in the seventeenth-century nonconformist's writings, explains that Baxter clearly devalues meditation in comparison to work in the world. Weber writes, "Because every hour not spent at work is an hour lost in service to God's greater glory, according to Baxter, time is infinitely valuable. Thus, inactive contemplation is without value and in the end explicitly condemned, at least if it occurs at the expense of work in a calling, for it pleases God less than the active implementation of His will in a calling" (*Protestant Ethic*, 160). In a footnote, Weber remarks that it is on this point that Puritanism differs sharply from Pietism, since for the latter the valuations are reversed, such that one's dedication to a worldly calling is reprehensible whenever it distracts one from God (373).[30] Crusoe evidently values inactive contemplation very highly, placing him at odds with the tenets of Puritanism, or English Calvinism, but in league with the Pietists, according to Weber's typology.[31]

In short, Crusoe shows himself to be more contemplative than diligent, more imaginative than vigilant, and more oriented toward ecstatic feeling than purposeful labor. Unlike the Puritan whose work in a calling is directed toward a transcendental end, Crusoe generally labors in order to satisfy a present need. He completely fills up his hours so as not to let them go to waste, yet he seldom has a consistent rationale for his choice of occupation. He illustrates how far he is from seeing the earthly realm as the proper arena of God-willed action when he proclaims, "I look'd now upon the World as a Thing remote, which I had nothing to do with, no Expectation from, and indeed no Desires about" (109). By his fourth year on the island, he has come to recognize that its natural resources are enough to supply him with each of his wants, so he no longer desires to increase his store by producing more corn or lumber than he can use at any given moment (110).

These contrasts should be understood not as categorical but as representing tendencies that, taken together, constitute distinct attitudes toward work and life in the world. That much of the difference between the exemplary teaching of Baxter and the novice Crusoe is a matter of degree and consistency in no way invalidates the conclusions drawn from such a comparison. Indeed, Weber differentiates between the offshoots of Calvinism precisely on the basis of the consistency with which they brought about a systematic attitude toward work as a calling. Thus, he considers Pietism, whose traits Crusoe seems to carry to a large extent, "a vacillation and instability in regard to the religious anchoring of its asceticism. The anchoring of Pietism in asceticism is considerably weaker than the iron-clad consistency of Calvinism's grounding in asceticism" (*Protestant Ethic*, 144). While Hunter attributes the vacillation in Crusoe's religious disciplining of his life to his everyman disposition, this tendency to waver finds an alternative explanation in the type of religiosity Crusoe expresses, namely one in which feelings of ecstasy, rather than public testimony and solemn acknowledgment of God's sovereignty, form the basis of one's conversion. The ethic associated with this religiosity has a weaker, though not altogether insignificant, impact on the rationalization of work and life. Furthermore, the asceticism that it demands is less stringent, allowing Crusoe to enjoy, at various reprieves, the pleasures of culinary delicacies and idle contemplation.

Through a consideration of Crusoe's religious and economic ethic starting from his prodigal flight from patrimony through to his ritualized religious activity on the island, we arrive at the conclusion that Defoe's protagonist is improperly held to be a Puritan ascetic and the prototype of the modern capitalist. The most that can be said for Robinson Crusoe as "economic man" is that he undergoes an incomplete apprenticeship in asceticism and the rational organization of work while he is on the island. Even so, he shows too much vacillation in this regard to be positively identified as a carrier of the work ethic that is inextricably tied to the expansion of capitalism.

The mischaracterization of Crusoe as a harbinger of modern capitalism may be due in part to a reductive understanding of Western capitalism in its historical specificity. Weber remarks that the form that capitalism has taken in the modern world must not be taken as the simple product of an acquisitive drive akin to greed or what was polemicized as Mammonism in the Middle Ages, since this drive is not unique to modernity. He makes this point as forcefully as he can, bringing apparent antinomies together to clarify the connection between them: "This naive manner of conceptualizing capitalism by reference to a 'pursuit of gain' must be relegated to the kindergarten of cultural history methodology and abandoned once and for all. A fully unconstrained compulsion to acquire goods cannot be understood as synonymous with capitalism, and even less as its 'spirit.' On the contrary, capitalism *can* be identical with the *taming* of this irrational motivation, or at least with its rational tempering" (*Protestant Ethic*, 237).[32] In effect, modern capitalism must be recognized as being preceded and conditioned by an ethic that curtails spontaneous impulses, bringing them to heel under a regime that makes hard work in one's worldly calling the highest of spiritual obligations. When readers of *Robinson Crusoe* heed this description of modern capitalism, they may quickly discover the mass of untamed, untempered motivations upon which the novel's protagonist acts, even following his dramatic conversion on the island. A pious convert of a contemplative-ecstatic brand of religion as well as an adventurer whose pattern of indiscretions does not constitute a complete reversal of his father's economic traditionalism, Crusoe makes small inroads toward a rationalized work ethic during his time on the island, but the improvised religion he adopts does not provide him a foundation firm enough to make his habits permanent. The picture of Crusoe as the isolated economic man is one that readers inherit from the philosophers and economists since Rousseau, who appropriated a sliver of the text as a model for individualism.[33] This limited picture obscures from view all of the ways in which Crusoe's actions resist the utilitarian interpretation. His ritual use of tobacco and penchant for inactive contemplation are not the exception but the rule of his behavior, before and after his conversion.

NOTES

1. Ian Watt aligns himself with Karl Marx and Charles Gildon in this view. Ian Watt, *The Rise of the Novel: Studies in Defoe, Richardson, and Fielding* (Berkeley: University of California Press, 1957), 79–81. More recently, Hans Turley takes a nuanced approach, arguing that Crusoe's religion is significant in its complicity with his capitalist and imperialist endeavors. Claims that "Crusoe evangelizes in order to profit" and "English Protestantism

cannot be separated from a desire for profit—spiritual or economic" are, however, not followed by an examination of the specifically religious sources of this insatiable desire (180, 186). Hans Turley, "Protestant Evangelicalism, British Imperialism, and Crusonian Identity," in *A New Imperial History: Culture, Identity, and Modernity in Britain and the Empire, 1660–1840*, ed. Kathleen Wilson (Cambridge: Cambridge University Press, 2004), 176–193.

2. J. Paul Hunter's examination of religious allegory in the novel remains the most authoritative. Hunter is able to explain some but perhaps not all of Crusoe's aberrant behavior as part of the process of his spiritual regeneration. J. Paul Hunter, *The Reluctant Pilgrim: Defoe's Emblematic Method and Quest for Form in Robinson Crusoe* (Baltimore: Johns Hopkins University Press, 1966), 175–184.
3. Watt and Maximillian Novak both engage significantly with Weber in their readings of *Robinson Crusoe*. Maximillian Novak, *Economics and the Fiction of Daniel Defoe* (Berkeley: University of California Press, 1962). Michael McKeon notes the tendency for materialist and spiritual readings of *Robinson Crusoe* to mutually exclude each other. Michael McKeon, *The Origins of the English Novel, 1600–1740* (Baltimore: Johns Hopkins University Press, 1987), 319. To present a less extreme interpretation, McKeon argues that Defoe's narrative mediates the contradictions inherent to a secularizing but still religious world view (332–333). Against this "middle ground" approach, John Richetti sees the narrative definitively moving from religious reverence to secular empowerment. John Richetti, "Secular Crusoe: The Reluctant Pilgrim Re-visited," in *Eighteenth-Century Genre and Culture: Serious Reflections on Occasional Forms*, ed. Dennis Todd and Cynthia Wall (Cranbury: Associated University Presses, 2001), 58–78, 58–59.
4. Max Weber, "The Social Psychology of the World Religions," in *From Max Weber: Essays in Sociology*, ed. H. H. Gerth and C. Wright Mills (New York: Oxford University Press, 1946), 267–301, 268–270. Weber's *Protestant Ethic* was meant as a corrective to "naïve historical materialism." Max Weber, *The Protestant Ethic and the Spirit of Capitalism*, trans. Stephen Kalberg (New York: Oxford University Press, 2011), 82. For this precise reason, it errs on the side of idealist explanations of historical phenomena (cf. 178–179).
5. Including Weber's own. Manuel Schonhorn's article admirably emphasizes Weber's insight regarding the significance of ascetic restraint for the development of capitalism. Manuel Schonhorn, "Weber, Watt, and Restraint: Robinson Crusoe and the Critical Tradition," in *Approaches to Teaching Defoe's Robinson Crusoe*, ed. Maximillian E. Novak and Carl Fisher (New York: Modern Language Association of America, 2005), 55–60. Schonhorn's larger point that "Defoe's narrative is subordinated to the larger perspective of a whole life, and this perspective is integrated into an evangelical frame that gives meaning and order to that experience" may be taking for granted how integral and coherent Crusoe's religious development is, overlooking his enduring lack of restraint and adventurous disposition (59).
6. G. A. Starr, *Defoe and Spiritual Autobiography* (New York: Gordian Press, 1971), 39.
7. D. Bruce Hindmarsh, *The Evangelical Conversion Narration* (Oxford: Oxford University Press, 2005), 44.
8. Daniel Defoe, *The Family Instructor* (London: S. Wright, 1715), 227–228.
9. I retain the chiastic construction of Defoe's phrase: "for in this Chest I found a Cure, both for Soul and Body, I open'd the Chest, and found what I look'd for, *viz.* the Tobacco; and as the few Books, I had sav'd, lay there too, I took out one of the Bibles which I mention'd before" (80).
10. After setting out from Hull, Crusoe's ship is caught in a storm. Crusoe "made many Vows and Resolutions, that if it would please God here to spare my Life this one Voyage, if ever I got once my Foot upon dry Land again, I would go directly home to my Father" (9).
11. James F. Turrell, "Anglican Liturgical Practices," in *A Companion to the Eucharist in the Reformation*, ed. Lee Palmer Wandel (Leiden: Brill, 2014), 273–292, 282–283.

12. Marcy Norton, *Sacred Gifts, Profane Pleasures: A History of Tobacco and Chocolate in the Atlantic World* (Ithaca, NY: Cornell University Press, 2008), 56.
13. King James I, *A Counterblaste to Tobacco* (1604).
14. F. W. Fairholt, *Tobacco; Its History and Associations; Including an Account of the Plant and Its Manufacture; with Its Mode of Use in All Ages and Countries* (London: Chapman & Hall, 1859), 63.
15. In 1690, Pope Innocent XII again enacted excommunication for takers of snuff or tobacco in St. Peter's Basilica (Fairholt, *Tobacco*, 78).
16. As Blackburn notes, Crusoe engages in another approximation of communion when he annually commemorates his arrival on the island with prayer and fasting followed by a meal of biscuit cake and grapes (103). Timothy C. Blackburn, "Friday's Religion," *Eighteenth-Century Studies* 18, no. 3 (1985): 360–382, 377. For Blackburn, Crusoe's sparse liturgy devoid of any reference to transubstantiation reflects a revised deism and a civil religion founded on the worship of power (381–382). Analysis of Crusoe's tobacco rites sheds light on the more baroque aspects of his religion.
17. Virginia Woolf, *The Second Common Reader* (1932; repr., San Diego: Harcourt, 1986), 31.
18. Lydia H. Liu, "Robinson Crusoe's Earthenware Pot," *Critical Inquiry* 25 (1999): 728–757, 738.
19. Romano Guardini, *Sacred Signs* (St. Louis: Pio Decimo Press, 1955).
20. Swetha Regunathan notes the semantic resonance between "idol" and "idle" in an article on Crusoe's polemic against China. The earthenware pipe combines idolatry with idleness, if the unproductive activity of smoking is also irreligious. Swetha Regunathan, "An Incongruous Monster: Idolatrous Aesthetics in Crusoe's China," *Digital Defoe: Studies in Defoe & His Contemporaries* 5 (2013): 45–64, 45–47.
21. Daniel Defoe, *The Farther Adventures of Robinson Crusoe* (London: W. Taylor, 1719), 298.
22. Daniel Defoe, *Serious Reflections during the Life and Surprising Adventures of Robinson Crusoe* (London: W. Taylor, 1720), 137.
23. The process that Weber calls rationalization of life occurs when all of one's daily activity becomes systematically oriented toward a goal, namely the attainment of a sacred value. "In general, all kinds of practical ethics that are systematically and unambiguously oriented to fixed goals of salvation are 'rational'" ("Social Psychology of World Religions," 294).
24. Hunter, *Reluctant Pilgrim*, 176.
25. The reason that Calvinism implies such strong systematization whereas Pietism does not "is that the inner motive [in Calvinism], deriving from the thought of having to testify over and over again from the beginning to a state of grace that gives security for an eternal *future*, has in Pietism been redirected onto the *present* as a result of its orientation to the believer's feelings" (Weber, *Protestant Ethic*, 144).
26. Robert W. Ayers, "*Robinson Crusoe*: 'Allusive Allegorick History,'" *PMLA* 82 (1967): 399–407, 405.
27. The dual typology that is most proper to Defoe's text is, of course, Puritan and Anglican. Hunter argues that Defoe's conciliatory tone in *The Family Instructor*, designed to appeal both to dissenters and the Church of England, is also the one he takes in *Robinson Crusoe* (176). This would not preclude that Defoe's charting out of a third way might take him through unexpected territory. Cf. Edward Dowden, *Puritan and Anglican* (London: Kegan Paul, Trench Trubner, 1900). Dowden was an important resource that informed Weber's conception of Puritanism. Peter Ghosh notes that Dowden's books are among the most often cited secondary sources in *The Protestant Ethic*. Peter Ghosh, "Max Weber's Idea of 'Puritanism': A Case Study in the Empirical Construction of the Protestant Ethic," *History of European Ideas* 29, no. 2 (2003): 183–221, 204.
28. Maximillian Novak, "Robinson Crusoe's Original Sin," *Studies in English Literature, 1500–1900* 1, no. 3 (1961): 19–29, 29.

29. Cf. Weber, *Protestant Ethic*, 136.
30. Weber overstates the case with regard to the condemnation of inactive contemplation, which, in Baxter at least, is held in relatively high esteem. In fact, a closer look at Baxter's work reveals that Weber's portrayal of it generally exaggerates the importance of turning a profit and plays down the religious motivations that always constitute the basis for action. In *A Christian Directory*, Baxter writes that for those who are overly concerned with business, "the world devoureth all the time almost that God and their souls should have; it will not give them leave to pray, or read, or meditate, or discourse of holy things: even when they seem to be praying, or hearing the word of God, the world is in their thoughts" (245). However, a certain amount of leeway should be permitted Weber in his representation of Puritan teaching, since his object is to locate the practical effects it had on the lives of congregants. Moreover, Weber's argument is logically consistent in its assessment of the different points of emphasis in Puritanism and Pietism as ideal types. Richard Baxter, *The Practical Works of Richard Baxter* (London: George Virtue, 1846).
31. Defoe himself practiced meditative reflections as a young man, as evidenced by his verse *Meditations*. Andrew M. Wilkinson, "The 'Meditations' of Daniel Defoe," *Modern Language Review* 46, nos. 3/4 (1951): 349–354. Wilkinson argues that Defoe's religious convictions evolved over time, moving from distrust to reverence of reason.
32. Schonhorn writes that Weber's insight regarding asceticism and capitalism is "only a passing thought" (58). In fact, Weber elaborates on this thought not only in the "Prefatory Remarks to Collected Essays in the Sociology of Religion," but also in the chapter of *The Protestant Ethic* on "Asceticism and the Spirit of Capitalism" (esp. 169–170), in *The Sociology of Religion* (esp. 182–183, 218–222, 269), and elsewhere. Whenever Weber uses the term "inner-worldly asceticism" (*innerweltliche Askese*), he is referring to the rational tempering of drives that is the precondition for modern capitalism. Max Weber, *The Sociology of Religion*, trans. Talcott Parsons (Boston: Beacon, 1963).
33. The tutor in *Emile* assigns only the portion of the novel dealing with Crusoe's life on the island to his pupil. Jean-Jacques Rousseau, *Emile, or On Education*, trans. Allan Bloom (New York: Basic Books, 1979), 184–185. In practice, the novel is only good for getting the pupil to imagine being cut off from society. Particularities of place and person are not only irrelevant but to be excised.

6

TAKEN BY STORM

Robinson Crusoe and Aqueous Violence

Jeremy Chow

> Of all Objects that I have ever seen, there is none which affects my Imagination so much as the Sea or Ocean. I cannot see the Heavings of this prodigious Bulk of Waters, even in a Calm, without a very pleasing Astonishment; but when it is worked up in a Tempest, so that the Horizon on every side is nothing but foaming Billows and floating Mountains, it is impossible to describe the agreeable Horrour that rises from such a Prospect.
>
> —*Spectator*, no. 489 (September 20, 1712)

In his journalistic *The Storm: or, A Collection of the Most Remarkable Casualties and Disasters Which Happen'd in the Late Dreadful Tempest, Both by Sea and Land* (1704), Daniel Defoe writes, "Histories are full of Instances of violent Tempests and Storms in sundry particular Places."[1] In a sort of self-fulfilling prophecy, *Robinson Crusoe*, published fifteen years after *The Storm*, encapsulates one such history. By focusing on "Instances of violent Tempests and Storms," this chapter embarks on an ecocritical reading of the novel, one that attempts to locate the distortions beget by Crusoe's tumultuous relationships with the sea and the inescapable storms. I do not use these two words or entities interchangeably, but as Crusoe realizes, the storms are contingent on the sea, and the sea's violent capacities are mediated and amplified by the recurrence of storms. I will characterize them, like Crusoe, as violent: "The Storm was so violent, I saw what is not often seen." Violence, visuality, the limits of the imagination, and the oceanic often go hand in hand in the novel, and I attempt here to understand their repeated interconnection. Eight storms punctuate the novel, each besetting our protagonist in new, unwieldy ways, and by patterning the occurrence, recurrence, and manifestation of these storms, I emphasize the violent relationality that Crusoe shares with these environmental inter-actors. In conversation with Christopher

Loar, my use of violence acknowledges the matrix of violent relations that permeate *Robinson Crusoe,* but extends that matrix to incorporate the nonhuman sea rather than just violence among humans.[2] Whereas Loar unpacks the technologies of violence that reflect an imperial political agenda, I seek to redirect our attention away from anthropocentric violence toward nonhuman violence. The novel, as I explore below, is not exclusively about violence between human actors, nor is the violence that human actors exhibit Crusoe's greatest fear.

This chapter exemplifies an investigation that complements the emerging field of the blue humanities—a call to humanities scholars to invoke, interpret, and ascertain the role that the ocean plays in our respective fields of study—and grounds it within eighteenth-century studies.[3] I emphasize the multiplicity and conjunction of the sea and storms so as to specifically conceptualize what I call "aqueous violence," a notion that locates violent nautical entanglements and repositions depictions of violence as one-sidedly anthropocentric. That is, I seek to avoid the fallacy that only humans can impart violent actions on the environment. The nonhuman can, of course, fight back. In concert with Stacy Alaimo's discussion of oceanic new materialisms in "States of Suspension: Trans-corporeality at Sea," I envision the interwoven and assembled nature of humans, nonhumans, and environmental interactors, while recasting these critical issues in Defoe's novel.[4] This chapter revamps the notion that a trans-corporeal state and human-nonhuman assemblage must somehow always be generative or welcomed. This is not the case for Crusoe and his oceanic interlocutors. Those familiar with tempests, hurricanes, typhoons, and extratropical cyclones (the nor'easter, for example) are well-versed in the ramifications of aqueous and environmental violence. Aqueous violence as a concept then considers how the physical, affective, and emotional intensities of violence become entangled with, within, and around water. To read aqueous violence within *Crusoe* is to read the oceanic fears, horrors, and scars that become marked on Crusoe's body and mind, which he ironically and repeatedly risks precisely so that he can escape aqueous threats.

The concept of aqueous violence may initially prompt incredulity, but as Rob Nixon's *Slow Violence* demonstrates, we need new ways of thinking about the relationship between violence and environment. Nixon's titular concept, "slow violence," encompasses "a violence that occurs gradually and out of sight, a violence of delayed destruction that is dispersed across time and space, an attritional violence that is typically not viewed as violence at all."[5] My use of aqueous violence is not a regurgitation of Nixon's—I, for example, do not emphasize the global or temporal displacements here—and yet aqueous violence does occur on the fringes of the novel and is not viewed as a typical form of violence by the majority of readers. The consequences of aqueous violence reframe and trouble Crusoe's sociality.

His violent experiences with the sea and the sea's storms reshape his relationship with self and human other and instill a new mode of being: one in which violent relationality is requisite. Aqueous violence is then a hermeneutic that illuminates the sea's capacity to segregate Crusoe from the boundaries of human sociality—that is, render Crusoe bereft of family, romance, and companionship.

I trace the extent of aqueous violence even further by contending that the systems of violence within the novel are deeply interconnected. In other words, violence is *contagious.* I do not use this word strictly metaphorically, and I do not intend to evacuate it from the sociomedical contexts, specifically the twentieth century's bacteriology with which it is most associated, or in the age of COVID-19 within which I author this. Violence is not a disease in the same way that most contagious entities are, but violence is catching, often retaliatory, and deeply embodied. For example, as Frantz Fanon insists in *The Wretched of the Earth*—where Crusoe and Friday are foundational examples—the process of colonization is an enactment of violence that must be radically combated with an equal if not greater violence so as to dispel the colonial legacy and stronghold on the minds of those subjected to colonization.[6] Fanon emphasizes the contagious nature of violence in the colonial sphere. Addressing the saturation of contagion discourses more contemporarily, Priscilla Wald, Nancy Tomes, and Lisa Lynch suggest that culture and contagion lexically operate as interchangeable entities; one can stand in for another to note exchange, contact, and the entanglement of bodies.[7] In *Robinson Crusoe,* we witness both a culture and a contagion of violence, and I pinpoint the sea as a violent entity, one that Crusoe must reckon with and a site that serves as a didactic reminder.[8] Crusoe's exercise of violence against the cannibals, I offer, stems from his earlier experiences with a violent sea, and his attempts to induce annihilation are echoes of violent oceanic experiences.

Considering the sea an actor is not merely anthropomorphism. As Bruno Latour notes, "Instead of always pointing out the danger of 'anthropomorphizing' natural entities, we should be just as wary of avoiding the oddity of 'phusimorphizing' them, that is, of giving them the shape of objects defined only by their causal antecedents."[9] He later contends that the problem with anthropomorphism or phusimorphism is not the prefix, it is the suffix: "morph." Attending to the semiotic rather than the ontological, Latour lucidly contends that morphism (shape and form of subjects and deemed objects) "*is a property of the world itself* and not only a feature of the language *about* the world."[10] I read Latour's invocation in mode with new materialisms, an approach that similarly realizes the potentiality of the nonhuman, and an intent to register the types of agencies, mobilities, and abilities of the nonhuman. Like Laura Brown in chapter 4 of this collection, I invoke a new materialisms approach; my new materialist bent seeks to access Crusoe's narration of the sea and its portent on the human. Diana Coole and Samantha Frost nicely sum up this vibrant field: "New Materialists emphasize the productivity and resilience of matter. Their wager is to give materiality its due, alert to the myriad ways in which matter is both self-constituting and invested with—and reconfigured by—intersubjective interventions that have their own quotient for materiality."[11] It is important, however, to disentangle the muddied perspective that new materialisms as an epistemology must necessarily import intent, cognition, *and* agency, which is to say that the "new" materiality must somehow embody all three. As Crusoe's narrative reveals, the ocean's waves seek to "swallow him up" thus reinforcing readings of intent and agency—the ocean intends to reclaim him—but neither the novel nor I envision aqueous sites or the storms as possessing cognition. As a central contention, the ocean need not have cognition in order to possess agency. Agentive possibility is not de facto a result of cognitive processing, which may very well reinforce anthropocentric views of and projections upon the nonhuman.[12] An oceanic new materialism, like the one this chapter offers, seeks to grapple with how the idea of an oceanic intent, registered by Crusoe's narrative, can avail different agencies (antagonistic ones, as demonstrated by my invocation of violence) that are not beholden to the cognitive. The fact that Crusoe envisions the sea's intent and narrates the agentive sea enacting violence lies at the core of being "taken by storm" in *Robinson Crusoe.*

On the evening of November 26, 1703, a category 3 hurricane (by today's meteorological standards) laid waste to London. With wind speeds of 100 to 140 miles per hour, the storm destroyed roofs, homes, and retaining walls and uprooted trees. The storm remains by historian Richard Hamblyn's assessment: "The worst in British history."[13] Eight thousand people perished, the majority of them sailors. Comparatively, Hurricane Jeanne, also a category 3 storm, ravaged the Caribbean and U.S. eastern seaboard in September 2004 and was responsible for three thousand deaths. For the 1703 storm, recovery would take years, but the trauma lingered. In 1710, some seven years after the storm, Queen Anne was still responding to financial pleas from widows whose sons and husbands were lost. The storm, Robert Markley argues, "reveals the complex ways in which our understanding of climate—in the twenty-first century as well as the eighteenth—both shapes and is shaped by a range of ecological, socioeconomic, and metaphysical values and assumptions."[14] Defoe's repurposing of the sea storms, by extension then, continues this coming to terms with climate and its intense realities.

Illustrations of The Storm—capital T, capital S—like the 1703 engraving depicted in figure 6.1, *England's Great Loss*, reverberated throughout early eighteenth-century popular culture as a result of what one survivor called, "A Prodigious damage to almost all sorts of People."[15]

Figure 6.1. Engraving of the Great Storm, November 26, 1703.

As the image emblematizes, we see a fleet of ships waylaid by the engulfing waves—a realization that is captivating for Defoe and employed throughout *Robinson Crusoe*—the Union Jack shredded by the winds yet still held steadfast, as ships and human bodies are relegated to an aqueous abyss. The humans are microscopic as they seek refuge on a lone rock with the undulating gyrus-like waves at their heels. Contemporaneous with this artistic rendering, popular literary documents like Defoe's periodical-based *The Storm* extended the fascination with this calamitous phenomenon. Undergirding the vast majority of these discussions was the immediacy of a religio-cultural need to expiate and an insistence upon humility; for many, the storm had been sent by God as a reminder to atone for wickedness. This gesture is felt by the epigraph to *The Storm*, which features an excerpt from the book of Nahum, a section of the Tanakh: "The Lord hath his way in the Whirlwind, and in the Storm, and the Clouds are dust of his Feet—." Such a sentiment is further echoed by *A Wonderful History of All the Storms, Hurricanes, and Earthquakes, &c That Have Happen'd in England for above 500 Years Past* wherein the anonymous author reminds readers, "Let us take these Omens as a fair warning, and consider how many Calamities have already ensued upon them, how

Plagues, Pestilence, and Famine want on his Commands to overthrow and devastate all that obstinately contend against him."[16] Four-years after the publication of *The Storm*, another Defoe-attributed work, *An Elegy on the Author of the True-Born-English-Man with an Essay on the Late Storm* (1708), dramatically describes the storm in heroic couplets:

It [The Storm] shook the Walls of Flesh as well as Stone,
And ruffl'd all the Nation. . . .
And Storms grew high within, as they grew high without
Flaming Meteors fill'd the Air,
But Asgil miss'd his Fiery Chariot there;
Recall'd his black blashpheming breath,
And trembling paid his homage unto Death,
Terror appear'd in every Face,
Even Vile Blackbourn felt some Shocks of Grace.[17]

The storm had taken hold of the popular imagination, and it was impossible to relinquish. As with *A Wonderful History,* Defoe's *The Storm* was published only a month after the catastrophe. But what separates *The Storm* is that Defoe solicited correspondence for first-person accounts of the near apocalypse. Some particularly graphic illustrations from the collection detail lives dashed out by falling chimneys and roof tiles; churches decimated and turrets found in counties over; and a mostly uncorroborated earthquake that seems to have followed the storm, inciting eschatological fear. In Defoe's words, "In short, Horror and Confusion seiz'd upon all, whether on Shore or at Sea: No Pen can describe it, no Tongue can express it, no Thought can conceive it."[18]

Within the past century, climate scientists and environmental historians have pinpointed the likely cause of this storm and others like it commemorated by countless early modern and eighteenth-century literatures: the Little Ice Age. Starting in the sixteenth century and ending around the middle of the nineteenth century, the Little Ice Age was a period of cooling, which troubled global transport and trade (especially to the north), induced famines, and introduced frightening weather phenomena. The Little Ice Age situated the Global North in the throes of climatological and environmental upheaval. As Defoe's *The Storm* and *Robinson Crusoe* model, eighteenth-century literatures are preoccupied with the storm, the sea, and the meeting of the two. Markley notes, "Defoe is very much a writer intent on describing the effects of the volatile climatic conditions that prevailed in northwest Europe during the Little Ice Age."[19] But because environmental factors are often aspects of setting, they are relegated to the backburner of literary criticism. Early modern and eighteenth-century texts—Shakespeare's *The Tempest*, *Pericles*, *Twelfth Night*, and *The Winter's Tale*, John Donne's "The Storm," and William Diaper's *Nereides; or, Sea-Eclogues*, to name only a few (there are countless more)—emphasize that the sea does, in fact, do something. The storm, likewise, does something. This essay homes in on those doings and somethings.

Like survivors of the 1703 storm who justify the disaster as a result of human sinfulness, many have read *Robinson Crusoe* and the storms therein as indicative of a providential reckoning, positioning the roles of religion and atonement as central to understanding the novel. I am neither interested nor invested in these readings, not only because they wholly allegorize Crusoe's experiences as some metonymic reiteration of Bunyan's *Pilgrim's Progress*,[20] but also because these perspectives place less weight in an emerging Enlightenment science that might realize the potentially for materiality and nonhuman actors. Jan Golinski illustrates the changing perspectives on eighteenth-century environmental phenomenon and the accompanying science that set out to explain it: "Their [British intellectuals of the time] consciousness of their climate reflected back to them an image of the society they inhabited . . . a culture that embraced science and technology while still exhibiting vestiges of magical thinking."[21] While the preface to *A Wonderful History of All the Storms, Hurricanes, and Earthquakes* offers a religious appeal, the body of the text provides scientific rationale for "the Cause of Winds and Stormy Tempests."

> Indeed the Winds how violently and stormy soever they are, are nothing else but the Air moved and driven with a more sudden and Tempestuous Motion, being pressed forward according as the Causes are great or less, composed of a Multitude of Early and Watery Atomes, that rushing upon one another, press with such Weight and Strength, that they man times bear down trees, Buildings and other weighty things before them. . . . Beating and bounding with strong concussions on the higher parts of the Earth, till driving to the lower they rush with impetuous Fury to gain a larger space. . . . And this is when we say A storm has spent its fury.[22]

As this suggests, an epistemological transformation was under way and foundational in establishing Enlightenment thought, which, in addition to setting the stage for myriad innovations, reoriented a focus on materiality and embodiment. This, of course, included the sea and other environments.

Defoe does not provide rationale for the climactic calamities that Crusoe experiences, but he does emphasize that environmental disasters, like sea storms, usher in violent distortions. Like the other seven storms that snake their way into *Robinson Crusoe*, the first storm is a breathless experience:

> The Ship was sooner gotten out of the Humber, but the Wind began to blow, and the Waves to rise in a most frightful manner: and as I had never been at Sea before, I was most inexpressibily sick in Body, and terrify'd

> in Mind: I began now to seriously reflect upon what I had done, and how justly I was overtaken by the Judgment of Heaven for my wicked leaving my Father's House, and abandoning Duty; all the good Counsel of my Parents, my Father's tears and my Mother's Entreaties came now fresh into my Mind, and my Conscience, which was not yet come to the Pitch of Hardness to which it has been since reproach'd me with the Contempt of Advice, and the Breach of my Duty to God. (9)

Crusoe's rambling here—it is only one sentence—epitomizes how the novel situates the storm as an experience of nature that is frantic and frenzied, despite the serious reflection that accompanies his retrospectively meditative narration. P. N. Furbank and W. R. Owens argue that Defoe's formal and narratological structures are deliberate; in other words, his prose is intentional and purposeful.[23] The narrative illustration of the storm emphasizes this deliberateness. The relentlessness of the long sentence seems to mirror the unceasing nature of the sea's waves. For Crusoe, the enduring waves extend his uncertainty about maritime life and travel and push him deeper and deeper into melancholic self-reflection. We, as readers, are brought along on this turbulent journey. Cynthia Wall notes that Defoe's narrative maintains a strange penchant: not only do the texts become a didactic lesson in reading semaphores, but "he re-enacts his behaviour in his storytelling; his method of storytelling explains his behaviour."[24] Wall, here, specifically refers to H. F., the narrator of *Journal of a Plague Year*, but her observation, I find, is equally appropriate to *Crusoe*. The method of storytelling describes the sea's behavior. The sea's behavior impels storytelling. And for those who opt to read this passage aloud, it is a tiring feat, which doubles down on the relentlessness of this experience. Despite the colons, semicolons, and commas, one gasps for breath while reading it, which metacognizes the experience of storm that so much troubles Crusoe. We experience the storm in situ. Contributors to *The Storm* similarly locate this breathlessness: "The Hurricane did not abate, but rather seemed to gather Strength. For Words were no sooner uttered, but they were carried away by the Wind, so that although those upon Deck spoke loud and close to one another, yet they could not often distinguish what was said; and when they opened their mouths, their Breath was almost taken away."[25] In reading Crusoe's first storm experience aloud, we don a Crusoe mask, feel the anxiety, and attempt to gather ourselves in moments of maelstrom.

Crusoe's description of being "most inexpressibily sick in Body, and terrify'd in Mind" during the first storm typifies the purgative distortions that he continues to encounter with each subsequent storm and sea voyage. The sea and storms offer varieties of distortion that test the limits of the body and Crusoe's survival. In the shift from the seventeenth to the eighteenth century, with the onset of the

Little Ice Age and the development of Defoe's career as a writer, relationships with the ocean were vitally shifting from spaces of wild abandon, to territories that facilitated and beset colonial endeavors. At the end of the eighteenth century these sentiments would be superseded by appreciation of the ocean as a manifestation of the Sublime. By Alain Corbin's assessment, prior to the eighteenth century, the sea was characterized as "demonic": a space ruled by "diabolical powers" and thus home to monsters plenty.[26] It is this depiction of the sea as "horrific" that Siobhan Carroll taps into by offering the eighteenth-century sea as an "atopia," a term she coins to signify "'real' natural regions falling within the theoretic scope of contemporary human mobility, which, because of their intangibility, inhospitality, or inaccessibility, cannot be converted into the locations of affective habitation known as 'place.'"[27] The sea as imagined atopia is a place that resonates with Crusoe's narrative: a place of inhospitality and lawlessness that both confounds and besets him.

While the winds are turbulent and frightening, it is the sea and rain in conjunction with the wind that truly foment cataclysmic destruction. As Anthony van Lauwenhoek writes to Defoe, as editor of *The Storm*, "Now, if we consider, what a quantity of Sea-water is spread all over the Country by such a terrible Storm, and consequently, how greatly impregnated the Air is with the same; we ought not to wonder, that such a quantity of Water, being moved with so great a force, should do so much mischief to Chimneys, tops of Houses, &c. not to mention the Damages at Sea."[28] A translation of this in *Robinson Crusoe* might look like Crusoe's admission that "I saw the Sea come after me as high as a great Hill, and as *furious as an Enemy* which I had no Means or Strength to contend with" (39, emphasis added). For Crusoe, the sea and subsequent storms repeatedly act upon him like an enemy and such an indictment engenders his convoluted, violent relationship with the sea.

The novel's first pages emphasize the sea's lure, though unlike Corbin's assessment, Crusoe's longing for the sea is predicated on dispossession, loss, and isolationism. Crusoe confesses, "I would be satisfied with nothing but going to Sea, and my Inclination to this led me so strongly against the Will, nay the Commands of my Father, and against all the Entreaties and Perswasions [*sic*] of my Mother" (5). Just three paragraphs into the account, Crusoe's impulse to experience the sea causes a schism with his parents. Crusoe seemingly must decide between biological or nonbiological kinship. Masculine familial abandonment might be a hallmark of maritime fictions, but the sea reinforces this separation and ensures that familial reunion is impossible; his extended sojourn on the Island of Despair ensures that he is unable to reunite with his parents (and any bequest due to him), who are deceased when he returns. To counteract what he reads as Crusoe's disobedience, Crusoe's father offers up an ultimatum: "he would do very kind things for me if I would stay and settle at Home as he directed . . . yet he would venture to say to me, that if I did take this foolish Step, God would not bless me, and I would have leisure hereafter to reflect upon having neglected his Counsel when there might be none to assist in my Recovery" (7). The dialogue here reinforces a binary between life on land (with his parents) and life at sea (without biological connection).

Defoe positions the spatiality of land as the locale for community, familial or otherwise, thus situating his life at sea as segregated from this human community, which reinforces his radical individualism, a concept I define more comprehensively below.[29] Later, when irreparably shipwrecked, Crusoe complains, "I seem'd banished from human Society, that I was alone, circumscrib'd by the boundless Ocean, cut off from Mankind, and condemn'd to what I call'd silent Life" (132). Crusoe's life at sea is replete with wreckages and drownings that repeatedly "condemn" him to solitary confinement. And though the island is populated by nonhuman animals who Crusoe enlists through animal husbandry, he recognizes neither them nor Xury or Friday as an equal that might constitute human community.[30] Sea life for Crusoe mandates this communal dislocation, which he willingly takes up, and the sea abducts Crusoe by way of storm and shipwreck, making it nearly impossible to form human social bonds.[31] This willingness, on Crusoe's part, and abduction, on the sea's, speaks to a fundamental entanglement between Crusoe and the sea. The sea's extensive ability to distort Crusoe is predicated on the fact that Crusoe cannot quit the lure of the sea. In addition to the formal breathlessness of Crusoe's first storm experience, he is woefully unprepared for the environmental chaos that awaits: "All this while the Storm encreas'd, and the Sea, which I had never been upon before, went very high, tho' nothing like what I have seen many time since; no, nor like what I saw a few Days after: But it was enough to affect me then . . . I expected every Wave would have swallowed us up, and that every time the Ship fell down, as I thought, in the trough or Hallow of the Sea, we should never rise more" (9). Like the first edition's title page, which foreshadows the consuming waves and shipwreck, Crusoe's greatest fears include the waves that will swallow him with a single gulp, a characterization of the ocean and its personified body that recurs throughout the narrative. Following this maelstrom moment, Crusoe "made many Vows and Resolutions, that if would please God here to spare my Life this one Voyage, if every I got once my Foot upon dry land again, I would go directly home to my Father, and never set it into a Ship again while I liv'd" (9). But Crusoe seems to have crossed his fingers behind his back—nullifying this vow and resolution—for "as the sea returned to its Smoothness of Surface and settled Calmness by the Abatement of the Storm," he narrates, "so the hurry of my Thoughts being over, my Fears and Apprehensions of being swallow'd up by the Sea being forgotten . . . I entirely forget the Vows and Promises that I made in my Distress" (10). The storms require that Crusoe make promises to himself and God that he otherwise would not. But like the ephemerality of the storms, so too are his vows.

Crusoe's mettle is once again tested when the second storm occurs two paragraphs later, an echo chamber of the first: "The Sea went Mountains high, and broke upon us every three or four Minutes: When I could look about, I could see nothing but Distress round us" (11). This storm ushers in Crusoe's final warning against a life at sea before he is ultimately wrecked. The second of only three fathers found in the text—the first is Crusoe's father, the second a sea captain, and the third Crusoe, himself, at novel's end—cautions Crusoe from pursuing the alluring call: "Young Man, says he, you ought never to go to Sea any more, you ought to take this for a plain and visible Token that you are not to be a Seafaring Man. . . . And young Man, said he, depend upon it, if you do not go back, where-ever you go, you will meet with nothing but Disasters and Disappointments till your Father's Words are fulfilled upon you" (14–15). These paternal warnings function as two strikes against Crusoe. The reminder of the storm and sea as an agent or actor lingers in these words.[32] The storm is a "plain and visible Token" of potential destruction to which Crusoe refuses to yield, and the destruction that awaits him is not just physical wreckage but also a dire toll on his relationships with others. He confesses, "But my ill Fate push'd me on now with an Obstinancy that nothing could resist. . . . I know not what to call this, nor will I urge, that it is a secret over-ruling Decree that hurries us on to be the Instruments of our own Destruction" (14). Crusoe cannot escape the lure of the sea, and yet his desire for the sea continues to stem from his self-aware fear of it. At the same time, Crusoe's sailing peers fear *his* desire to remain at sea.[33] Seemingly they realize he carries a curse: "You made this Voyage for a Trial, you see what a Taste Heaven has given you of what you are to expect if you persist; perhaps this is all befallen us on your Account" (15). Inasmuch that Crusoe realizes the sea as a frightening entity—an observation he makes during the first storm—he becomes just as frightening to others in his refusal to yield these maritime warnings. Like the frightening sea, Crusoe becomes both frightened *and* frightening. He is frightened for his own well-being, and he makes his companions afraid not only for his well-being, but their own given that storms seem to follow him wherever he goes to sea. The lure that materializes in storms and wreckage then dispossesses Crusoe from his own mental faculties while simultaneously distorting his relations with his sailing brethren and his family.

Two more storms beset Crusoe before he arrives on the Island of Despair, and like the first two, the third and fourth storms push Crusoe deeper into radical individualism and closer to death, further segregating him from community. As Crusoe and his peers attempt to flee from this fourth storm, the sea's effective power becomes abundantly clear: "In a word, it took us with such a Fury, that it overset the Boat at once; and separating us as well from the Boats, as from one another, gave us not the time hardly to say, O God! for we were all swallowed up in a Moment" (39). Again, the sea then operates as a voracious maw that swallows, satiated only by destruction and human offerings. This characterization of the sea has an antecedent in *The Storm*, wherein Henry Barclay recounts, "Soon after our Ship struck upon the Sands: the Sea broke over us, we expected every minute that she would drop to pieces, and that we should all be swallowed up in the Deep."[34] In the fiction of *Crusoe*, the sea's hunger is sated by the death of Crusoe's peers—none can survive but him—which, again, forcibly exiles Crusoe from human community and familiarity.

The sea, though, resists expelling Crusoe and, more compellingly, Crusoe realizes it: "Nothing can describe the Confusion of Thought which I felt when I sunk into the Water; for tho' I swam very well, yet I could not deliver my self from the Waves so as to draw Breath, . . . I got upon my Feet, and endeavoured to make on towards the Land as fast as I could, before another Wave should return, and take me up again" (39). Crusoe's rough and nonconsensual baptism exemplifies the sea's abilities to familiarize him with modes of tactile violence. Crusoe's omission of his original baptism in the first paragraph imposes this forceful experience as a cathartic awakening. But these incessant, consumptive waves—Crusoe states in the following paragraph, "The Wave that came upon me again, buried me at once 20 or 30 Foot deep in its own Body"—wash over Crusoe to induce in him a new way of being (40). His resilience springs from his survival of violence and the foreclosure of his human community. Crusoe eschews the consuming sea that attempts, and yet fails, to reconcile him with his lost, deceased peers. He states, "I must have been strangled in the Water; but I recover'd a little before the return of the Waves . . . I clamber'd up the Clifts of the Shore, and sat me down upon the Grass, free from Danger, and quite out of the Reach of the Water" (40). The "Reach of the Water" implies that the sea reaches toward Crusoe, attempting to grasp him with every untempered wave. Crusoe implicitly visualizes the sea with hands (and opposable thumbs) as it "strangle[s]" and "reach[es]" for him. Crusoe, we know though, makes landfall and thus escapes the sea's attempts at annihilation. But this escape is not without effect: Crusoe's sociality is rendered devoid of human peers. Upon recovering his senses, Crusoe takes stock of the loss: "I cannot describe, reflecting upon all my Comerades [*sic*] that were drown'd, and that there should not be one Soul sav'd but my self" (40). Crusoe cannot free himself from the sea's immersive tendrils, and thus the immersion ushers in a binary that constitutes the sea's effect: providing opportunity and survival while also potentially foreclosing all opportunities and survival.

The sea's violence imparts isolation and spurs Crusoe's radical individualism: he is constantly the only survivor. I refer to Crusoe's identity as "radically individual" to acknowledge how the sea dislocates him while simultaneously underscoring his survival as an exceptional individual. Peter Hulme defines Crusoe's radical individualism as "one which staggers backwards into the future, lacking in self-understanding, full of guilt, self-contradictory, tearful, violent."[35] Hulme's acknowledgment of Crusoe's violent individuality is apposite in thinking through the immersive and contagious quality of aqueous violence. The radical individualism promoted by the sea and accompanying shipwreck is one exclusively founded on separation from a community, as evidenced by the first two and all subsequent storms. Crusoe is rarely harmed by the storm, which contrasts the overwhelming death of his sailing peers: "Where are the rest of you? Did not you come Eleven of you into the Boat, where are the Ten? Why were not they sav'd and you lost? Why were you singled out? Is it better to be here or there? and then I pointed to the Sea" (54). The storms foreclose human community by eliminating Crusoe's sailing peers altogether. In making impossible particular forms of human community, the storms and sea regulate his isolation and instill in him a violent readiness. That is, the "violent" storms that have expelled Crusoe to the Island of Despair—"I am without Defence or Means to resist Violence of Man or Beast" (58)—prepare Crusoe to wield his own form of violence on others like the cannibal. While this is assuredly a survival method, I see the distortive experiences the sea has wrought as a didactic methodology that Crusoe borrows by way of interaction with the cannibals: single out, violate, and similarly distort. He confesses to this mutualistic contingency, "the Storms and Tides, by which I have so long been nourish'd and supported" (212), which structure his relationship with an aqueous environment as well as prepare him for the violent interactions with the cannibals. In this way, Crusoe can mirror the sea's didactic violence and thus effect a violent, powerful assault.

The revelation of the cannibal, whom Crusoe finds strange and abhorrent, provides the perfect outlet for Crusoe to wield the violence that he has been forced to reckon, in his relationship with the aqueous environment. And since Crusoe understands the cannibal as existing outside the parameters of a Protestant/English/European humanity and thus more animalized or naturalized—"I spent my Days now in great Perplexity, and Anxiety of Mind, expecting that I should one Day or other fall into the Hands of these merciless *Creatures*" (155)—the violence he sets out to impart is retaliatory. While it is true that Crusoe does not exclusively use the moniker "creature" to describe the cannibals, I have argued elsewhere that

Crusoe's use of this term, which is bestowed on animals, Friday, and, in a lone moment, himself, registers his recognition of a racialized and animalized affinity. The use of "creature" does not disregard the acknowledgment of Friday and here the cannibals as belonging to human embodiment, it does however "signal a radical otherness that incites violent engagement and results in the dispossession of stable identity categories: human, colonist, racialized companion."[36] His growing indignation and fear results in violent thinking: "I made no doubt, but that if there was twenty I should kill them all: This Fancy pleas'd my Thoughts for some Weeks, and I was so full of it, that I often dream'd of it; and sometimes that I was just going to let fly at them in my Sleep" (143). Crusoe cannot erase the obsession with the cannibal. And while Crusoe cannot exterminate the sea that has so much abused and violated him, he *can* effect great harm against the otherness of the cannibal.

After fifteen years in isolation, the infamous footstep in the sand jars Crusoe, morphing his relationship with self and other. Crusoe remarks that such a footstep consumes him "as if I had seen a Apparition" (130). Whereas before Crusoe's frustration arose from isolation—"I was alone, circumscrib'd by the boundless Ocean, cut off from Mankind, and condemn'd to what I call'd silent Life" (132)—the introduction of the ghostly footprint positions Crusoe as longing for that silent Life that once plagued him. Crusoe's frustration with both sea and human-other results from his inability to fully understand either entity. He cannot be happy with isolation, and he cannot be happy with the potential of human sociality, largely because he does not understand the cannibal as belonging to the same category of human by which he understands himself: "I could think of nothing but how I might destroy some of these Monsters in their cruel bloody Entertainment" (142). His sense of relationship is so distorted by the sea that has policed his prolonged isolation that he desires neither the solitary nor the possibility of the communal. His distorted relationship with both emphasizes his radical individual state in which he cannot be reconciled with either.

In *Robinson Crusoe*, violent thinking is both the fear of being violated and the desire to violate. The inter-flux of violence mimics the constant flux of the sea: Crusoe's state becomes informed by the sea. This is a connection that Crusoe of course cannot make or recognize himself because of his deeply seated fear of "the Fury of the Sea, which came pouring in after me" (40). The littoral space, home of the footprint and the first interaction with the cannibals, becomes the arena for violence to unfold and the "fury" to be resituated. Crusoe recognizes the shore as the cannibal's territory, "for certain it is, that these Savage People who sometimes haunted this Island, never came with any Thoughts of finding any Thing here; and consequently never wandered off from the Coast" (147). The characterization of the sea as violent, condemning, and deliberate seems to generate a genealogy of violence that moves from nonhuman environment to human. Carol Houlihan Flynn provides a way of seeing Crusoe's relationship with the island landscape as one connected to his hatred of the cannibal: "The idea of the savage causes him to limit the size of his economy, for his physical safety depends upon his relative invisibility. . . . Greater visibility requires more bodies to defend against encroaching 'enemies.' Yet he cannot risk becoming too insular or he will become 'swallowed up' by a self-enclosing, self-reflective landscape."[37] The landscape that can engulf is more indicative of the ocean, corroborated by the title page, and the storms that Crusoe retrospectively narrates. Both the sea and the cannibal seemingly work in tandem to limit Crusoe, and thus the modes of violence that he witnesses generate his radical response to reject enclosure. Crusoe cannot see that he has become like the sea (or the cannibal), but his ignorance does not nullify the similitude.

And it is this similitude that spurs violent entanglement. His fear of the cannibal growing, Crusoe observes, "I walk'd every where peeping, and peering about the Island . . . what a Surprise should I have been in if when I discover'd the print of a Man's Foot, I had instead of that, seen fifteen or twenty Savages, and found them pursuing me . . . no Possibility of my escaping them" (147). His solution to combating these fears is to prepare for an unavoidable battle: "I was laying all my blood Schemes for the Destruction of innocent Creatures" (146). The sea's violence and the potential cannibal violence are, then, different sides of the same coin, especially given that the cannibals body forth from the shore: "They had two Canoes with them, which they had haled up upon the Shore; and as it was then Tide of Ebb, they seem'd to me to wait for the Return of the Flood, to go away again; it is not easy to imagine what Confusion this Sight put me into" (154). Not only do the cannibals seem to operate on the shore—amplifying both Crusoe's fear of the littoral and its connection to loss—but their ability to navigate the tides and sea confuses Crusoe. Crusoe's insecurity with the cannibal is not only their potential violence against him, but their ability to read the tides in a way that he cannot, suggesting a superiority that he cannot abide. Crusoe's palpable fear recognizes a violence that intends to totally eradicate and erase—stamping out memory, record, and embodiment—which is mirrored in the ocean that consumes the deceased sailors in its own body. The cannibals who Crusoe observes feasting on human flesh replicate this behavior. In this way, the cannibal connection with the sea further distances them from Crusoe, and thus seemingly justifies his violence against them. In accepting both violent entities as unavoidable and threatening, Crusoe, in his suffocating fear, must violently react. Crusoe's violence is not only learned but becomes a preventative measure: ironically, to protect himself from the violence of others Crusoe must assume the offensive.

In beholding the cannibal on "my Side of the Island," Crusoe remarks, "During all this Time, I was in the murthering Humour; and took up most of my Hours, which should have been better employ'd, in contriving how to circumvent, and fall upon them" (154–155). Suddenly, Crusoe's work ethic becomes fixated on murder, and the contagion of violence spreads.

Upon finally witnessing the cannibals in action, Crusoe reveals the similarities between these different kinds of violence: one, the sea's and thus a seemingly "natural" one, and, two, a separate "natural" violence that seems immanent in the cannibals.[38] I employ "natural" in scare quotes here to reinforce several readings: first, to acknowledge the sea as an environmental, natural biome; second, to recognize the types of inborn incivility that Crusoe pinpoints within the cannibals; and third, to gesture toward figures of nature in the novel that Crusoe aligns as being violent and oppositional. Put simply, the naturalness of violence in the novel is immersive, and this also recognizes Crusoe's violence against others as equally naturalized. He narrates, "In short, I turn'd my Face from the Horrid Spectacle [the consumption of human flesh]; my Stomach grew sick, and I was just at the Point of Fainting, when Nature discharg'd the Disorder from my Stomach; and having vomited with an uncommon Violence, I was a little reliev'd" (140). Like the ocean's emesis of Crusoe earlier in the novel, here, he reenacts this violent expulsion. This aping of projectile vomiting bespeaks the slippage—the fluidity—between his body and other bodies. In vomiting "the Disorder," Crusoe mirrors the sea's consuming and emetic habits. Afterward, he vomits with "uncommon Violence." The cannibal violence he surveys—the dehumanization of the human body—is too much to bear for Crusoe. Whereas he has borne witness to the sea's violence on the human, it appears as though human against human violence physically repulses him, thus suggesting a hierarchy of violence. His violent machinations then manifest both mentally and bodily. But unlike his mind's obsession, his body cannot withhold this obsession. Crusoe must bodily jettison the appearance of the cannibal and the display of bodily violence. The revolt that Crusoe literally bodies forth here comforts him and works to distinguish the superior colonizer from the forces that necessitate colonization: "I look'd up with the utmost Affection of my Soul, and with the Flood of Tears in my Eyes, gave God Thanks that had cast my first Lot in the Part of the World, where I was distinguish'd from such dreadful Creatures as these" (140). As Anglo-colonizer, Crusoe prays with both gratitude and pride and, in so doing, consolidates his superiority over the cannibal other. Yet the violent measures that he intends to enact on the cannibal do not surface in his prayers, which suggests a deliberate concealment. Crusoe suggests that certain forms of superiority and violent behaviors are more acceptable to God than others, thereby indemnifying himself. However, even in his abilities to successfully expel the violent experience, what remains is the trace of violence.

At the close of *The Storm*, we are left with a frightful account:

> One unhappy Accident I cannot omit, and which is brought us from good Hands, and happen'd in a Ship homeward bound from the *West-Indies*. The Ship was in the utmost Danger of Foundring; and when the Master saw all, as he thought, lost, his Masts gone, the Ship leaky, and expecting her every moment to sink under him, fill'd with Despair, he calls to him the Surgeon of the Ship, and by a fatal Contract, as soon made as hastily executed, they resolv'd to prevent the Death they fear'd by one more certain; and going into the Cabbin, they both shot themselves with their Pistols. It pleas'd God the Ship recover'd the Distress, was driven safe into—and the Captain just liv'd to see the desperate Course he took might have been spar'd; the Surgeon died immediately.[39]

So fearful of the uncertain and painful death that the sea and storm might institute, the captain and the surgeon commit suicide. The extremity of stormy experiences weigh unimaginably on the sailors, and the preferred violence is a self-violation—one that both the captain and surgeon can control—rather than an environmental violence that is unknowable, uncontrollable, and unpreventable.

The ending of *Robinson Crusoe* also features a murderous shot to the head, painted in similar tones of escapism: violence appears as the only way for Crusoe to truly escape the Island of Despair. Following the mutiny on the English ship and Crusoe's heroic emancipation of the prisoners, the newly assembled group intends to lure the mutineers to their demise on the shore. Crusoe assures his new converts that they must kill or be killed, which echoes his Faustian bargain for Friday: "If they [the mutineers] escaped, we should be undone still; for they would go on Board and bring the whole Ship's Company, and destroy us all. Well then, says I [Crusoe], Necessity legitimates my Advice" (215–216). Crusoe does not offer amnesty but rather insists on a gesture that intends to murder before being murdered. The waylaid sailors agree to these terms. "Watching from the Shore," Crusoe bears witness to even more gruesome violence by which the mutineer captain is assassinated: "shot thro' the head, the Bullet entering at his Mouth, and came out again behind one of his Ears" (229).

As the experience of the Island of Despair draws to a close, it is clear that the contagion of violence in *Robinson Crusoe* continues to spread with proximity to the sea. Violence is the means of both entry and exit to the island, just like the sea. An ecocritical new materialist reading, like the one I have offered here, acknowledges plural systems of violence that saturate Defoe's novel and considers how modes of transcorporeal relationality manifest with regard to environmental agents such as the sea and natural disasters. At novel's end, despite Crusoe's familiarity with the sea's turbulent and mercurial nature, his residual fear remains: "I had been accustom'd enough to the Sea, and yet I had a strange Aversion to going to *England* by Sea at that time; and though I could give no Reason for it, yet the Difficulty encreas'd upon me so much" (242). His gut instincts take over: "I had been very unfortunate by Sea, and this might be some of the Reason: But let no Man slight the strong Impulses of his own Thoughts in Cases of such Moment" (242). There's good reason, Crusoe clarifies, both of the ships "miscarry'd": one overwhelmed by pirates and on the other "all the People drown'd except three" (242–243). He has narrowly avoided yet another maritime disaster. Resigning himself to sea travel only between Calais and Dover—"resolv'd to travel all the Way by Land"—Crusoe narrates his sea aversion: "In a Word, I was so prepossess'd against my going by Sea at all" (243). As this chapter has demonstrated, Crusoe's prepossession with the sea materializes as horror, disgust, fear, and loathing. The sea frightens Crusoe because it can do damage, both immediately and gradually, and such immersive processes are wholly transformative. Truly, this is sea power.

NOTES

1. Daniel Defoe, *The Storm*, ed. Richard Hamblyn (New York: Penguin, 2005), 18. All citations are to this version.
2. Christopher Loar, "How to Say Things with Guns: Military Technology and the Politics of Robinson Crusoe," *Eighteenth Century Fiction* 19, nos. 1–2 (2006): 1–20.
3. John R. Gillis, "The Blue Humanities," *Humanities* 34, no. 3 (May/June 2013), https://www.neh.gov/humanities/2013/mayjune/feature/the-blue-humanities. Margaret Cohen, Killian Quigley, and Jason Payton, among others, have also begun to explore what I consider an eighteenth-century blue humanities. Margaret Cohen and Killian Quigley, eds., *The Aesthetics of the Undersea* (New York: Routledge, 2018); Jason Payton, "Of Water, Winds, and Storms: The Elemental Regimes of the Buccaneer Journal," in *Eighteenth-Century Environmental Humanities*, ed. Jeremy Chow (Lewisburg, PA: Bucknell University Press, forthcoming).
4. "Transcorporeality," by Alaimo's definition, "is a new materialist and posthumanist sense of the human as substantially and perpetually interconnected with the flows of substances and the agencies of environments." Stacy Alaimo, "States of Suspension: Transcorporeality at Sea," *Interdisciplinary Studies in Literature and the Environment* 19, no. 3 (2012): 476.
5. Rob Nixon, *Slow Violence and the Environmentalism of the Poor* (Cambridge, MA: Harvard University Press, 2011), 2.
6. Frantz Fanon, *The Wretched of the Earth*, trans. Richard Philcox (New York: Grove Press, 2004).
7. Priscilla Wald, Nancy Tomes, and Lisa Lynch, "Introduction: Contagion and Culture," *American Literary History* 14, no. 4 (2002): 617–624. See also Cynthia Davis, "Contagion as Metaphor," *American Literary History* 14, no. 4 (2002): 828–836.

8. For an eighteenth-century investigation of disease contagion and its association with reading, see Annika Mann, who pinpoints contagion in Defoe's *Journal of a Plague Year*. Annika Mann, *Reading Contagion: The Hazards of Reading in the Age of Print* (Charlottesville: University of Virginia Press, 2018).
9. Bruno Latour, "Agency in the Time of the Anthropocene," *New Literary History* 45 (2014): 11.
10. Latour, "Agency in the Time of the Anthropocene," 13.
11. Diana Coole and Samantha Frost, eds., *New Materialisms: Ontology, Agency, and Politics* (Durham, NC: Duke University Press, 2010), 7.
12. Cognitive literary studies is a vibrant field that has beneficially troubled what constitutes cognition and cognitive processing. See, for only one of myriad examples, N. Katherine Hayles's recent *Unthought: The Power of the Cognitive Unconscious* (Chicago: University of Chicago Press, 2017).
13. Richard Hamblyn, "Introduction," in *The Storm*, x.
14. Robert Markley, "'Casualties and Disasters': Defoe and the Interpretation of Climatic Instability," *Journal for Early Modern Cultural Studies* 8, no. 2 (2008): 103.
15. Defoe, *The Storm*, 104.
16. *A Wonderful History of All the Storms, Hurricanes, and Earthquakes, &c That Have Happen'd in England for above 500 Years Past* (London: Oxford Arms, 1704), i. Courtesy of the Clark Library.
17. Though *The Storm*'s genre (especially its fictionality) has been debated, *An Essay on the Author* is self-pronounced satire, and the description of the storm is couched in religious and political allegory. Daniel Defoe, *An Elegy on the Author of the True-Born-English-Man with an Essay on the Late Storm* (London, 1708), 21. Courtesy of the Clark Library.
18. Defoe, *The Storm*, 53.
19. Markley, "'Casualties and Disasters,'" 110.
20. The connectedness between *Pilgrim's Progress* and *Robinson Crusoe*, as Leopold Damrosch Jr. shows, was an intertextuality that Defoe seems to have intended, which he explains in his subsequent *Serious Reflections*. See "Myth and Fiction in *Robinson Crusoe*." Leopold Damrosch Jr., *God's Plot and Man's Stories: Studies in the Fictional Imagination from Milton to Fielding* (Chicago: University of Chicago Press, 1985).
21. Jan Golinski, *British Weather and the Climate of the Enlightenment* (Chicago: University of Chicago Press, 2007), 76.
22. *Wonderful History of All the Storms*, 54.
23. P. N. Furbank and W. R. Owens, "Defoe and the 'Improvisatory' Sentence," *English Studies* 67, no. 2 (1986): 157–166.
24. Cynthia Wall, "Introduction," in *Journal of a Plague Year* (New York: Penguin, 2003), xxx.
25. Defoe, *The Storm*, 144.
26. Alain Corbin, *The Lure of the Sea: Discovery of the Seaside in the Western World, 1750–1840*, trans. Jocelyn Phelps (Berkeley: University of California Press, 1994), 7.
27. Siobhan Carroll, *An Empire of Air and Water* (Philadelphia: University of Pennsylvania Press, 2015), 6.
28. Defoe, *The Storm*, 112–113.
29. The familial community provided by land is also mapped onto Defoe's other seafaring novels like *Moll Flanders* and *Captain Singleton*.
30. Markman Ellis suggests that Crusoe "creatively dehumanises" Friday and the other cannibals. Markman Ellis, "Crusoe, Cannibalism and Empire," in *Robinson Crusoe: Myths and Metamorphoses*, ed. Lieve Spaas and Brian Stimpson (New York: St. Martin's, 1996), 54.
31. For discussions of Crusoe's nonhuman animal communities, see Lucinda Cole's *Imperfect Creatures*, Heather Keenleyside's *Animals and Other People*, and my "Crusoe's Creature Comforts." Lucinda Cole, *Imperfect Creatures: Vermin, Literature, and the Sciences of Life,*

1600–1740 (Ann Arbor: University of Michigan Press, 2016); Heather Keenleyside, *Animals and Other People: Literary Forms and Living Beings in the Long Eighteenth Century* (Philadelphia: University of Pennsylvania Press, 2016); Jeremy Chow, "Crusoe's Creature Comforts," *Digital Defoe* 10, no. 1 (2018), http://digitaldefoe.org/2018/11/01/crusoes-creature-comforts/.

32. Discussions of the actant are broad and philosophically far-reaching. I employ it here to specifically think about Jane Bennett's extension of Bruno Latour and Gilles Deleuze. Bennett defines the actant as "neither an object nor a subject but an 'intervener'" and as a "substitute word for what in more subject-centered vocabulary [is] called agents." Jane Bennett, *Vibrant Matter: A Political Ecology of Things* (Durham, NC: Duke University Press, 2009), 9.
33. Samuel Taylor Coleridge imitates this palpable fearfulness in his *Rime of the Ancient Mariner* (1798): "I Fear thee, ancient Mariner! / I fear thy skinny hand / And thou are long, and lank, and brown, / As is the ribbed sea-sand. / 'I Fear thee and thy glittering eye, / And thy skinny hand, so brown.'" Samuel Taylor Coleridge, *The Rime of the Ancient Mariner*, ed. Millicent Rose (New York: Dover, 1970), lines 224–229.
34. Defoe, *The Storm*, 167.
35. Peter Hulme, *Colonial Encounters* (New York: Methuen, 1986), 215.
36. Chow, "Crusoe's Creature Comforts," 2.
37. Carol Houlihan Flynn, *The Body in Swift and Defoe* (Cambridge: Cambridge University Press, 1990), 153.
38. Ellis locates this latter type of "natural" violence—that is, something inborn in cannibal cultures—within an eighteenth-century context. He suggests that Defoe repurposed Montaigne's "On the Cannibals," which elides the "savage," racialized other as cannibal. Ellis also notes that like Crusoe, Cook's popular reports of cannibalism in the Antipodes "remain either circumstantial, secondhand or dramatic." Ellis, "Crusoe, Cannibalism and Empire," 58.
39. Defoe, *The Storm*, 180.

7

LIFE GETS TEDIOUS

Crusoe and the Threat of Boredom

Pat Rogers

The sun comes up 'n the sun goes down,
The hands on the clock keep goin' around;
I just get up 'n it's time to lay down,
Life gets tee-jus don't it?
—Carson Robison, "Life Gets
Tee-Jus Don't It" (1948)

For the last seventy-five years the good and great have been dispatched on a radio program from a stuffy BBC studio to a tropical paradise. The signature tune of "Desert Island Discs" is a piece by Eric Coates, "By the Sleepy Lagoon," which suggests that these guests have landed up in Polynesia. The castaways are armed only with a book (along with the default choices, the Bible and Shakespeare), a luxury item, and eight pieces of music. When asked by the presenter how they would fare, the guests usually put on a brave face. Some admit that they might feel lonely, perhaps frightened at times. One thing they seldom mention is boredom. Yet most of us would find the daily routine indescribably wearisome. Guests do talk about the ways they would keep busy. But, as everyone knows, some of the busiest activities in which people engage—housework, gardening, manual labor, shuffling papers in an office—can also be some of the most mind-numbing. If you have to do everything entirely by yourself, the weight of repetitive tasks grows even more destructive of the spirit.

Crusoe, once recast as the epitome of the Victorian Englishman with his stiff upper lip, can hardly have failed to have been bored stiff much of the time. He does freely express many emotions, particularly when first arriving at the island: shock, fear, isolation, a sense of being out of his element, a feeling of confinement, wonder at the surroundings, guilt for his past actions. Some of these are dissipated in time, with the help of his new religious awareness. Despite that, his fears never really go away, whether the threat is that of wild animals, cannibals, or pirates.

But of course he gets by. This resilience perhaps owes something to his can-do personality and the energetic way of life he led up to the time that he was shipwrecked. Yet his very productivity and globetrotting would make it all the harder for him to adjust to existence on a tiny atoll lying somewhere off a great continent. No one was ever less able, in Pascal's celebrated phrase, to sit in a quiet room alone—or, as La Bruyère rephrased it, "Tout notre mal vient de ne pouvoir être seuls." Yet Crusoe does not directly address the boredom that he must have felt alongside other emotions. It is a feeling that never wholly goes away throughout the two volumes of his adventures, though he finds ways to allay its effects through compensatory devices such as hyperactivity and obsessive recording of his daily tasks.

Much has been said about the hero's original sin, usually traced back to his refusal to follow the injunctions that his father gave him when he was young. Crusoe senior warns his son against the "secret burning Lust of Ambition for great things" (7), and counsels him to follow a more settled path in the middle station, because it will promote a more virtuous, enjoyable, and even tranquil way of life.[1] The passage can be interpreted theologically, in terms of Calvinist doctrine; sociologically, in terms of emerging attitudes toward class; or economically, in terms of capitalist ideology. But apart from all this, Crusoe's decision to break away from his family values has a psychological dimension. He has in effect quit his ancestral church, turned away from solid respectable business to become an adventurer and slave trader, and abandoned his native land. The mode of living that he now has to practice on the island is in many ways more restrictive, rule-bound, and unvaried socially than the one he would have experienced if he had stayed to perch on a stool at a counting house in York. At eighteen, the fate he had most dreaded was to have gone "Apprentice to a Trade, or Clerk to an Attorney," as he was sure that if so obliged he would "run away from my Master before my Time was out, and go to Sea" (8). The paradox is that after his bid for freedom, he ultimately finds himself condemned to a more demanding routine than these jobs would have entailed. How could he not be resentful, as well as terminally bored?

Less familiar than the passage just cited is the self-description Crusoe gives at the start of the *Farther Adventures*. Feeling restless in England after his return, and plagued by dreams of his life on the island, he tries to find new objects on which he can focus: "I resolv'd to divert my self with other Things, and to engage in some Business that might effectually tye me up from any more Excursions of this kind; for I found that Thing return upon me chiefly when I was idle, and had nothing to do, nor any Thing of Moment immediately before me" (*FA* 6).[2] Following the death of his wife, he suffers from what he calls "a deep Relapse of the wandring Disposition, which, as I may say, being born in my very Blood, soon recovered its Hold of me" (*FA* 7). The notion of "rambling" recurs throughout the second installment of the novel. The hero has "a native Propensity to Rambling," while his wife had checked his "rambling Genius"; he sees that "if Trade was not my Element, Rambling was" (*FA* 1, 8, 230). In the most striking instance, Crusoe compares his attitude to mercantile ventures with that of a staid fellow traveler: "My new Friend . . . would have been content to go like a Carrier's Horse, always to the same Inn, backward and forward, provided he could, as he call'd it, *find his Account in it*: On the other hand, mine was the Notion of a mad rambling Boy, that never cares to see a thing twice over" (*FA* 233).

> The only Means of living comfortably, I mean Diligence, for a Life of Sloth and Idleness, is not Happiness or Comfort; Employment is Life, Sloth and Indolence is Death; to be busy, is to be cheerful, to be pleasant; to have nothing to do, is all Dejection, dispiriting, and in a word, to be fit for nothing but Mischief and the Devil.
>
> —Daniel Defoe, *A Plan of the English Commerce* (1728)

The injunction to keep busy came from several quarters. We think that Crusoe's ceaseless efforts to build a life on the island go back to his Puritan upbringing. But long before Protestants had a work ethic, Catholics had inscribed in the works of the fathers a similar insistence on the value of an active involvement in the world for the sake of benefiting others. As everyone knows, sloth was accounted one of the seven deadly sins, and *acedia* prompted a range of other vices.[3] In his *Purgatorio* Dante portrayed the penance for *acedia* as running "continuously at top speed," which again reminds us of the way Crusoe led his early life. There was a more desirable firm of idleness, that is *otium*—time devoted to constructive leisure, educational, or philosophical meditation, often seen as a boon of retirement in the wake of a life of public service. But such a retirement is not something Crusoe can experience: he never approaches the repose that the term sometimes implied. Rather, the absence of the business that had previously occupied him is one of the things that soon drives him to distraction on the island, and then leads him to engage in occasionally pointless activity to sublimate his now unquenchable urges.

Theologians and moralists of every persuasion inveighed against idleness. Among them regularly we find the influential Latitudinarian divine John Tillotson, for instance, enjoining "diligence" to be inculcated in children:

> Children that are bred up in laziness are almost necessarily bad, because they cannot take the pains to be good; and they cannot take pains, because they have never been inured and accustomed to it; which makes their

> Spirits *restive,* and when you have occasion to quicken them and spur them up to business they will stand stock still.
>
> Therefore never let your Children be without a *Calling,* or without some useful, or at least innocent employment that will take them up; that they may not be put upon a kind of necessity of being *vicious* for want of something better to do. The *Devil* tempts the active and vigorous into his service, knowing what fit and proper instruments they are to do his drudgery: But the slothful and idle, no body having hired them and set them on work, lie in his way, and he stumbles upon them as *he goes about;* and they do as it were offer themselves to his service, and having nothing to do they even tempt the *Devil* himself to *tempt* them, and to take them in his way.[4]

Who better fits the definition of a restive spirit than the young Crusoe?

> Life is first boredom, then fear.[5]
>
> —Philip Larkin, "Dockery and Son"

The etymological history of the keyword gives limited help. The phrase *Tædium vitæ* is found on many Roman tombstones, but it was not in general usage: *tædium* meant disgust, not boredom, and the stock expression was *tædet me vitæ*. The word was employed sometimes by patristic writers. As for "tedium," this was brought into English in the seventeenth century. *Tædium vitæ* is first recorded in an English prose context in Edward Young's *Conjectures on Original Composition* in 1759.

Approaching the eighteenth century, we encounter a vestigial Spenserian element in Samuel Garth's treatment of Sloth in *The Dispensary* (1699) and Alexander Pope's of Dulness in *The Dunciad* (1728). In *The Castle of Indolence* (1748), James Thomson provides a secular version of the trope, in which industry triumphs over the seductions of indolence. There is not much doubt where Defoe stands on this issue, with his hyperactivity as a man and a writer. His *Complete English Tradesman* (1725–1726) could have served as a model for Hogarth's industrious apprentice in the prints of 1747, while it supplied a warning not to fall into the ways of his idle colleague. A tradesman is "always stirring and bustling, never idle . . . all Life and Spirit, is continually in a brisk Motion."[6] He inveighed against idleness in several places, for example in *A New Voyage round the World* (1725), where the narrator deplores what he sees as the indolence of the people of Chile, both native and Spanish.[7]

Then there are concepts such as ennui and spleen, which we think of as a product of the post-Romantic era embodied in the work of Baudelaire, the symbolists, and decadents—as when Villiers de l'Isle Adam depicted Axël in his castle turning away from the world. Or consider Bouvard and Pécuchet, brought together by a common emptiness, "un même ennui." Most discussions of the topic trace a long trajectory in which ennui reaches its apogee in the nineteenth and twentieth centuries.[8] In addition they tend to see ennui as self-generated, with an existential rather than an environmental causation. However, well before modern life could be blamed for feelings of lassitude, such notions had been given full scrutiny even in Defoe's lifetime. They were thoroughly medicalized in works such as William Stukeley's *Of Spleen* (1723), Sir Richard Blackmore's *Treatise on the Spleen and Vapours* (1726), and George Cheyne's *The English Malady: or a Treatise of Spleen and Vapours* (1733). Conveniently the spleen could be seen as an "idle" organ, since it is not essential for human beings to survive. The message of these works has a clear relevance to Crusoe's low spirits on the island. Cheyne claimed that "*Nervous* Disorders are the Diseases of the Wealthy, the Voluptuous, and the Lazy." The remedy lay partly in diet, preferably the plain fare favored by "the middling Rank" of society. But just as important was *activity*, promoted by regular exercise such as horseback riding (not available to Crusoe), and the avoidance of luxury (not a problem for Defoe's hero). Cheyne belabors the "unactive" and lazy with some energy. As Anita Guerrini puts it, "Too much leisure depressed the spirits."[9] It was physical diversion that alleviated troubles of the mind, and by inference warded off the idleness that provoked boredom. By this date, clearly, depression had ceased to be a purely behavioral issue, as it could now exhibit a respectable set of symptoms and prompt a diagnosis that looked impressive. A medical man in fiction, Lemuel Gulliver, agreed with his Houyhnhnm master that hard work was the infallible cure for spleen, "which only seizes on the *Lazy*, the *Luxurious*, and the *Rich*."[10]

Nobody much has investigated this subject as it affects literature of the period, except Patricia Spacks in her intriguing study of *Boredom* (1995). She shows that satiety and vacuity became emblems of a certain kind of gentility in the middle decades of the century. Spacks suggests that boredom was essentially invented around 1700, and the threat grew still more potent fifty to a hundred years later when "interest" became the touchstone.[11] She analyzes this development with learning and panache. There is a parallel shift in meaning that has not been so thoroughly explored. When Pope wrote his mock epic, "dul(l)ness" meant primarily stupidity, secondarily drowsiness, and thirdly low spirits. As for the main modern sense of tediousness, *OED* records no example prior to a usage by Johnson in *Rambler* 141 in 1751. Even the easily bored Boswell employs the word in one of the older senses. When he first came to London, he needed contact with the outside world, he reports in his journal on February 8, 1763, to keep his spirits from sinking into "lethargic dulness." The word applied to his mental condition, not the properties of the life he was leading.[12] But increasingly people found things outside themselves to be the cause of the tedium they felt.

A closely related trend was the growing search for novelty, as scientific innovations enabled people to indulge in fresh experiences, while increasing prosperity meant they could savor unfamiliar foods. Travel gradually got safer and faster, so that there were more remote places to go.[13] Curiosity is a good thing, but its flip side can be apathy if the desired stimulation does not occur. Outside literature, the coming of industrialism led to a spike in the number of mindless jobs that required concentration on repeated tasks over a long stretch. It is of course easy to see how you could be bored at a factory bench, or at a kitchen sink—not so obvious if you are in a tropical paradise with no children to care for, no deadlines to meet, and no overseer with a stopwatch.

The very word "boredom," in its modern sense, did not enter the language until quite recently. The earliest example cited in *OED* is from *Bleak House*, chapter 28, "The Ironmaster." Here Dickens contrasts the "strong and active" self-made industrialist Robert Rouncewell with the rotting Dedlock clan whom he visits at Chesney Wold. The poor relations hanging on to Sir Leicester are described as "plated links upon the Dedlock chain of gold," but in their fruitless existence it would have been better for them "to have been made of common iron at first and done base service." The worst case of aristocratic languor is that of the châtelaine herself, surrounded by her idle relatives: "My Lady, whose chronic malady of boredom has been sadly aggravated by Volumnia this evening, glances wearily towards the candlesticks and heaves a noiseless sigh."[14] Displayed in the body language of lassitude, world weariness among the upper classes could be used by this date as the emblem of exhaustion, bred from an enfeebled genetic pool.

What does all this have to do with Crusoe? A great deal, in my view. His original mistake was to reject his father's advice for a prudent life, enticed by the false lures of travel, adventure, and riches. Intended for the role of Francis Goodchild, he has chosen the way of Tom Idle, who is "turn'd away, and sent to Sea" in Hogarth's prints. He started out easily bored, and now his apprehensions have come true on the island. What motivated him had been the same "chronic malady" that Lady Dedlock endured, the often frustrated need for a rush of excitement. In other words, a fear of boredom.

> I know most People have an Aversion to a Tedious Subject,
> and the *Beauty of Novelty* is very taking.
> —Defoe, *Review*, July 12, 1705

For the first eight months of his captivity on Juan Fernàndez, Alexander Selkirk had felt terror and despair in his solitary state. "After he had conquer'd his Melancholy," Woodes Rogers tells us, "he diverted himself by sometimes cutting his

Name on the Trees, and the Time of his being left and Continuance there." He gradually got used to his place of captivity, so that he became "very easy" with his surroundings.[15] Richard Steele's account differs slightly: he reports that Selkirk suffered melancholy for eighteen months, after which he grew reconciled to his condition, and started to take delight in everything around him.[16] The key word here is "diverted." People went on seeking ways to charm away boredom, as when Hester Piozzi determined to "study Hebrew to divert Ennui & pass the Summer Months away."[17] In his illuminating study of "the rhetoric of diversion," Darryl P. Domingo has shown how a variety of cultural practices grew up in the later seventeenth and early eighteenth centuries "to stave off boredom and satiety." These included a number of commercial undertakings that provided "reigning diversions of the town," an explicitly urban form of provision that would be impossible for a lone castaway to replicate.[18]

To divert oneself implies being able to evade one's present condition, that is, to move in a different direction, physically or mentally—something much harder for someone who has to endure solitary confinement, as Crusoe does in effect. It is interesting that Schopenhauer, who regarded pain and boredom as the two opposite forces threatening happiness, condemned such a form of punishment for criminals, on the grounds that it had no deterrent element. It threatens someone tempted to crime by want or hardship with the opposite pole of human misery, that is, boredom. Schopenhauer quotes a couplet from Goethe, which might be roughly translated, "If a real torture is imposed on us, we long for boredom."[19] (This contrasts with the famous dictum of Kierkegaard, that boredom is to be shunned as the root of all evil—the gods were bored and so they created the human race.) Actually Schopenhauer's condemned prisoners, like Crusoe, might see their situation in a different light, since boredom is a crucial part of the torture imposed on them. Idleness is easy to philosophize about when you are busy writing.

Like Selkirk on his lonely planet, Crusoe is not all business. After one frightening experience at sea, when he rashly attempted an escape in his primitive canoe, he determines not to carry out any ambitious trips in the boat, although "sometimes I went out in her to divert my self" (130). Similarly he begins to go out every day with his gun, "as well to divert myself, as to see if I could kill any thing fit for Food" (53). But even in his earliest period of activity he had ordered his day, dividing up the hours between his shooting expeditions, sleep, and "time of Diversion" (62). Already the utilitarian is accompanied by a need to alleviate the stresses imposed by his unvarying routine: paradoxically, the answer is to take up a kind of hobbyist pastime of shooting, then combine it day after day with the quest for food. When he finally starts to explore and discovers a more pleasant location on the other side of the island, he reports that he was "exceedingly diverted with this Journey" (93). He forges a close relation with his pets and stock, to assuage loneliness but also diversify his occupations. Milking the goats becomes his "Evening Diversion" (134). He acknowledges that "all the while I was at work I diverted my self with talking to my Parrot" (102). After twenty-two years, he admits to having "some little Diversions and Amusements, which made the Time pass more pleasantly with me a great deal, than it did before" (152). The first such pastime involves conversations with the parrot, who learns to talk in a seemingly articulate manner.

As he gradually reconciles himself to his situation, he realizes that tedium is an unavoidable part of his efforts to survive on the island:

> This want of Tools made every Work I did go on heavily, and it was near a whole Year before I had entirely finish'd my little Pale or surrounded Habitation. The Piles or Stakes, which were as heavy as I could well lift, were a long time in cutting and preparing in the Woods, and more by far in bringing home, so that I spent some times two Days in cutting and bringing home one of those Posts, and a third Day in driving it into the Ground; for which Purpose I got a heavy Piece of Wood at first, but at last bethought my self of one of the Iron Crows, which however tho' I found it, yet it made driving those Posts or Piles very laborious and tedious Work.
>
> But what need I ha' been concern'd at the Tediousness of any thing I had to do, seeing I had time enough to do it in, nor had I any other Employment if that had been over, at least, that I could foresee, except the ranging the Island to seek for Food, which I did more or less every Day. (56–57)

On the island Crusoe takes up a number of "projects," but with no one else to benefit and no fortune to acquire, the usual aim of projects, these ultimately shade into make-work exercises. Of course, Defoe himself had always been something of a projector, and like his creation he had come up with some useless and unproductive schemes. As for Crusoe, he overdoes the furbishing of his cave, almost as though he is expecting visitors, and puts up shelves with the zeal of a DIY enthusiast.

Having started with the most basic tasks to ensure self-preservation, his activities gradually move toward less essential undertakings. A case in point is his creation of his bower or "Country-House." He takes a positive pleasure in building it, and when it is completed he rejoices: "About the Beginning of *August, as I said,* I had finish'd my Bower, and began to enjoy my self" (87). Absurdly, he compares his possession of this retreat with that of "any Lord of a Mannor in *England*" (85). To write like this is to ape the mores of the leisured classes, and Crusoe has a long way to go before he can indulge himself in extensive periods of leisure. I do not think it trivializes this episode to see in it a foreshadowing of summer vacation homes. This can be said because Defoe appears to be the only English writer of this period who refers to the *bastides* used by merchants of Provence. As he says in the *Tour* about the new mansions going up in Surrey: "These are all Houses of Retreat, like the *Bastides* of *Marseilles*, Gentlemen's meer *Summer-Houses*, or Citizen's *Country-Houses*; whither they retire from the hurries of Business, and from getting Money, to draw their Breath in a clear Air, and to divert themselves and Families in the hot Weather."[20] Of course, Crusoe doesn't have any business to do on the island, and he has no way of getting money. The thirty-six pounds he does retain must lie growing "mouldy with the Damp of the Cave" (110).

This identification with prosperous merchants at home may look grotesque. But we can perhaps understand Crusoe's need to abridge the longueurs of his stay on the island by dreaming of a cozy second home. As part of his quest for gentility, Defoe himself had moved out from the city to what was then the rising suburb of Stoke Newington, described in 1720 as "pleasantly situated, and full of fine Country Houses for Citizens, being about 3 or 4 Miles from *London*."[21] There he had built "a very handsom House, as a Retirement from London, and amused his Time either in the Cultivation of a large and pleasant Garden, or in the Pursuit of his Studies."[22] The castaway lacked his creator's large store of books to study; but otherwise some of his ways of amusing his time are not so different from those of Defoe. Certain aspects of Crusoe's existence, once he has made himself a secure lodging place, do start to resemble the conditions of retirement, rather than the hectic life of trade that he formerly led.[23]

> Ah! que la vie est quotidienne.
> —Jules Laforgue, "Complainte sur certains ennuis"

Crusoe recounts in the form of a journal his earliest days of isolation. Journals are usually seen as based on Puritan diary keeping, and primarily as a vehicle for reflecting on spiritual progress. They are that, but they also serve a more normal "modern" function of keeping track of events, weather, spending, and the like. Along with navigation Crusoe had been taught by his first mentor, the plain-dealing sea captain, something about "how to keep an Account of the Ship's Course" (17). Obviously a ship's log would be a routine exercise for him, but he would have also been familiar with the kind of bookkeeping practiced in forms such as the shop and trading journals, which as Stuart Sherman has shown in his brilliant book *Telling Time* (1996, 61–68), provided one of the models for the spiritual journal and for domestic diaries in the mode of Samuel Pepys.[24] Naturally it was a key part of the diurnal schedule of *The Complete English Tradesman* to "keep his day-book duly posted."[25] Another mode of personal record keeping existed in the shape of almanacs, which left convenient spaces for users to fill with daily events, and which marked in the accompanying text the passage of weeks and seasons. Paradoxically the castaway might have been more aware of these things than most ordinary people in England would have been.

Sherman quotes from a section in Defoe's *Tour* where the journal keeping of two travelers is compared, one drafting entries that are functional and selective, the other fussy, meticulously detailed, and gossipy.[26] The difference of opinion in what constituted an "exact" journal echoes through the century, but it is clear that Defoe was deeply influenced by the Baconian injunctions given to travelers to keep a close record of what they observed on their progress, another means of defining experience in a temporal framework.[27] All this comes to a head in Crusoe's decision to keep a journal, and in the entries that he inserts into his narrative. His delay in beginning on this task is explained along lines suggested by the contrast set out in the *Tour*: "Indeed at first I was in too much Hurry, and not only Hurry as to Labour, but in too much Discomposure of Mind, and my Journal would ha' been full of many dull things: For Example, I must have said thus, *Sept.* the 30th. After I got to Shore and had escap'd drowning, instead of being thankful to God for my Deliverance, having first vomited with the great Quantity of salt Water which was gotten into my Stomach" (60). Let no one claim that Defoe did not give Crusoe a sense of humor.

We may suspect that, once the first few weeks of frenzied activity had gone by, Crusoe started to find his days a little empty, and so it became a sort of repetitive therapy to transcribe his experiences since he landed on the island. He admits that this retrospective form of keeping a journal means going over for a second time the "Particulars" of his life after the shipwreck (60). But he seems compelled to give a shape to his experiences by logging them, dull times and washed-out days included. (This is in addition to the bare calendar he has created by cutting notches on a post, something he began to do very soon after arrival.) Eventually, after just over a year, his ink gives out, and his journal disappears from the text. While it lasts, this is for many readers one of the most compelling sections of the entire story. It dramatizes Crusoe's initial feelings of fear, despair, and hopelessness more vividly than anything else, until a measure of routine and familiarity sets in. His fears for his safety never go away completely, as noted earlier, but they recede over the years. Routine and familiarity are the prerequisite of a settled existence, but they are the enemy of intense living, and often their accompaniment is boredom.

Taken together, the *Strange and Surprizing Adventures* and the *Farther Adventures* provide a longitudinal survey of an obsessive personality. The young Crusoe rejects the prospect of "a Life of Ease and Pleasure," preferring to copy the way of "Men of desperate Fortunes . . . who went abroad upon Adventures, to rise by Enterprize, and make themselves famous in Undertakings of a Nature out of the common Road" (6). He embarks on his first voyage from Hull to London on mere whim, and after passing through a big storm his ship lies becalmed for seven or eight days in the dangerous Yarmouth Roads, the scene of many maritime disasters chronicled in the *Tour.*[28] When the wind rises again, the ship sinks and he barely escapes with his life. He recognizes that he ought to take this as a sign and do what most people would do—abandon his dreams of a life at sea. But "my ill Fate push'd on me now with an Obstinacy that nothing could resist" (14), and he rejects the dictates of reason. Once the die is cast, he cannot go back. Over the next five decades he pursues a quest that will take him ultimately "round three Parts of the Globe," as the title page of the *Farther Adventures* has it. Once he is captured by Barbary pirates and imprisoned at Salé on the coast of Morocco for two years. But this is one of the few periods of stasis in all his journeying. Much later he is marooned in Bengal, while he suffers some delays through the weather in his trek across Siberia. By this time his survival techniques must have been unequaled. But nothing deters him from seeking further worlds to explore and exploit. The drive to move on will always consume him.

How could such a restless soul as Crusoe not feel pangs of despair at his confinement on his island? How could the international trader not resent his immobility? How could a student of navigation and geography like Defoe not visualize such inertia in an unmapped locality as a very death in life?[29] Soul-destroying boredom (for the hero and his creator) would result, unless some activity—of more or less any kind—could be brought into the narrative; and there is a limit to the plausibility of useful actions he could perform. His investigation of the island is curiously belated, as though he is for once reluctant to encounter novelty; but when it comes, it is another way of staving off monotony.

One reason that Friday (named from the calendar) is so welcome an intruder, plainly, lies in his utility as a loyal helpmate: "in a little Time *Friday* was able to do all the Work for me, as well as I could do it my self" (179). He is thus totally unlike the unwilling laborers whose work-shy behavior Defoe laments elsewhere: "*In a Glut of Trade* they grow saucy, lazy, idle, and debauch'd." Crusoe would not have countenanced any shirking on Friday's part, any more than his creator would put up with a servant or apprentice who was guilty of "neglecting his Business."[30] At the same time, the mere presence of Friday acts to abridge the sameness of the hero's previous existence. After his arrival, Crusoe found that his own life "began to be so easy, that . . . could I but have been safe from more Savages, I cared not, if I was never to remove from the place while I lived" (177). Expressions of lassitude disappear from the text. Boredom has been effaced.

Unquestionably Crusoe had plenty to fill his days when he first arrived on the island. He worked like a Stakhanovite in order to satisfy the bare necessities of existence. But materially the conditions of his life grew less demanding over time, while existentially his religious conversion gave him a stability of mind he had lacked at first. He comes to recognize that he "had enough to eat, and to supply my Wants, and, what was all the rest to me?" (110). As year follows year, he has less to report, and whole chunks of his sojourn go without any record in the text. Almost without realizing it, we move on from the eleventh year to the fifteenth, which is reached halfway through the novel, and then on to the twenty-third and twenty-fourth, before Friday at length shows up. To chart incidents we now need a five-year calendar: Crusoe's old post would have worn thin with notches—around ten thousand of them, by the end. There must have been many hours of idleness.

A prolonged stay in this restricted space must give rise to a variety of psychological effects. But one that is partly disguised is the lassitude that overcomes the hero at times, especially when he needs to embark on repetitive labor such as that involved in building his stockade, or when he succumbs to cabin fever after the weather confines him to barracks in his little cave. He admits to depression after the failure of some of his bright ideas, like a plan to repair the ship's boat to make his escape. Looking closely again at the narrative, we can see that his activity often served as a coping mechanism, to create a "diversion" in the absence of escape routes, and to deflect from the stodginess of his diurnal routine. As the sun came up and the sun went down, boredom can never have been very far away.

NOTES

1. An influential reading of the passage on "original sin" is that of Maximillian E. Novak, *Economics and the Fiction of Daniel Defoe* (Berkeley: University of California Press, 1962), 32–48.
2. Text and references follow *The Farther Adventures of Robinson Crusoe, Being the Second and Last Part of His Life, and Strange Surprizing Accounts of His Travels round Three Parts of the Globe*, 2nd ed. (London, 1719), abbreviated here as *FA*.
3. For the background, see Siegfried Wenzel, *The Sin of Sloth: Acedia in Medieval Thought and Literature* (Chapel Hill: University of North Carolina Press, 1967).
4. *The Works of the Most Reverend Dr. John Tillotson* (London, 1696), 627.
5. It is noteworthy that Defoe had a particular fondness for the expression "it would be tedious" (to mention, etc.), which he uses at least twenty times in books and periodicals.
6. Daniel Defoe, *The Complete English Tradesman* (London, 1725–1726), 2:73–74.

7. *A New Voyage round the World, by a Course Never Sailed Before* (London, 1725), 2:46.
8. See esp. Reinhard Kuhn, *The Demon of Noontide: Ennui in Western Literature* (Princeton: Princeton University Press, 1976).
9. *The English Malady: or, A Treatise of Nervous Diseases of All Kinds, as Spleen, Vapours, Lowness of Spirits, Hypochondriacal, and Hysterical Distempers, &c.* (London, 1733), iv, 158. For an excellent discussion of the work, see Anita Guerrini, *Obesity and Depression in the Enlightenment* (Norman: University of Oklahoma Press, 2000), 143–152, 148.
10. *Gulliver's Travels*, ed. David Womersley, in *The Cambridge Edition of the Works of Jonathan Swift*, vol. 16 (Cambridge: Cambridge University Press, 2012), 396.
11. Patricia Meyer Spacks, *Boredom: The Literary History of a State of Mind* (Chicago: University of Chicago Press, 1995), esp. chaps. 2 and 3.
12. *Boswell's London Journal 1762–1763*, ed. Frederick A. Pottle (London: Heinemann, 1950), 183.
13. On the new ways in which curiosity could be satisfied, see Al Coppola, *The Theater of Experiment: Staging Natural Philosophy in Eighteenth-Century Britain* (Oxford: Oxford University Press, 2016), esp. chaps. 1 and 5, along with the valuable pioneering study by Barbara M. Benedict, *Curiosity: A Cultural History of Early Modern Inquiry* (Chicago: University of Chicago Press, 2001), esp. chap. 2.
14. Charles Dickens, *Bleak House*, ed. Stephen Gill (Oxford: Oxford University Press, 1995), 411–414. Spacks, *Boredom* (192–198) provides a subtle analysis from a different perspective of "Lady Dedlock's emotional deadness."
15. Woodes Rogers, *A Cruising Voyage Round the World* (Santa Barbara, CA: Narrative Press, 2004), 72–73.
16. Richard Steele, *The Englishman*, no. 26, December 3, 1713.
17. Hester Lynch Thrale, *Thraliana*, ed. Katharine C. Balderston (Oxford: Clarendon, 1951), 2:1065.
18. Darryl P. Domingo, *The Rhetoric of Diversion in English Literature and Culture, 1690–1763* (Cambridge: Cambridge University Press, 2016), 214, summarizing the argument of the book as a whole (see esp. chap. 3).
19. Arthur Schopenhauer, *Die Welt als Wille und Vorstellung*, Band 2 (Leschberg: Verlag Jürgen Beck, 1996), 472.
20. Daniel Defoe, *A Tour thro' the Whole Island of Great Britain*, ed. John McVeagh (London: Pickering & Chatto, 2001), 1:202. There is also a reference to the *bastides* in *Atlas Maritimus & Commercialis* (London, 1728), 239, a work for which Defoe was almost certainly responsible.
21. John Stow, *A Survey of the Cities of London and Westminster*, ed. John Strype (London, 1720), 2:131.
22. The description by Defoe's son-in-law, first printed from the original by George Reuben Potter in "Henry Baker, F.R.S. (1698–1774)," *Modern Philology* 29 (1932): 308–317, 310.
23. According to Alain Corbin, "Robinson Crusoe's island features all the characteristics of the Garden of Eden after the Fall: there is a prospect of serene happiness provided man does not spare his sweat, organizes his time, and carefully orders his labour." See *The Lure of the Sea: Discovery of the Seaside in the Western World, 1750–1840*, trans. Jocelyn Phelps (Berkeley: University of California Press, 1994), 15.
24. Stuart Sherman, *Telling Time: Clocks, Diaries, and English Diurnal Form, 1660–1785* (Chicago: University of Chicago Press, 1996), 56–58, 61–68. The whole book is relevant to themes discussed here in relation to *Robinson Crusoe*, but see esp. chap. 5 on travel writing.
25. Defoe, *English Tradesman*, 1:324.
26. Defoe, *Tour*, 3:10–11.

27. See Ilse Vickers, *Defoe and the New Sciences* (Cambridge: Cambridge University Press, 1996), 152–153.
28. Defoe, *Tour,* 1:112–115. See also remarks collected by Defoe in *The Storm* (London, 1704), 64–67, 210–211, 281–282.
29. See Daniel Defoe, *The Compleat English Gentleman*, ed. Karl D. Bülbring (London: David Nutt, 1890), 227–228, for Defoe's lofty expectations of geographical knowledge. Few individuals then living would have scored more highly on this test than Crusoe.
30. Daniel Defoe, *The Great Law of Subordination Consider'd* (London, 1724), 82, 219.

Part Three

CHARACTER AND FORM

8

CRUSOE'S RAMBLING

Benjamin F. Pauley

The year 1719 saw the publication of a great many books, but *Robinson Crusoe* was not one of them. It was, rather, two of them: first, *The Life and Strange Surprizing Adventures of Robinson Crusoe* published on April 25th (with three more editions to follow in that year alone); and then, just four months later, *The Farther Adventures of Robinson Crusoe* (which also appeared in a second edition before the year was out).[1] While Defoe and his publishers must have been pleased by the rapid success of the first Crusoe novel, *The Farther Adventures* does not seem to have been prompted by the response to *The Life*, as such. The closing pages of *The Life* provide a reasonably full (if rushed) précis of the first half of the second novel's plot, suggesting that Defoe had, at the very least, a detailed mental outline of much of the second novel before the first was completed.[2] While *The Farther Adventures* is a sequel, then, it is not simply an addendum, but belongs to Defoe's original (though not necessarily initial) conception of his larger work. The same cannot be said, it should be noted, for *The Serious Reflections of Robinson Crusoe*, published the following year. Defoe claims, in "Robinson Crusoe's Preface" to the third book, that "the present Work is not merely the Product of the first two Volumes, but the two first Volumes may be called the Product of this: The Fable is always made for the Moral, not the Moral for the Fable."[3] But while *The Serious Reflections* may serve, as Robert Markley suggests, as a "meta-commentary" on the first two volumes, it is not really continuous with them in narrative terms.[4] As Melissa Free has shown, the first two Crusoe texts almost invariably appeared together throughout the eighteenth and nineteenth centuries, but the two-book *Robinson Crusoe* quickly parted company with *The Serious Reflections*. The tendency to confine the label "*Robinson Crusoe*" to the text of the first novel alone, Free finds, is a twentieth-century one, beginning around the end of the First World War. As Free suggests, "The Crusoe that we assume our forebears to have known is a character whose life we have since, in effect, halved."[5]

While *The Farther Adventures* has never been entirely neglected by scholarship, it has not yet been widely assimilated into critical understandings of *Robinson Crusoe*, specifically, or of Defoe's oeuvre, more generally.[6] Readers familiar only with *The Life* will find *The Farther Adventures* a strange, surprising departure, indeed. The two parts of Crusoe's story are not simply different, they are *systematically* different. Where, in the first book, Crusoe is solitary and, for twenty-eight years, fixed in one spot off the coast of South America, the second book finds him almost perpetually in motion (traveling, in the words of the title page, "Round three Parts of the Globe"). Where, in *The Life*, Crusoe learns that "all the good Things of this World, are no farther good to us, than they are for our Use; and that whatever we may heap up indeed to give others, we enjoy just as much as we can use, and no more" (110), he spends much of the second half of his *Farther Adventures* heaping up good things. Where, in the first novel, Crusoe comes to a truer possession of himself as he cultivates his dominion over the island, he spends the second pointedly lamenting his lack of fixity and his inability to master his "native Propensity to rambling."[7]

In his introduction to the Crusoe novels for the Pickering & Chatto edition of *The Works of Daniel Defoe*, W. R. Owens suggests that stopping our reading at the end of the first volume, as most readers have done for the last hundred years, tends to provide "a satisfying sense of closure, with the island episode forming the imaginative core of the work, and Crusoe back home in England having expiated his 'original sin' of wanderlust."[8] Including *The Farther Adventures* in our reading of *Robinson Crusoe*, as Owens suggests we must, makes for a stranger and messier book: one that unsettles any sense of closure it might offer; one that second-guesses—perhaps even openly repudiates—its own "imaginative core"; one that leaves us questioning whether its narrator has learned anything at all. That stranger, messier book, however, is the one that Defoe actually wrote and published—in two parts—in 1719. While I will focus primarily on the second novel, part of my contention is that reading the larger *Robinson Crusoe* entails rethinking some commonly held ideas about the first novel. One commonplace view that comes under particular pressure, I think, is the notion that Defoe's fiction represents a brief for modern individualism. This is a view articulated influentially by Ian Watt, of course, who saw Crusoe as the archetypal hero of modern "economic individualism," and it is a view that still informs general opinion of the novel, despite convincing critiques offered by careful readers of Defoe's larger oeuvre like Maximillian Novak.[9] When we take *The Farther Adventures* into account, our sense of Crusoe as heroic individual comes to be tempered by an insistence on the claims of national interest—claims that Crusoe, in large measure, fails to recognize. In *The Farther Adventures*, Crusoe's individualism comes under greater scrutiny, first as he neglects to convert his island possession into a colony yoked to the interest of England, and second as he pursues a (to him) lucrative circuit of trading around the ports of Asia. In both cases, it is precisely Crusoe's individualism—his abstraction from English national identity, his tendency toward the deracinated pursuit of individual gain—that comes in for judgment.

Crusoe's return to England at the end of *The Life* should be something like a homecoming, but even the account in the first novel is equivocal. When Crusoe returns to Yorkshire, he finds that he has scarcely any family remaining, and—since he had long been presumed dead—no estate or legacy awaits him. With no particular tie holding him to England, he considers returning to Brazil to reclaim his plantation there, since he was, "as it were, naturaliz'd to the Place" (241), but is restrained by uncertainty over how to secure his newfound wealth and by some misgivings about embracing Catholicism. Crusoe is, in a sense, at home nowhere: he has lived the greatest part of his life on an island from which he was grateful to be delivered; he is a property owner and naturalized resident of a country to which he cannot bring himself to return; and he feels alienated from the country of his birth. The beginning of *The Farther Adventures* develops this picture of Crusoe's uneasy homecoming in greater detail, and it becomes clear that his wanderlust (the "sin" that Owens suggests we might have thought was "expiated" by the end of the first novel) continues unabated. Though his wife's expostulations rouse him to correct his "wandring Fancy" for a time, her death proves to be a "Blow from unforeseen Providence." Without her steadying presence, Crusoe finds that there is no resisting his "Distemper of Wandring," and he falls in with his nephew's proposal to carry him to his island in the course of a trading voyage to the East Indies.

Waving off the advice of his longtime counselor, the captain's widow, Crusoe makes his will and settles his estate "In such a Manner for my Children, and placed in such Hands, that I was perfectly easy and satisfy'd they would have Justice done to them, whatever might befal me."[10] In a symmetrical counterpart to the beginning of the first book, Crusoe the sometime prodigal son becomes a prodigal father, leaving his children (none of whom can be as old as seven) in order to revisit the island he had longed to escape.[11] Crusoe's desire to see his island again does not, however, translate into any lasting attachment to it: after a few weeks' stay, he abandons his initial plan and opts to continue instead on his nephew's trading voyage to the East Indies. The reader is drawn up short by Crusoe's reflections upon his island after his second (and final) departure: "I have now done with my Island, and all Manner of Discourse about it; and who ever reads the rest of my Memorandum's, would do well to turn his Thoughts from it, and expect to read of the Follies of an old Man, not warn'd by his own Harms, much less by those of other Men, to beware of the like; not cool'd by almost fourty Years Misery and Disappointments, not satisfy'd with Prosperity beyond Expectation, not made cautious by Affliction and Distress beyond Imitation."[12] This passage enunciates a decisive break with all that has come before in Crusoe's story. Defoe exploits formal characteristics of spiritual autobiography, accentuating the difference and the distance between Crusoe the character *in* the story and Crusoe the narrator *of* the story. In his role as narrator, Crusoe takes pains to identify and to condemn the failings of perception and the errors of judgment committed by his earlier self. At the same time that it highlights the imprudence of his decision, the retrospective voice of Crusoe's narration also proleptically condemns everything that is still to come in the second novel: his commercial ventures in the East Indies and his stupendous overland trek across China and Russia are here anticipated as merely the "Follies of an old Man."

Owens suggests that Crusoe's expressions of remorse here are of a piece with his reflections in the first novel on his rejection of his father's counsel and on his heedlessness in leaving his Brazilian plantation for a slaving voyage to Guinea, but seems to suggest that none of these moments of self-judgment is to be taken especially seriously: "As Crusoe's self-recriminations these are all entirely in character, but they should not be regarded as moralisings by Defoe or be regarded as the 'message' of the book."[13] To minimize such statements, however, seems to me to risk losing sight of Crusoe's own judgments of himself, expressed pointedly throughout both novels. Time and again, he takes himself to task for his "rambling Thoughts" (5), his "meer wandring Inclination" (5), his "rambling Designs" (35), his "native Propensity to Rambling," and so on.[14] One consequence of including *The Farther Adventures* in our reading of *Robinson Crusoe*, as Owens implies, is that our sense of the island episode as the text's "imaginative core" begins to slip. What the second novel throws into sharp relief is that the real issue at the novel's imaginative core is Crusoe's rambling disposition, itself.[15] Crusoe is a far less settled hero, I would suggest, than he is generally taken to be. Reading *The Farther Adventures* together with *The Life* makes *Robinson Crusoe* less a triumphant narrative of conversion and self-possession than a record of sustained irresolution and frequent tergiversation.

Given the language of patriarchal monarchy that Crusoe always employs with regard to his island subjects (he styles himself "the Father of the whole Family," for instance), his decision to leave the island figures as yet another instance of Crusoe's vexed relationship to the ideological claims of the family: he chooses, ultimately, to leave the islanders (much as he did his children) seemingly persuaded in his own mind that he has made adequate arrangements for their welfare. But Crusoe's reflection on his abandonment of the island is also strongly colored by the language of national belonging. In a string of rueful subjunctive clauses, Crusoe suggests what he might have done instead of sailing to the East Indies:

> Had I taken a small Vessel from *England*, and went directly to the Island; had I loaded her, as I did the other Vessel, with all the Necessaries for the Plantation, and for my People, took a Patent from the Government here, to have secur'd my Property, in Subjection only to that of *England*; had I carry'd over Cannon and Ammunition, Servants and People, to plant, and taking Possession of the Place, fortify'd and strengthen'd it in the Name of *England*, and encreas'd it with People, as I might easily have done; had I then settled myself there, and sent the Ship back, loaden with good Rice, as I might also have done in six Months Time, and order'd my Friends to have fitted her out again for our Supply; had I done this and stay'd there myself, I had, at least, acted like a Man of common Sense.[16]

By failing to bring the island into the circulatory system of English trade, Crusoe misses at once the chance to extend England's national prosperity and the surest means to solidify his own possession of the island. In imagining a more prudent course of action, Crusoe emphasizes not independence and rulership, but rather subjection—his property is best "secur'd," is most his own, when it is "in subjection only to that of England."

These retrospective reflections stand, confusingly, in sharp contrast to what had seemed to be Crusoe's sentiments at the time of his departure (given just a few pages earlier in the text) and thus serve to highlight how ill-founded his decision to proceed on his nephew's East Indies voyage really was. As he prepares to leave the island for the final time, Crusoe seems confident in the colony's prospects. The Spaniards and Englishmen appear to be fully capable of governing themselves and of setting aside the differences of Protestant and Catholic to "teach [the savages] the general Knowledge of the true God; and of their Saviour Jesus Christ."[17] This emerging multinational community would seem to confirm Aparna Dharwadker's observation that Crusoe's story minimizes the distinctions between European nationalities in the face of racial difference. Members of otherwise rival European nations, Dharwadker suggests, are quick to recognize "a collective racial, religious, cultural, and political identity which becomes the basis for separating Europeans *from the non-white, non-Christian other.*"[18] As Crusoe, notes, however, this multinational collective does not, in fact, thrive after his departure. In his absence, the settlers grow "Male-content with their long Stay there," prompting five of the Spaniards to leave the island; Will Atkins dies and the survivors beg Crusoe's partner at Brazil to write to remind him "of the Promise I had made, to fetch them away, that they might see their own Country again before they dy'd."[19] Though he allows that, had he stayed at the island, his personal presence might have held the people together, Crusoe must confess that his "paternal" authority was not really a sufficient foundation on which to build and sustain his multinational colony: "I never so much as pretended to plant in the Name of any Government or Nation; or to acknowledge any Prince, or to call my People Subjects to any one Nation more than another; nay, I never so much as gave the Place a Name; but left it as I found it belonging to no Body; and the People under no Discipline or Government but my own."[20]

As is frequently the case, *The Farther Adventures* here presents difficulties for some otherwise cogent readings of *The Life*. Manuel Schonhorn's account of Defoe's ideal of kingship in *Defoe's Politics* is compelling in its treatment of Defoe's political writings and of *Jure Divino*, and his closing chapter is persuasive where *The Life* is concerned, but it deals only rather awkwardly with *The Farther Adventures*. Schonhorn closes his treatment of Crusoe's theory of kingship by turning briefly to Crusoe's description of his absolute rule in the island, offered in a conversation with the exiled Muscovite prince he meets in Tobolski.[21] But Crusoe's grandiose claims are pointedly undermined by the fact that the dominion he describes is one he had abandoned. If *Robinson Crusoe* articulates a model of kingship, it is one that is observed in the breach, as Crusoe fails to occupy it. Similarly, Crusoe's hypothetical remarks about establishing his island as an English colony do seem to indicate a sense, as Anna Neill suggests, that his island "will only become properly civil once it participates in the English Atlantic trade." It is not clear, however, that Crusoe *actually* experiences the transformation "from colonizer-king to responsible English merchant" that Neill suggests he does (and that, I think Neill is correct in thinking, Defoe thought his protagonist *ought to* have experienced).[22] While Crusoe "recognizes that a place might be found for his island colony in the arena of foreign trade," it is a recognition he articulates—as with the model of kingship that Schonhorn derives from the work—in the act of lamenting his failure to pursue it.[23] Rather than offering its protagonist as a model for emulation, the two-book *Robinson Crusoe* is a text structured by ironies that expose how imperfectly Crusoe learns the lessons of his own life.

This is a dynamic, it is worth noting, that is already present in the first book, but our tendency to read *The Life* as a self-contained story can make Crusoe's "conversion" seem more solid than it really is. It is certainly true that Crusoe's island experience brings him, at times, to express a calm acceptance of Providence. But he is also easily discomposed, and his reliance on the disposal of Providence is readily shaken, as when the sight of a man's footprint produces a degree of fear that he confesses "banish'd all my religious Hope" (132). Even in cases less dramatic than his understandable fear of death at the hands of cannibals, Crusoe sees in himself a certain unsteadiness that never really leaves him. Certainly, Crusoe's struggles with his own inclinations are in large measure what give the book its spiritual and psychological interest.[24] There is a danger, however—perhaps exacerbated by his prosperity at the end of *The Life*—of reading Crusoe's story as more triumphant than it really is. In what is perhaps his most direct articulation of what he takes to be the "moral" of his story, Crusoe himself describes his narrative (and I quote, advisedly, from the first novel, rather than the second) as "a *Memento* to those who are touch'd with the general Plague of Mankind, whence, for ought I know, one half of their Miseries flow; I mean, that of not being satisfy'd with the Station wherein God and Nature has plac'd them" (164). This is not the verdict of a narrator secure in his mastery of his own rebellious nature, but of one acutely aware of how readily he has been mastered by his own restless dissatisfaction. It is a perspective that is perhaps hard to reconcile with the generally triumphant tone of the end of *The Life*, but is more obviously consistent with the larger, far more equivocal story that includes *The Farther Adventures*.

I would suggest that we can profitably read *The Farther Adventures* as a cautionary unraveling of what had appeared (but only appeared) to be the didactic certainties of *The Life*. Whatever the imaginative attractions of the exotic rambling it records, *The Farther Adventures* prompts us to see Crusoe as a man who never learns. He neglects repeatedly, in Christopher Flint's phrase, to "put his own self-interest aside" in service of any broader collective: as a son, and later as a father to his natural families; as a patriarchal monarch to the settlers at his island; and also, I would argue, as a subject of the British nation.

Robert Markley sees in Crusoe's turn away from his island colony a repudiation of a colonialist ideology that had structured the first book and a corresponding turn, in his pursuit of the East Indies voyage, toward a new ideology of commerce unencumbered by "the social, theological, and administrative headaches" of territorial possession.[25] In Markley's account, Crusoe's embrace of "visions of an infinitely profitable trade to the East Indies and South Seas" participates in the elaboration of a fantasy of English economic self-reliance. Markley's reading of the Chinese episodes in *The Farther Adventures* as defensive and compensatory assertions of English cultural supremacy strikes me as very persuasive.[26] In common with Owens's warning not to take Crusoe's self-recrimination as an articulation of the book's "message," however, Markley's account of the trading portion of the book demands that we set aside Crusoe's own overt judgments. Crusoe's condemnation of his failure to establish the island as a colony seems to me too clear and too pronounced to be dismissed as mere "moralistic rhetoric."[27] Markley argues that Crusoe's moralizing is quickly drowned out by our sense of the wealth that he accumulates as an independent trader, but I would suggest that Crusoe's trading comes in for more critical scrutiny than Markley allows for, and we are brought to see the ways that, in his Asian adventures, Crusoe fails to recognize and maintain ties to a larger, collective, national interest.

It is certainly true that Crusoe prospers materially from his Asian trade—the end of *The Farther Adventures*, like the end of *The Life*, features an accounting of his profits, which are considerable.[28] Crusoe and the independent English merchant he meets in Bengal trade from port to port around India, Malaysia, Indonesia, China, Japan, and the Philippines, handling a dizzying variety of exotic goods, each answering to the appetites of a different market. Their canny arbitrage of these Asian commodities is lucrative enough for Crusoe's partner to say that he "would have been content to have gone like a Carrier's Horse, always to the same Inn, backward and forward, provided he could, as he call'd it, *find his Account in it*."[29] Though Crusoe's own temperament is less that of the steady merchant than that of "the mad rambling Boy," he admits that even he was liable to have been converted to his partner's way of thinking by the sheer magic of accumulation.[30]

While the account of Crusoe's lucrative trading in the East Indies may have primed English readers to approve of the pursuit of gain in Asia, as Markley and J. A. Downie argue, Defoe's nonfiction writings suggest that Crusoe's trade is not necessarily one that Defoe would have favored. The commerce in which Crusoe and his partner engage is a wholly Asian one: Sumatran spices are bartered for Siamese opium, which is sold in China, with the proceeds plowed back into Sumatran spices, and so on. Endlessly circular, it is a trade that may indeed enrich two private Englishmen, but not one that holds any promise of reconnecting with English commerce or the fortunes of the English nation. Like Crusoe's unsubjected island, this is not a trade that is connected to the circulatory system of English commerce.[31] Crusoe and his partner transmute the valuable silks, spices, and furs they had purchased in Asia and Russia into cash at Hamburg, rather than bringing them back to England, and so may avoid some of the opprobrium Defoe aimed at the East Indies trade for filling Europe with only "Gaiety and Trifles."[32] But their trade doesn't serve to promote English exports, either, and so would seem to do good only for themselves.

Beyond such economic considerations, Crusoe offers more personal critical reflections on his East Indies venture, insisting that he really had no business doing what he was doing:

> Had I been twenty Year younger, I should have been tempted to have staid here and sought no farther, for making my Fortune; but what was all this, to a Man on the wrong Side of threescore, that was rich enough, and came

> abroad, more in Obedience to a restless Desire of seeing the World, than a covetous Desire of getting [in] it . . . I say, what was this Gain to me? I was rich enough, nor had I any uneasie Desires about getting more Money and therefore, the Profit[s] of the Voyage to me, were Things of no great Force, for the prompting me forward to farther Undertakings.[33]

Crusoe here echoes observations he had made at the beginning of the novel, where he had noted that "the common Motive of foreign Adventures was taken away in me; for I had no Fortune to make, I had nothing to seek: If I had gain'd ten thousand Pound, I had been no richer; for I had already sufficient for me, and for those I had to leave it to."[34] Crusoe suggests, then, that he does himself no real good in this pursuit.

Crusoe's material gains must, moreover, be balanced against other kinds of losses and failings that *The Farther Adventures* registers through several pronounced ironies in the final phase of his travels, after he has left the island. On more than one occasion during this stage of his travels, Crusoe finds himself in situations that echo earlier episodes of his story. In some cases, Crusoe notes and meditates upon these parallels; in others, he appears oblivious to them, leaving readers to remark his inconsistencies.

I will turn, in closing, to one such irony that is, on its own, perhaps, rather minor, but which I believe chimes with the broader concern with matters of national identification that I have been tracing. In an oddly revealing moment as Crusoe prepares to leave his island, he imagines an alternative formation for his multinational island colony. When planning their voyage, Crusoe and his nephew had resolved to carry the partially assembled frame of a sloop to the island. Thus, Crusoe's nephew could leave Crusoe at the island and continue his East Indies voyage without leaving his uncle "just reduced to the Condition [he] was in before."[35] Once he has decided to continue with his nephew on the East Indies voyage, however, Crusoe's explanation of the sloop appears to have changed. He says that, while he had thought of leaving the sloop to the islanders, the stories of the dissensions among them that he had heard upon first coming back to the island had changed his mind: "I saw it plainly had I set up the Sloop, and left it among them, they would upon every light Disgust have separated, and gone away from one another, or perhaps have turn'd Pirates, and so made the Island a Den of Thieves, instead of a Plantation of sober and religious People, so as I intended it."[36] Crusoe's reasoning here is never really explained. His decision, as he notes, was based on his first impressions of the islanders' state ("I found, *at least at my first coming*, such Seeds of Divisions among them"), but his subsequent conversations with the Spaniards and Englishmen showed that those early dissensions were behind them.

In this moment of narrative incongruity, Crusoe imagines some troubling alternatives to the peaceable multinational, multiconfessional colony that he had prided himself on forming. On the one hand, if the islanders were not to bond together sufficiently, the colony might simply dissolve, with some of them leaving in disgust (as seems to have been the case for five of the Spaniards). The other alternative, however, is perhaps still worse: they (or at least some of them) might, indeed, make common cause with one another, but by becoming pirates.

The figure of the "pirate" appears as a European analogue to the cannibal or savage: a nationless man who is held to be *hostis humani generis*—an enemy of all mankind—and hence liable to be hunted and brought to summary justice by anyone.[37] Crusoe, himself, had insisted that he would have been justified in executing the English sailors who had mutinied against the captain of the ship that was his rescue from the island—first at the end of *The Life*, when he uses the possibility of hanging as an inducement to persuade the men to accept the clemency of staying at his island (217), instead, and again at the beginning of *The Farther Adventures*, when he has vivid dreams of the Spaniards telling him of the outrages of the English.[38] It is, therefore, a curious reversal of positions when Crusoe and his partner, themselves, fall under suspicion of piracy while trading in Asian waters. He and his partner have purchased a ship from a crew of Dutch sailors who prove to have absconded with it after the death of their captain. As Crusoe learns from an English and a Dutch sailor who approach him while his crew repairs a leak on the coast of Cambodia, the story of the Dutch ship sold "at *Bengale*, to a Set of Pirates, which were gone a Cruising in her" has spread through an apparently quite efficient (if inaccurate) network of professional gossip among both Dutch and English ships' captains and crews. Should they be caught by any Dutch or English ship, they conclude, they must expect no quarter: "we could have expected nothing from them, but what Rage would have dictated, and an ungoverned passion have executed."[39]

These two passing invocations of the specter of piracy highlight the equivocal place of a multinational community in a world (as Dharwadker suggests) otherwise organized by "national" interests. By venturing into Asian waters without any attachment to the East India Company, Crusoe appears suspiciously disconnected from the ties of national identity. To be sure, Defoe was hardly a supporter of the East India Company, and Crusoe's vulnerability while in Asia is not an endorsement of the national monopoly company. (Crusoe, after all, chides himself not for neglecting to become a servant of the East India Company before rambling around Asia, but for rambling around Asia *at all*.) But it is notable that, in taking up with an independent English trader and assembling a multinational crew, Crusoe finds himself liable for the second time in the two parts of the novel to what he terms "the Fear of Man"—the same phrase he had used to describe his apprehensions after seeing a single human footprint in the sand (138).[40] In that well-known episode in the first book, Crusoe had remarked on the unaccountable irony of his newfound apprehension: "How strange a Chequer Work of Providence is the Life of Man! . . . For I whose only Affliction was, that I seem'd banished from human Society, that I was alone, circumscrib'd by the boundless Ocean, cut off from Mankind . . . *I say,* that I should now tremble at the very Apprehensions of seeing a Man, and was ready to sink into the Ground at but the Shadow or silent Appearance of a Man's having set his Foot in the Island" (132–133). Crusoe's circumstance after learning that he is presumed to be a pirate marks an intriguing inversion of this earlier case. While the coast of Cochinchina is a "wild and barbarous" place inhabited by "savage" others, the real source of terror for Crusoe and his partner is actually the captains and crews of English and Dutch ships who sail those waters—their nominal "countrymen." In an inversion that equates the pirate-hunting Europeans with pirates, themselves, Crusoe notes that he found himself "as much afraid of being seen by a *Dutch* or *English* Merchant Ship, as a *Dutch* or *English* Merchant Ship in the *Mediterranean* is of an *Algerine* Man of War."[41] Crusoe, of course, is *not* a pirate (to the disappointment, as it happens, of the two European sailors who had warned him of his danger at Cambodia: Crusoe learns that they had come in hopes of joining a pirate crew and "going a Roguing").[42] But his continued imprudent rambling has brought him to the point where he is easily mistaken for one.

As was the case with *The Life, The Farther Adventures* ends with Crusoe's return to England by a perilous overland journey (though the danger Crusoe faces comes not from the wild beasts of Languedoc, but from the "savage" Tartars of China and Siberia). In the course of this journey, Crusoe encounters an uncanny double in the person of a Muscovite nobleman exiled by the Czar to the remote garrison town of Tobolski. When their conversations turn to "the Greatness, the Magnificence, the Dominions, and the absolute Power of the Emperor of the *Russians,*" Crusoe cannot help boasting of his dominion over his own island, which he claims is still more absolute than the Czar's.[43] This encounter thus redirects attention to the island that Crusoe had said, categorically, that he had "had done with" at the novel's midpoint. Crusoe's boasts about his dominion in the island ring hollow, however, in light of his earlier reflections on his failure to secure it for himself and for England: we know that that neglect has left the island as much a "no-man's-land" as the forsaken Siberian steppes through which Crusoe has been traveling, which, though nominally the Czar's dominions, are, practically speaking, controlled neither by the Czar nor by the Chinese. Crusoe's story elicits in turn the Muscovite's account, in language that recalls passages from *The Life,* of the victory his exile has allowed him to achieve over the vanities of worldliness. Though Crusoe admires the man's wisdom, he is surprised when the nobleman rejects his offer of assistance in escaping from captivity and insists that he is better off in exile, secure from the temptations of the world.

On the one hand, the nobleman's religious and philosophic calm in retirement throws into relief the extent to which Crusoe himself has let slip the spiritual gains that his island solitude had afforded him. But it is not clear that the Muscovite's choice to remain in seclusion is one that Defoe would have us endorse.[44] As is the case with many of the novel's episodes, Crusoe never clearly settles the questions raised by his encounter with the Muscovite prince. He carries on his way back to England, and the novel ends—rather abruptly—with Crusoe's declaration that he resolves to "harass" himself no more, and that he is "preparing for a longer Journey than all these."[45] Though it is true that, unlike *The Life*, the ending of *The Farther Adventures* projects no more travels in this world, Crusoe's closing declaration that he has learned "the Value of Retirement, and the Blessing of ending our Days in Peace" seems suspect: Crusoe's rambling inclination appears to have been not so much exorcised as merely curtailed. If we can rationalize the restlessness of the first novel's ending as a function of being the "center" of Crusoe's adventures, the comparative lack of resolution at the end of the second novel is more problematic. When we read both parts of Crusoe's story, the self-made convert of *The Life*—alert to the ways of providence, achieving mastery over his environment as he achieves mastery over himself—slips from view, to be replaced by a man who remained a "mad rambling Boy" until his seventy-second year, never settled and nowhere at home.

NOTES

1. See John Robert Moore, *Checklist of the Writings of Daniel Defoe* (Bloomington: Indiana University Press, 1960). Throughout, I will have occasion to refer to these novels both singly and collectively. In general, I distinguish between the two novels by using their individual titles (*The Life* and *The Farther Adventures*). On those occasions when I refer to "*Robinson Crusoe*," I have in mind a notional whole comprising both novels together.
2. Maximillian Novak observes that while Defoe ends other novels with hints of sequels (like *Moll Flanders*, for instance), the projection at the end of *The Life* is so thorough as to suggest that "he was already at work on the sequel before the original was printed." Maximillian E. Novak, *Daniel Defoe: Master of Fictions* (Oxford: Oxford University Press, 2001), 555. W. R. Owens concurs in his introduction to the two Crusoe novels, suggesting, "It is clear that even before the first part had been published Defoe had planned out a sequel in some detail." Defoe, *The Novels of Daniel Defoe*, ed. P. N. Furbank and W. R. Owens (London: Pickering & Chatto, 2008), 1, 15.
3. Defoe, *Novels*, 3, 51.
4. See Robert Markley, *The Far East and the English Imagination, 1600–1730* (Cambridge: Cambridge University Press, 2006), 181. In his introduction to *Serious Reflections*, George

Starr has suggested that the text can best be thought of not as "an anticlimactic final instalment" of *Robinson Crusoe*, but rather as "a fascinating early draft" of a line of Defoe's thought on the supernatural, the occult, and the potential dangers of deviation from sound belief that he developed in the late 1720s with *The Political History of the Devil*, *A System of Magick*, *An Essay on the History and Reality of Apparitions*, and *A New Family Instructor*. See Defoe, *Novels*, 3, 1.

5. Melissa Free, "Un-Erasing Crusoe: Farther Adventures in the Nineteenth Century," *Book History* 9 (2006): 89–130, 97. The twentieth-century critical assessment of the second novel is captured nicely, because unselfconsciously, in Benjamin Boyce's offhand remark qualifying Sir Walter Scott's good opinion of *Memoirs of a Cavalier*: "Sir Walter's judgment in these matters loses some of its authority when we discover that he or his friends the Ballantynes thought it a good idea, in their 1810 edition of the *Novels of Daniel DeFoe*, to delete the last six and a half paragraphs of *Robinson Crusoe* and attach to it, without warning, the much less interesting *Farther Adventures of Robinson Crusoe* as if they constituted a single work of art. One wonders how many nineteenth-century readers knew Defoe's work only in the Scott-Ballantyne version." Boyce, "The Question of Emotion in Defoe," *Studies in Philology* 50, no. 1 (January 1953): 45–58, 48n3.
6. Roxann Wheeler, for instance, cites the revision of Friday's nationality in *The Farther Adventures* (his people are not really "Caribs") in order to complicate the novel's sense of the "savage." See "'My Savage,' 'My Man': Racial Multiplicity in *Robinson Crusoe*." *ELH* 62, no. 4 (1995): 821–861. Robert Markley attends to *The Farther Adventures* as a distinct, free-standing novel in order to suggest that Defoe redirects his attention from dreams of colonization to fantasies of mercantile accumulation in the Far East. A notable exception is Maximillian Novak, whose treatment of Crusoe's character and story has taken both novels into account since *Economics and the Fiction of Daniel Defoe*. More recently, scholars like Anna Neill, Jason Pearl, and Colby Dowdell have begun to include *The Farther Adventures* in broader readings of the Crusoe story. See Anna Neill, *British Discovery Literature and the Rise of Global Commerce* (New York: Palgrave Macmillan, 2002); Jason Pearl, "Desert Islands and Urban Solitudes in the Crusoe Trilogy," *Studies in the Novel* 44, no. 2 (Summer 2012): 125–143; and Colby Dowdell, "'A Living Law to Himself and Others': Daniel Defoe, Algernon Sidney, and the Politics of Self-Interest in *Robinson Crusoe* and *Farther Adventures*," *Eighteenth-Century Fiction* 22, no. 3 (Spring 2010): 415–442.
7. Defoe, *Novels*, 2, 5.
8. Defoe, *Novels*, 1, 17.
9. See Ian Watt, *The Rise of the Novel: Studies in Defoe, Richardson, and Fielding* (Berkeley: University of California Press, 1957); and, especially Novak, *Economics and the Fiction of Daniel Defoe*. Neill and Dowdell also offer strongly anti-individualist readings of Crusoe's story that take *The Farther Adventures* into account.
10. Defoe, *Novels*, 2, 11–12.
11. As Christopher Flint has noted, *Robinson Crusoe*, like Defoe's other novels, places the pursuit of individual desire in vexed relationship with the ideological claims of the family. See Flint, "Orphaning the Family: The Role of Kinship in *Robinson Crusoe*," *ELH* 55, no. 2 (Summer 1988): 381–419, esp. 395–406, which addresses *The Farther Adventures* as well as *The Life*.
12. Defoe, *Novels*, 2, 125.
13. Defoe, *Novels*, 1, 33.
14. For Crusoe's "native Propensity to Rambling," see Defoe, *Novels*, 2, 5, also 7 and 9, among many others. All told, some form of the word "ramble" appears at least nineteen times, and some form of "wander" appears more than twenty times in the two books.
15. Novak identifies Crusoe's "wandring Spirit" as his "original sin" in an important reading that takes both novels into account, attributing Crusoe's tribulations to "his lack of economic

prudence, his inability to follow a steady profession, his indifference to a calm bourgeois life, and his love of travel." Novak, *Economics and the Fiction of Daniel Defoe*, 32. George Starr has cautioned that, in Crusoe's rejection of his father's counsel, Defoe is taking aim at "the wildness that [he] found characteristic of unregenerate man in general, and of youth in particular, rather than the 'personal characteristics' suggested by . . . Novak." Starr, *Defoe and Spiritual Autobiography* (New York: Gordian Press, 1971), 77. While Crusoe allows that the inability to be satisfied with one's situation is "ordinarily the Fate of young Heads" and that "Reflection upon the Folly of it, is as ordinarily the Exercise of more Years, or of the dear bought Experience of Time," his "wandring Spirit" does not appear to be a function merely of his youth. Defoe, *The Life*, 164.

16. Defoe, *Novels*, 2, 125. Dennis Todd notes that the Caribbean location of Crusoe's island doesn't make it an especially promising candidate for being folded in to any system of English colonial trade. Todd argues that Defoe's focus in the Crusoe novels is on the psychological and spiritual dimensions of conversion, rather than the economic prospects of settlement and planting. See Todd, *Defoe's America* (Cambridge: Cambridge University Press, 2010), 61–64.
17. Defoe, *Novels*, 2, 113.
18. Aparna Dharwadker, "Nation, Race, and the Ideology of Commerce in Defoe," *The Eighteenth Century: Theory and Interpretation* 39, no. 1 (Spring 1998): 63–84, 75.
19. Defoe, *Novels*, 2, 125–126.
20. Defoe, *Novels*, 2, 125.
21. See Manuel Schonhorn, *Defoe's Politics: Parliament, Power, Kingship and "Robinson Crusoe"* (Cambridge: Cambridge University Press, 1991), 163–164.
22. Neill, *British Discovery Literature*, 55.
23. Neill, *British Discovery Literature*, 56, 65. J. A. Downie sees at the heart of Defoe's travel narratives a tension between the allure of exploration and the colonial imperative to settle and develop. Crusoe's rambling nature, Downie notes, "makes him . . . ill-fitted as a man of business," but the exploration and description of exotic locales provided by characters like the adventuresome Crusoe serve the ideological function of "[clearing] the ground for the level-headed, hard-working settler to follow." J. A. Downie, "Defoe, Imperialism, and the Travel Books Reconsidered," *Yearbook of English Studies* 13 (1983): 66–83, 74–75, 76.
24. Starr rightly notes that, in keeping with the spiritual tradition in which Defoe was working, "conversion was not seen as providing immunity to spiritual turmoils, but rather a new strength with which to resolve them." Starr, *Defoe and Spiritual Autobiography*, 115. I would suggest that *The Farther Adventures* (which Starr does not substantively address in this discussion) calls pointedly into question the extent to which Crusoe actually resolves his spiritual turmoils.
25. Markley, *Far East*, 181.
26. Betty Joseph argues along similar lines, suggesting that we can read Crusoe's statements about China as signs of the "frustrations" that one mode of (European, mercantile) capital encountered when meeting a different and incompatible system. Such "moments of cultural friction, when the flow of commodity exchange is interrupted," Joseph suggests, can reveal "the distinctions (or unevenness) that emerge among capital's various forms (whether mercantilist, manufacturing or industrial) as well as their role vis-à-vis specific historical contexts." Joseph, "Capitalism and Its Others: Intersecting and Competing Forms in Eighteenth-Century Fiction," *Studies in Eighteenth-Century Culture* 45 (2016): 157–173, 159–163.
27. Markley, *Far East*, 185.
28. Though Maximillian Novak downplays Crusoe's profits, arguing that the profits from the sale of his Brazilian plantation leave him "moderately wealthy, but not rich," David Spiel-

man's treatment of the relative values of the sums involved suggests that Crusoe, even by the most modest computation, would have found himself in the upper 5 percent of British society by income, ca. 1688. Nevertheless, Novak's broader contention that "there is no reason to believe that he would not have been as rich [if] he had not left York. It is certain that he would have been wealthier if he had remained in Brazil to cultivate his garden" remains plausible. See Novak, *Economics and the Fiction of Daniel Defoe*, 46, 163n29 and Spielman, "The Value of Money in *Robinson Crusoe, Moll Flanders*, and *Roxana*," *Modern Language Review* 107, no. 1 (January 2012): 65–87, esp. 70–76.

29. Defoe, *Novels*, 2, 146.
30. Defoe, *Novels*, 2, 145–146.
31. Defoe was notably ambivalent about the East Indies trade, as, for instance, in *The Trade to India, Critically and Calmly Consider'd*. Defoe, *Political and Economic Writings of Daniel Defoe*, 8 vols., ed. W. R. Owens and P. N. Furbank (London: Pickering & Chatto, 2000), 7, 83–104. For the importance of the circulation of goods to Defoe's sense of English commerce, see Earle, *The World of Defoe* (New York: Atheneum, 1977); and Schmidgen, "*Robinson Crusoe*, Enumeration, and the Mercantile Fetish," *Eighteenth-Century Studies* 35, no. 1 (Fall 2001): 19–39. For discussions of Defoe's attitudes toward the importation of Asian textiles, see Smith, "'Callico Madams': Servants, Consumption, and the Calico Crisis," *Eighteenth-Century Life* 31, no. 2 (Spring 2007): 29–55; and Cahill, "Realist Latitudes: Textilic Nationalism and the Global Fiction of the 1720s," *Digital Defoe: Studies in Defoe & His Contemporaries* 7, no. 1 (Fall 2015): 66–91. For a broader discussion of the entanglement of economics and trade with questions of national identity in Defoe's writings, see Abunasser, "Daniel Defoe and the Economic Production of English National Identity," *New Perspectives on the Eighteenth Century* 5, no. 1 (Spring 2008): 3–12.
32. Defoe, *Political and Economic Writings*, 7, 100.
33. Defoe, *Novels*, 2, 145. The Pickering & Chatto text does not have the word "in" that I have supplied in square brackets. That missing word appears in what Henry C. Hutchins calls the "second issue" of the first edition, which in current parlance should really be considered a new edition, as it was, with the exception of sheet B, fully reset (evidently from printed copy, as Hutchins plausibly argues). Hutchins, *Robinson Crusoe and Its Printing 1719–1731: A Bibliographical Study* (New York: Columbia University Press, 1925), 97–112. Owens notes Hutchins's characterization of the variants that appear in the "second issue" as "numberless errors in the printing and in the setting of the type which could only come from hasty work." Defoe, *Novels*, 2, 247. In this particular case, however, the reading from the later setting strikes me as preferable.
34. Defoe, *Novels*, 2, 5.
35. Defoe, *Novels*, 2, 11.
36. Defoe, *Novels*, 2, 119.
37. Joel Baer offers a survey of the laws concerning pirates in the eighteenth century, with reference to *The Farther Adventures*, among other works. Baer, "'The Complicated Plot of Piracy': Aspects of English Criminal Law and the Image of the Pirate in Defoe," *The Eighteenth Century: Theory and Interpretation* 23, no. 1 (Winter 1982): 3–26.
38. See Defoe, *Novels*, 2, 6–7.
39. Defoe, *Novels*, 2, 153.
40. Defoe, *Novels*, 2, 165.
41. Defoe, *Novels*, 2, 159. There is perhaps also an inexact echo here, as well, of Crusoe's capture and enslavement by the "Turkish Rover" of Sallee in *The Life* (see Defoe, *The Life*, 17.)
42. Defoe, *Novels*, 2, 172.
43. Defoe, *Novels*, 2, 205.

44. In *Serious Reflections*, Crusoe argues that "solitude," rightly understood, need not imply a withdrawal from the world (and indeed, that mere withdrawal from the world does not constitute "solitude" in the proper sense). See Defoe, *Novels*, 3, 57–66. As David Blewett argues, Defoe's sense of "retirement" is more aligned with the Puritan tradition than with classical sources. Retirement from the world when we find ourselves unequal to the task of resisting its temptations is, on this view, certainly better than worldly sin; but it is, at best, a negative virtue. Blewett, "The Retirement Myth in Robinson Crusoe: A Reconsideration," *Studies in the Literary Imagination* 15, no. 2 (Fall 1982): 37–50. See also Beesemyer, "Crusoe the Isolato: Daniel Defoe Wrestles with Solitude," *1650–1850: Ideas, Aesthetics, and Inquiries in the Early Modern Era* 10 (2004): 79–102; and Pearl, "Desert Islands."
45. Defoe, *Novels*, 2, 217.

9

CRUSOE'S ENCOUNTERS WITH THE WORLD AND THE PROBLEM OF JUSTICE IN *THE FARTHER ADVENTURES*

MAXIMILLIAN E. NOVAK

AT THE BEGINNING OF HIS section of *Atlas Maritimus & Commercialis* (1728), a survey of the entire world, mostly in economic terms, Daniel Defoe wrote, "I have study'd Impartiality thro' the Whole; and have therefore avoided all fulsome Panegyricks, all Bluster and Rhodomontades, in the Description of any Country."[1] It would hardly be a work by Defoe, about whom his enemies complained that he was unbearably opinionated, if he could have actually obeyed this injunction. There are passages in which he almost weeps over the destruction of Carthage by the Romans, and his portrayal of British commerce reveals much the same enthusiasms as his nearly contemporary writing in *A Tour thro' the Whole Island of Great Britain* (1724–1727 [for 1726]) and *A Plan of the English Commerce* (1728). Nevertheless, in his description of China in the *Atlas*, while expressing some doubts, he yields to the opinions of so many travelers and accepts the truth of these accounts. He expresses his admiration for the Grand Canal and for the regularity of the plan of Nanking. Fiction was another matter. As I will indicate, in *The Farther Adventures of Robinson Crusoe*, Defoe's protagonist subjects almost everything about China to severe criticism. In that work of world travel, we see things through the eyes of a character whose unreliable enthusiasms color all of his experiences.

Admittedly, as Jacques Derrida's recent reading of the first volume of the *Robinson Crusoe* trilogy has demonstrated, a critic is capable of experiencing the maximum intellectual play with Defoe's character in dealing with a kind of Cartesian Crusoe, isolated and having to deal with his inner thoughts.[2] Indeed, decades earlier, Crusoe's isolated situation had become a central point of illustration for Ludwig Wittgenstein's beliefs about private language.[3] There is no question that philosophers and economists have preferred a Crusoe who has no one or, at best, only a few people with whom he can speak. On the other hand, taking him merely on the island risks failing to see how much his is a tale of travel and encountering other peoples, not merely Friday and his fellow Cannibals, but the inhabitants of northern Africa, Brazil, Portugal, and Spain. And these experiences appear merely in the first volume of the series. In the second volume, usually read along with the first until the middle of the twentieth century, Crusoe travels away from his farm in England through the world—back to his island and to Brazil, and then to Madagascar and Bengal, through the West Indies to China, and then across Siberia and back to England.

What I want to do in this essay is to consider some aspects of Crusoe's encounters with other peoples, especially those encounters involving matters of justice and ethics. I want to emphasize how much Crusoe, when not carried away by his passions, his personal religious beliefs, and his often overly active imagination, tries to understand how people around the world tend to think, and, for the most part, to sympathize with them and their differences from the notions he absorbed in growing up in York during the seventeenth century. Most famous, of course, is his difficult acceptance of the humanity of the cannibals who threaten his existence—his overcoming of the rage he feels toward them and his gradual use of his reason to control his passions. His was hardly a commonplace stance, however much it might have owed to the paradoxes of Michel Montaigne.[4] Whenever possible, I want to avoid the complications implied in considerations of colonialism and it evils, however obvious those evils are to the modern mind.[5]

The important point to remember is that Crusoe is not Defoe but rather a literary character and an often unreliable narrator. It is easy enough to illustrate this with a crux in Defoe's rendering of the notion of a crusade against the entire pagan world. In his journal, *The Commentator*, published during 1720, Defoe assumed the persona of a sensible, modern thinker. In the issue of June 17, 1720, Defoe raised the question of a new worldwide Crusade on behalf of Christianity, only to dismiss such a notion as a harebrained scheme. "I am no Man for Crusadoes," he wrote, "nor am I a Man for a general War against the Infidel World, by way of Mission *ad propaganda. fid.*"[6] If the "Commentator" poses as an eminently sensible person, how would we describe Robinson Crusoe, who, in *Serious Reflections . . . of Robinson Crusoe*, a work written in the same year as *The Commentator*, proposed just such a scheme.[7] This would involve Christian nations waging unjust wars against the rest of the world. Small wonder that the writer who calls himself the Commentator settles for a war to eliminate the Barbary Pirates. This contradiction should lead us to conclude that although Crusoe has his notable moments of clear thinking, Defoe wanted his readers to view him as an enthusiast and an imaginist.[8] The passions, which often lead him astray, will frequently overwhelm his reason and his sense of justice. Indeed, we start *The Farther Adventures* with

Crusoe in a frenzy to return to his island—a frenzy accompanied by vivid dreams, daydreams, and what Crusoe calls "Extasies of Vapours . . . that I actually suppos'd my self, often . . . at my old Castle."[9] Only his wife's offer to travel with him, along with the difficulties that would be involved in journeying at a time when she is pregnant, allows him to struggle with "the Power of . . . [his] Imagination" (2:115) and to conquer his irrational urges.

I want to start the main part of my discussion with Crusoe in a kind of no-man's-land between China and Siberia, but nominally controlled by China. Defoe sets the stage for Crusoe's brief moment of enlightenment. He has just finished his view of China as an impoverished country with a subservient population. Dismissing the concept of the wise Chinese, he nevertheless finds himself willing to praise a house he visits that is made entirely of porcelain, but as for the Great Wall of China, he thinks that it is constructed only to keep out the Tartars, not for anything like a European army with contemporary artillery.[10] But now, on his way out of China, he decides to buy a camel at one of the outlying fortresses. Accompanied by the owner, he is attacked when returning to the caravan by five Tartars on horseback. The camel is lost in the skirmish, and Crusoe feels that he should not be forced to pay for it.

> We made no great Gain however by this Victory, for we lost a Camel, and gained a Horse; but that which was remarkable, when we came back to the Village, the man demanded to be paid for the Camel; I disputed it, and it was brought to a hearing before the *Chinese* Judge of the Place; that is to say, in *English*, we went before a Justice of the Peace: Give him his due, he acted with a great deal of Prudence and Impartiality; and having heard both Sides, he gravly ask'd the *Chinese* Man, that went with me to buy the Camel, whose Servant he was? I am no Servant, says he, but went with the Stranger. At whose Request, says the Justice? At the Stranger's Request, says he. When then, says the Justice, you were the Stranger's Servant for the Time, and the Camel being deliver'd to his Servant, it was delivered to him, and he must pay for it. (3:173)

Crusoe reluctantly admits the "just Reasoning upon the Consequence," pays for the lost camel, and buys another, this time keeping at a considerable distance from the place of purchase.

This example of Chinese justice is revelatory of a number of things. Crusoe's previous dismissal of concepts of Chinese greatness "Glory, (as some call it)" (3:151) is an attempt to correct what he feels to be exaggerated descriptions of Chinese civilization. He insists the praise lavished on China arose mostly from low expectations—that is from the little that might be expected from a nation beyond the sphere of European culture. It is only because so little is expected of what, in

Crusoe's words, is "a barbarous nation of Pagans, little better than Savages" (3:152) that travelers had praised aspects of their culture. Too many of these travelers were accustomed to authoritarian forms of government.[11] Crusoe, on the other hand, analyzes China from the standpoint of Whiggish concepts of society and politics, revealing the people to be what he calls "a contemptible herd or Crowd of ignorant sordid Slaves, subjected to a Government qualified only to rule such a People."[12] He adds that, as a state, China appears acceptable only because the Russian Empire, which adjourns it, is "almost as rude, impotent, and ill govern'd a Crowd of Slaves as they." At this point, Crusoe shows off that aspect of his character that is illustrative of British thickheadedness and insularity that Defoe had satirized to great effect in his *True-Born English Man* (1700). But there is another side to him, the side that is more open and willing to accept new ideas when experience shows his prejudices to be either wrong or inadequate to deal with reality, what Defoe liked to call "the Thing Itself."[13]

Despite his occasional longings for absolute sovereignty, during his island experience, Crusoe is confident that a government based on the agreement of the governed is the most reasonable one, yet the Chinese Justice of the Peace, who judges against him, is as capable of using his reason as any other human being. And the Chinese magistrate's notion of how property is transferred shows a sagacity that Crusoe hardly expects. Whatever else may be wrong with China, its system of judges appears to operate better than the British system of which Defoe often complained. We experience a number of hints that Crusoe's initial judgment about China is not entirely objective. Amid all of his criticism, Crusoe praises the roads as excellent. And in his attack on Chinese "Glory," he admits that nothing irks him so much as the "Pride" (3:157) that he observes in a Mandarin being fed by the local population. Crusoe perceives this the equivalent of a country gentleman in England being fed by his servants. His daydreams of a European army and navy easily destroying the Chinese armed forces come as a reaction to what he feels to be the Chinese sense of superiority. Thus, when faced with the rationality of the Chinese Justice of the Peace, he finds himself reluctantly admitting something good about China. It is the more convincing because he loses the case. Despite his prejudices, then, Crusoe is occasionally willing to admit to excellence in foreign countries when he encounters it.

This concern with justice is a major theme throughout *The Farther Adventures*. Crusoe leaves England to return to visit his island, partly because of his not entirely rational compulsion to see what had happened to his island and partly because he has strong doubts about the justice of a society such as that of the England to which he has returned in which "the Men of Labour spent their Strength in a daily struggling for bread . . . , so being in a daily Circulation of Sorrow, living but to Work, and working but to live" (2:117–118). Compared to this grim assessment of economic life in civilization, the island, with its inherent restrictions on luxury and excessive labor and relative equality, represents a form of utopia.

That justice will be a major motif is clear from the beginning of his new journeying. On the voyage out, in encountering two ships that had experienced difficulties, Defoe has Crusoe experience what may be seen roughly as the dramatization of two natural law case studies about self-preservation. One had caught fire and had to be abandoned; the other had been rendered unnavigable by a storm. Both raised questions about justice and natural law. In the latter ship, the passengers had been allowed to go without food and water for days, resulting in the death of a passenger, the mother of a young man. In the former, the passengers were saved before being forced to resort to cannibalism, but it was a matter of time before such a grim prospect would have become a reality. In these situations, self-preservation, the first law of nature in Defoe's system, seemed to abrogate all forms of justice.[14] It is significant that, having fled from the economic injustice of society, the first scenes he encounters are demonstrations of the artificiality of justice, scenes in which the laws of society collapse into a Hobbesian state of nature.

In delineating these two scenes, Defoe emphasizes the way human beings respond to these situations. In the instance of the ship that has caught fire, he has Crusoe observe the passions of those who have been saved—the extravagant behavior, the cries of joy and violent gestures. Defoe has Crusoe note that some of this might be explained by their French nationality, but it allows Defoe to reveal the basic passions that dominate human behavior. Similarly, by way of displaying emotion recollected in tranquility, he has the maid recall at considerable length the feelings aroused in her by her hunger—how she would have been willing to devour anything or anyone and even considers biting her own arm. The crew has allowed these passengers to starve, placing the demands of their own bodies before those they regard as outsiders.[15] Thus the themes of human necessity—the demands of the body—along with the passions and their conflict with reason and justice are introduced at the beginning of *The Farther Adventures.*

Once on his island, Crusoe hears from the Spanish Captain the tale of war between the settlers on the island and the cannibals who land there with the intent to destroy them. This story of self-defense and self-preservation is essentially about the laws of warfare. The settlers, with their superior firepower, are able to kill dozens of the cannibals, but this is what they have to do. There is no apology offered here. Warfare is horrible, but the cannibals invade the island with the intention of destroying and indeed devouring the settlers.

Before this invasion, three of the Englishmen had been in continual conflict with the Spaniards, but as in Defoe's concept of the way societies tend to consolidate through the need for self-defense, the war against the cannibals brings with it a relatively peaceful society—a society that Crusoe might easily have helped toward becoming a well-governed island state. Nevertheless, Crusoe does not remain on his island. He thinks, after he discovers sometime later that the colony is floundering, that he might have remained to be a patron to these people. He might also have attempted to mediate between the various groups on the island, to have ruled as a just leader, but it is as an observer of the world, and to a certain extent as an observer of justice in that world that he decides to pass the remainder of his days.

Shortly after leaving his island for a brief stay in Brazil, Crusoe encounters the kind of justice meted out by the Inquisition. He secretly rescues a family that has been persecuted and impoverished by the Inquisition as "Heretick[s]" (3:78). We never learn what kind of heresy has brought on this treatment, but Crusoe permits them to be smuggled on board a sloop that is heading toward his island. So if Crusoe once boasted of the religious tolerance existing on his island, he adds to it some unnamed religious heresy.

Perhaps the most vivid scene in *The Farther Adventures* involves misunderstanding and revenge, which Defoe tends to view as the opposite of justice. Crusoe's ship stops at Madagascar. The confrontation between the natives and the sailors results in a violent encounter in which the sailors burn down the native village and indulge in a brutal slaughter of the inhabitants. The cause of the quarrel was the rape of one of the native girls by one of the sailors. The natives succeeded in taking revenge on the sailor guilty of the crime, a Thomas Jeffry, but this only angered the other sailors. That they also thought that they might find some treasure among the natives made their desire for revenge all the more exciting. They refer to the natives as "Dogs" and engage in a mass slaughter of the natives after finding the body of Thomas Jeffry displayed in the village. Coming upon the natives when they are asleep, the sailors set fire to their huts and kill them indiscriminately.

> In short there were such Instances of a Rage altogether barbarous, and of a Fury, something beyond what was human, that we thought it impossible our Men could be guilty of it, or if they were the Authors of it, we thought they ought to be every one of 'em put to the worst of Deaths. But this was not all, we saw the Fire encreas'd forward, and the Cry went on just as the Fire went on; so that we were in the utmost Confusion. We advanc'd a little Way farther, and behold to our Astonishment, three Women naked, and crying a most dreadful Manner, come flying, as if they had indeed had Wings, and after them sixteen or seventeen Men, Natives, in the same Terror and Consternation, with three of our *English* Butchers, for I can call them no better, in their Rear. (3:96)

I have discussed Defoe's rendering of this scene from the standpoint of its painterly quality, based on an imagined painting of the horrific rape of the city of Magdeburg during the Thirty Years' War.[16] But here I would like to consider it from the standpoint of justice and ethical behavior.

Like Conrad's Lord Jim, some one hundred eighty years later, Crusoe, the European, is often puzzled by the relationship between himself and the natives he encounters. Are they to be considered as living according to their own schemes of justice, or are they to be held to schemes of justice of which they had no knowledge at all? Is there a natural law that governs all humans? Or was one to rely on a law of nations that often seemed as various as human society itself?[17] On one point, Defoe is fairly consistent. Acting "the Spaniard" as Defoe calls it in his section of *Atlas Maritimus* (291), by which he means slaughtering some forty to fifty million natives in the Spanish conquest of America, is something that should never be repeated.[18]

In this case, the sailors take the revenge of the strong against the weak. They have a cause. They raise the punishment meted out to Thomas Jeffry as a justification for their massacre. But had Jeffry not raped a native girl? Was that not a crime punishable by death in many Western countries? Was his punishment by the natives sufficient justification for a general massacre by Jeffry's fellow sailors? Crusoe appears to be the only one who feels sympathy for the natives as he finds his efforts at restraining the crew are futile. "I seeing it quite out of my Power to restrain them, came away pensive and sad," he writes, "for I could not bear the Sight, much less the horrible Noise and Cries of the poor Wretches that fell into their Hands" (3:99). The Boatswain disputes Crusoe's claim, insisting that "Justice" was on their side. He excuses Jeffry's rape as simply taking "a little Liberty with a Wench" (3:101), and justifies the massacre of the natives as proper punishment for their murder. Crusoe's Nephew provides a different explanation. On seeing the body of Thomas Jeffry, "he was not Master of himself, neither could he govern his Passion," and that "as he was a Man, and Nature mov'd him, he could not bear it" (3:100).

Crusoe refuses to accept that form of colonial mentality that would consider the notion that the natives having taken the life of one of "us" would be sufficient justification for a general slaughter of "them." He completely rejects his Nephew's claim to being unable to control his passions, and finds the Boatswain's claim to "Justice" untenable. He quotes Jacob's judgment on Simeon and Levi (Genesis 49:7) for the slaughter of so many in revenge for the rape of Dinah: "*Curse be their Anger, for it was fierce; and their Wrath for it was cruel*" (3:98). He regards the "Murther" of a hundred fifty natives as unpardonable. The empathy that he demonstrates for the natives reveals that his experience with Friday has indeed shaped his sense of justice both for Europeans and for the natives of what we now call the Developing World. What Crusoe calls the "*Massacre of Madagascar*" (3:103) and his constant upbraiding of the crew for their cruelty leads eventually to his being put ashore at Bengal.

At this point in recounting Crusoe's adventures, Defoe apparently thought he would take the opportunity to explore another aspect of justice, the kind of justice with which a pirate, or supposed pirate, is treated by a mob. As James Kelly has suggested, Defoe looked back to a time when an innocent English Captain and his crew were hanged in Scotland after judgment by what today would be called a "kangaroo court." The so-called "Worcester Affair" was a major scandal in 1704, coming a few years before the Union of the England and Scotland.[19] Of course, Defoe shaped the story differently, providing a happy ending for Crusoe, but the events are much the same. Crusoe has been trading throughout the Far East with a ship that, unknown to him or his partner, once belonged to pirates—pirates who had murdered the rightful captain and three of the crew.

The battle with the boats that tried to overtake Crusoe's ship occurs in the area around present-day Cambodia. Having successfully made their escape, Crusoe and his crew learn about the rumors that had surrounded their ship. Crusoe's Partner points out that "they had such a Prepossession against us beforehand, it had been in vain for us to have defended our selves, or to hope for any good Quarter at their Hands, and especially considering that our Accusers had been our Judges, and that we could have expected nothing from them, but what Rage would have dictated, and an ungoverned Passion have we executed" (3:121–122). Although Crusoe's Partner wants to go back to Bengal to find "proper Judges" to provide "some Justice, and not be hang'd first, and judg'd afterward" (3:122), Crusoe considers this expectation of finding such judges overly optimistic and convinces his Partner that it would be safer to rid themselves of the ship in China.

Robert Markley remarked on the connection between this event and Crusoe's fear of the Dutch and of injustice at their hands—a fear that Markley associates with the massacre of English merchants at Amboyna in 1623 at the hands of members of the Dutch East India Company.[20] Indeed John Dryden's mercantile tragedy, *Amboyna*, performed in the 1670s, made the English merchant, Gabriel Towerson, into an heroic figure, resisting Dutch oppression. In his nightmare following the incident of the boat chase, Crusoe finds himself lashing out against a Dutch sailor and actually damaging his hand in the process. But although the ship Crusoe and his partner had purchased had apparently been illegally taken in a mutiny in Batavia, controlled by the Dutch, the area in which the chase occurs was the "River of Cambodia" and the sailors chasing them appears to have been a mixed lot of English and Dutch sailors. Two of the boats in the lead "were English" and "outsailed the rest" (3:119). Why then the apparent awakening of what Markley calls the "trauma" of Amboyna?

One reason is Crusoe's discomfort of discovering that the ship that he and his partner bought was in fact stolen. He remarks on the danger he and his partner are in:

> For whatever ill Circumstances I had been in, I was never pursu'd for a Thief before; nor had I ever done any Thing that merited the name of Dishonest or Fraudulent, much less Thievish. I had chiefly been my own Enemy, or as I may right say, I had been no Body's Enemy but my own: But now I was embarrass'd in the worst Condition imaginable; for tho' I was perfectly innocent, I was in no Condition to make that Innocence appear: And if I had been taken, it had been under a supposed Guilt of the worst Kind; at least a Crime esteem'd so among the People I had to do with. (3:123)

Feeling guilty, despite his own sense of innocence, Crusoe displaces his uneasiness by blaming the Dutch and the "cruel usage" he and his crew might suffer: "the Story of *Amboyna* came into my Head, and the Dutch, might perhaps torture us" (3:141) and force them into false confessions.

Crusoe's irrational anxieties—his mixture of fear, guilt, and aggression—contribute toward establishing the main point of this episode, which appears to be directed toward the failure of justice where it is directed by passion rather than reason. The sailors in the ships pursuing Crusoe's ship wanted revenge against a crew they considered to be pirates. Even if there had been some kind of trial, like that which condemned the Captain and crew of the Worcester, it would have amounted to revenge rather than justice—revenge of much the same kind that motivated the sailors who had retaliated against the natives in Madagascar, which is to say, revenge given an edge by the profit motive. Those involved in the "Massacre of Madagascar" hoped to find valuables in the huts of the natives, and the sailors attacking Crusoe's ship in Cambodia would have profited by capturing the ship and its cargo.

On the way to China, Crusoe and his crew put in at a place to search for a leak in their ship. The natives, thinking that the ship was actually a wreck, attempt to get loot from the vessel. They are driven off successfully, but only after Crusoe's crew pour hot pitch on the natives. Such an action could be justified as self-defense and under the laws of self-preservation, which Defoe thought to be a universal right. Nevertheless, it is significant that Crusoe is not entirely satisfied:

> . . . for I was sick of killing such poor Savage Wretches, even tho' it was in my own Defence, knowing they came on Errands which they thought just, and knew no better; and tho' it may be a just Thing, because necessary, for there is no necessary Wickedness in Nature, yet I thought it was

> a sad Life, which we must be always oblig'd to be killing our Fellow-Creatures to preserve, and indeed I think so still; and I would even now suffer a great deal, rather than I would take away the Life, even of that Person injuring me. (3:129)

It is not entirely clear how much Crusoe (or Defoe for that matter) fully understood the grimmer aspects of colonialism—of going about the world to impose one's power on a native population—but it is clear enough that at this point in traveling through the world, Crusoe has seen enough of these encounters to give him some sense of what would be involved.

His future Partner had enticed him to action with an appeal to the necessity of human activity: ". . . you shall be Captain, I'll be Merchant, and we will go a trading Voyage to *China*; for what should we stand still for? The whole world is in Motion, rouling round and round; all the Creatures of God, heavenly Bodies and earthly are busy and diligent, Why should we be idle? There are no Drones in the World but Men, Why should we be of that Number?" (3:108). Crusoe has his doubts. He is rich enough. He is not really interested in making more money. But movement—going to new lands—that, he admits, excites his interest.

This leads to the final section of *The Farther Adventures* that I want to discuss in detail. Like some of the others, it is ambiguous in its import, particularly on the matter of justice. Crusoe takes offense at the appearance of a kind of idol worshipped by the Tartars of Siberia, a god called *Cham-Chi-Thaugnu*. Crusoe writes,

> I confess, I was more mov'd at their Stupidity and brutish Worship of a Hobgoblin, than ever I was at any Thing in my Life; to see God's most glorious and best Creature, to whom he had granted so many Advantages, *even by Creation*, above all the rest of the Works of his Hands vested with a reasonable Soul, and that Soul adorn'd with Faculties and Capacities, adapted both to honour his Maker and be honoured by him, sunk and degenerated to a degree so more than stupid, as to prostrate it self to a frightful Nothing, a meer imaginary Object dressed up by themselves, . . . that this should be the Effect of meer Ignorance, wrought up into hellish Devotion by the Devil himself; . . . should shock Nature it self. (3:184)

Crusoe works himself into a "Rage." He does some violence against the idol, but eventually decides to blow it up. He describes his plan to a Scots merchant, who is amused at Crusoe's "Zeal." He asks what Crusoe proposes by this, and Crusoe says "to vindicate the Honour of God" (3:183). The Scotsman warns Crusoe that it could start a war with the Tartars that might cause a revolt against the Czar.

But Crusoe is adamant. He says that he will destroy the idol "tho' I were to be deliver'd up to them for satisfaction" (3:184). What punishment Crusoe has in mind is never clear, but the Scottish Merchant tells Crusoe of the terrible punishment that the Tartars inflicted on a Russian who affronted their worship—how they shot arrows into him and then burned him as a sacrifice to this idol. Interestingly enough, in response to this story, Crusoe tells the Scottish Merchant the story of the Massacre of Madagascar, now drawing the moral that they ought to exact the same revenge for that Russian victim as the sailors inflicted on the villagers in Madagascar. Crusoe describes how the Scottish Merchant finds it difficult to make a connection between the two events. And seemingly to cool Crusoe's ardor he explains that although they sacrificed the "poor *Russian*" (3:184) to the same idol, it was a different village that was involved. Clearly the Scots Merchant is concerned that Crusoe wants to replace the "Massacre of Madagascar" with his own "Siberian Massacre." Relenting, Crusoe insists that he just wants to destroy the idol; and with the help of another Scotsman, they do indeed blow it up.

This results in a crisis for the Governour of the region, as thirty thousand Tartars gather at Nertinskay, the town where the caravan has stopped, to demand justice. Since the Czar has charged the Governour to treat the Tartars "with Gentleness and Civility" (3:189) to avoid a war with them, the Governour suggests that he will try to discover if anyone in the caravan might have destroyed the idol, at the same time giving the caravan notice to make haste in departing. Crusoe notes that no one in the caravan had any notion of the matter; "and as for us that were guilty, we were the least of all suspected" (3:190). Although the caravan succeeds in escaping for a brief time, they do have to fight a battle with the Tartars on the third day. The Tartars demand that the leader of the caravan give up those who had blown up the idol, *Cham-Chi-Thaungu*, but the perpetrators manage to deceive the other members of the caravan. The ensuing battle, with its shower of arrows, fails to hurt anyone, and the caravan manages to escape by a subterfuge, using a "meer Tartar" (3:193) who has been part of the caravan, to give the army of Tartars false information about another caravan to the south, suggesting that the guilty parties belonged to that caravan. As a result, Crusoe's caravan manages to escape.

G. A. Starr has recently suggested that Defoe expected the reader to approve of Crusoe's actions, that so far from being an unreliable narrator, he was a trustworthy gauge of Defoe's opinions.[21] On some level, had Crusoe been acting on his island where he alone would have had to endure the consequences of his action, this might have been true. But in Siberia Crusoe is part of a commercial caravan. His action involves everyone in the caravan, a not inconsiderable part of the Tartar nation, and the possible future of Russia's relations with the people of Siberia.

It throws light on Crusoe's discomfort with life in England after his twenty-eight years on the island—his creation of his self-sufficient farm and his seeming inability to live comfortably among his neighbors.

Crusoe's own language gives us the clue to how we should read this adventure. The desire to blow up the idol takes its place among Crusoe's uncontrollable desires—similar to the "wandering Fancy" that seizes him at various times and his rage against the cannibals who visit his island. His inability to govern the "Rage" that he feels at seeing the idol reveals to the reader that once more Crusoe finds himself governed by impulse. As mentioned previously, the Scots Merchant is somewhat puzzled by Crusoe's "Zeal" (3:183), warning him that the Tartars will demand revenge of the Governour of Nertsinskay. This only leads to Crusoe's determination to do the demolition at night and in the disguise of a Tartar. Although Crusoe and the two Scotsmen who engage in the act reveal no "guilt" in their faces, they know that they are entirely guilty of an action that had the possibility of causing a war. It is not clear who appointed Crusoe as the defender of the "Honour of God." And in raising the image of the "Massacre of Madagascar," Crusoe suddenly draws a completely wrong moral from his objections that brought about his being put ashore in Bengal. This is not like Crusoe's most famous failure of reason—what Tony Brown describes as the way his entire world becomes distorted with horror on discovering the footprint in the sand.[22] Rather the demolition of the idol has the feel of a boy's prank of the kind that Defoe discussed in his *An Account of the History and Reality of Apparitions* (1727).[23] And there is no question that at this stage in his development, Crusoe, who, as Geoffrey Sill suggested, showed some ability to restrain his passions in *The Life and Strange Surprizing Adventures*, slides backward badly.[24]

When he asks his commercial Partner to join them in the action against the idol, the Partner refuses: ". . . he said, he was ready to assist me to the utmost, and upon all occasions for my defence; but that this was an Adventure quite out of his way" (3:185). As mentioned previously, his Partner had stirred Crusoe to action as a trader throughout the Far East, but it was all for the sake of action itself and of making money. What part should he have played in this adventure? Risking the start of a war was hardly advantageous for the cause of making a profit from their goods in the caravan, and that was all that governed his interests. In this, Crusoe's Partner appears to be carrying out the proper providential role of the merchant and trade. In his *A General History of Trade* (1713), Defoe had argued that "we know no other Interest in Commerce but Gain," punctuating this statement with a fierce rejection of any qualms about religion in such matters: "We Trade with *Turks*, Infidels, Idolaters, Gentiles, Heathens, Savages, it matters not what Gods they serve, so they serve our end, and we can serve our Interest by Trading with them; what if they Worship the Sun or the Moon, this Idol or that; Visytly-pustly, Teckoacoman, Mahomet, or Lucifer? Getting Money is the only Idol that Trade Worships, and it is nothing to the Merchant who he trades with, if he can make a good Return."[25] Crusoe's Partner might also have had some hesitations about what amounted to a criminal act. Defoe found in trade a form of openness and liberation. To the contrary, the guilt involved in this surreptitious act in the dark of night hardly seems part of such a scheme. In comparing himself to his Partner, Crusoe might have temporarily enlisted the sympathy of the reader in judging his Partner as going "like a Carrier's Horse, always to the same inn, backward and forward, provided he could as he call'd it, *find his Account in it*" as opposed to Crusoe's description of himself as being like "a mad rambling Boy, that never cares to see a Thing twice over" (3:111). The naive reader might reject the dull merchant for the adventurous Crusoe, but in the end, the Partner was benefiting the world by his drudgery. Led by his passions, Crusoe causes trouble.

Defoe provides sufficient clues for the reader to recognize that Crusoe is once more being controlled by his passions. By his action, Crusoe may have put to rest the frenzied rage that suddenly governed him, but clearly justice is not done in this case. The Tartars have their idol destroyed, and no one is punished. On his island, before the coming of Friday, Crusoe does a number of foolish things, but he is the only person victimized. Out in the world, he has the potentiality of making tens of thousands of people unhappy. Although he provides a religious motivation for his action—the defense of true religion—in some ways the destruction of the idol is a partial fulfillment of the European artillery that he imagines blowing up the Great Wall of China—not an action taken in defense of true religion but rather the result of a violent colonialist impulse he finds difficult to govern.

The self-indulgence characterized by this episode stands in sharp contrast to Crusoe's encounter at Tobolsk with the victims of Peter the Great's often paranoid punishment of some of the best servants of his state. Those who have not been executed have been exiled to Siberia. In Defoe's fictional Tobolsk, they manage to live better than many of the real victims of Peter's justice, but they are still being victimized by an absolutist state with an arbitrary system of justice. Before he returns to England, Crusoe succeeds in smuggling out of Siberia to Europe one victim, the son of an exiled Prince. Although it is a gesture that might have been expected of any Englishman indignant at the injustices of absolute monarchy, whether in China or Russia, it is still fraught with danger, and Crusoe once more emerges as a defender of justice. But at times Crusoe is indeed, like another of Defoe's protagonists, Moll Flanders, too "indifferent" (or unreliable) a guide for the alert reader to follow.[26]

NOTES

1. *Atlas Maritimus & Commercialis* (London: James and John Knapton . . . , & Executors of William Taylor deceased, et al., 1728), iii. John Robert Moore's *Checklist of the Writings of Daniel Defoe* (Bloomington: Indiana University Press, 1960), 215–218 (item 501), gives an excellent explanation for Defoe's role in writing this section of this work. P. N. Furbank and W. R. Owens's insistence on giving this work a kind of problematic status in their *Critical Bibliography of Daniel Defoe* ([London: Pickering & Chatto, 1998], 276–279) is difficult to explain.
2. See Jacques Derrida, *The Sovereign and the Beast*, vol. 2 (Chicago: University of Chicago Press, 2011).
3. See Saul Kripke, *Wittgenstein on Rules and Private Language* (Oxford: Blackwell, 1982); and Ludwig Wittgenstein, *The Philosophical Investigations*, ed. George Pitcher (London: Macmillan, 1968), 54–112, 257–266, 267–288, 286–323.
4. Defoe was fond of his own paradoxes. When he was released from captivity, after spending time in prison and standing on the pillory three times, he almost immediately began his news sheet of opinions—the *Review of the Affairs of France*. It was an attempt to explain the reasons for the greatness and power of France to the English at a time when England was at war with that country. Sidney Godolphin, the Lord Treasurer, considered Defoe's journal to be a seditious text. He wrote to Robert Harley, then secretary of state, condemning Defoe's work and suggesting that it should be suppressed. Given considerable leeway by Harley, Defoe persevered and kept the paper going for ten years. See Defoe, *Letters*, ed. George Healey (Oxford: Clarendon Press, 1955).
5. Ann Marie Fallon deals with the postcolonial approach to *Robinson Crusoe* in *Global Crusoe: Comparative Literature, Postcolonial Theory and Transnational Aesthetics* (Farnham: Ashgate, 2011).
6. In *Religious and Didactic Writings of Daniel Defoe*, 10 vols., ed. P. N. Furbank and W. R. Owens (London: Pickering & Chatto, 2012), 9:206 (no. 48).
7. In *Romances and Narratives by Daniel Defoe*, 14 vols., ed. George Aiken (London: Dent, 1895), 3:206–235.
8. Of course Defoe plays on Crusoe's name to include crusader, in addition to the obvious notion of one who cruises about the world.
9. *The Farther Adventures of Robinson Crusoe*, in *The Shakespeare Head Edition of the Writings of Daniel Defoe*, 14 vols. (Oxford: Blackwell, 1927), 2:173. Subsequent citations to *The Farther Adventures* will refer to this edition and be included within parentheses in the text.
10. Lydia Liu connects Crusoe's interest in Chinese porcelain to his manufacture of clay pots on the island. Defoe always admired technological advances, and there is no question that he viewed this highly profitable industry and its importation into Europe with considerable admiration. See Liu, "Robinson Crusoe's Earthenware Pot," *Critical Inquiry* 25 (1999): 728–757.
11. Defoe drew many of his allusions to China from the work of Louis Le Comte, who was both a Frenchman at the time of Louis XIV as well as a Jesuit, accustomed to the hierarchical structure of the Catholic Church and of the French state.
12. For some other comments on Defoe's dislike of China as a tyrannical nation, see G. A. Starr, "Defoe and China," *Eighteenth-Century Studies* 43, no. 4 (2010): 435–454.
13. See my *Transformations, Ideology, and the Real in Defoe's* Robinson Crusoe *and Other Narratives: Finding the Thing Itself* (Newark: Delaware University Press, 2014).
14. For Defoe on self-preservation, see his *Jure Divino* (London, 1706), bk. 3, p 10.
15. For a fuller discussion of these problems as part of natural law, see my *Defoe and the Nature of Man* (Oxford: Clarendon, 1963), 65–88. Jean Barbeyrac's notes to Hugo Grotius's *De*

Jure belli et pacis presented specific examples of cannibalism among survivors of shipwrecks and its justification.

16. See my *Transformations, Ideology, and the Real*, 53–54. Writing seven years after the disastrous siege of Magdeburgh in 1631, Franciscus Junius maintained that the sacking of a city provided painters the widest range for displaying the passions. Although Ann Marie Fallon (*Global Crusoe*, 44) is probably right in thinking that Defoe intended an "elevation" in comparing a scene involving a skirmish between sailors and natives to sieges of European cities, the rendering of the passions—the central point for Junius—would have been the same.
17. Samuel Pufendorf's attempt to establish a normative law relating to marriage ran to over forty-five folio pages in some editions without his coming to any firm conclusion. See *Of the Law of Nations*, trans. Basil Kennett (Oxford, 1703), 75–121.
18. Crusoe's surprising defense of the actions of the Spanish toward the natives of the New World in *Serious Reflections . . . of Robinson Crusoe* may be seen as a shift in his thinking from that of the isolated seaman dealing with a particular human situation to that of a writer on religion and morality involved in contemplating the theological implications of the massacre of millions of natives at a particular time in history. Since God permitted this terrible slaughter to occur, Crusoe feels that it would be verging on the irreligious to question it too closely. He notes the terrible sacrifices committed by the Aztecs with blood a "foot thick" in their temples as a partial justification. The main point is that although, from the standpoint of human ethical behavior, the actions of the Spaniards "must be abhorred by us," we are not in a position to question God's sense of justice. See *Serious Reflections* (3:214–216).
19. James Kelly, "The Worcester Affair," *Review of English Studies* 51 (2000): 1–23.
20. Robert Markley, *The Far East and the English Imagination, 1600–1700* (Cambridge: Cambridge University Press, 2006), 185–186.
21. See G. A. Starr, ed., *Christianity Not as Old as Creation*, by Daniel Defoe (London: Pickering & Chatto, 2012), xxi.
22. Tony C. Brown, *The Primitive, the Aesthetic, and the Savage* (Minneapolis: University of Minnesota Press, 2012), 159–161.
23. *An Account of the History and Reality of Apparitions*, ed. Kit Kincade (1727; New York: AMS Press, 2007), 269–270. Robert Markley also finds this action suspect, noting its resemblance to "juvenile acts of 'heroism.'" See *Far East*, 203.
24. Geoffrey Sill, *The Cure of the Passions and the Origins of the English Novel* (Cambridge: Cambridge University Press, 2001), 86–106.
25. *A General History of Trade*, no. 3 (July 1713): 47 [46].
26. See *OED*, s.v. "indifferent, adj. 1, n., and adv." Accessed October 12, 2020, http://www-oed.com.

10

"TO US THE MERE NAME IS ENOUGH"

Robinson Crusoe, Myth, and Iconicity

ANDREAS K. E. MUELLER

IT IS A CRITICAL COMMONPLACE that Daniel Defoe's *The Life and Strange Surprizing Adventures of Robinson Crusoe* (1719) generated one of the "great myths of our civilization."[1] Defoe's story of shipwreck, colonial mastery, religious conversion, and endurance and acquisition has created what is widely recognized as the "Crusoe phenomenon."[2] Over the past three hundred years, stories of isolation and survival, real or imagined, have rarely failed to elicit a reference to Defoe's book and its eponymous "character of archetypal significance."[3] As a result, scholars regularly resort to superlatives when assessing the ongoing cultural resonance of Defoe's story: "It can be rightly said that *Robinson Crusoe* has been and is everywhere," observes one commentator, while another asserts that the novel is a "touchstone fable" that remains "unrivalled in western literature."[4]

The transformation of Crusoe into a modern cultural myth has to a significant extent depended on visual representations of the character and his adventures. The first edition of the book included, unusually for the period, a "haunting portrait" of a dejected Crusoe in his goat-skin clothes (figure 10.1), and illustrations that visually interpreted elements of the Crusoe story consistently remained a feature of subsequent editions into the twentieth century.[5] Pantomime versions of *Robinson Crusoe*, which reached a peak in the nineteenth century, offered additional visualizations of the story, or at least specific aspects of it, and the twentieth century saw many screen versions of the book, especially around the middle of that century. The actual text of the book has receded into the background over the course of the centuries: Geoffrey Sill notes that "playgoers in the 1870s interpreted theatrical performances in visual terms derived from book illustrations, rather than from the text of the novel itself,"[6] while Robert Mayer has pointed out that "in the twentieth century more people encountered Defoe's most famous narrative in screen versions than read the novel," adding that "the Crusoe story

Figure 10.1. Frontispiece of Daniel Defoe, *The Life and Strange Surprizing Adventures of Robinson Crusoe*, 1719. Public domain image.

remains a *popular* narrative in the late twentieth and early twenty-first centuries to an important degree because of its varied career on screen."[7] Visual interpretations have thus played a central role in the perpetuation of Defoe's story and the development of the Crusoe myth: as one scholar has noted, "*Crusoe* survives through its images,"[8] especially images that have circulated widely in popular culture, such as the quintessential Crusoe image of the isolated individual in a desolate place.

Of course, much condensation and reduction has occurred in the process of mythologizing the figure of Robinson Crusoe. Beginning with the very first illustration, the Crusoe myth as conveyed via visual images almost exclusively centers on the protagonist's long-term survival on his "island of despair." Subsequent versions of *Robinson Crusoe* as well as the so-called Robinsonades—derivative stories inspired by Defoe's book—have effectively reduced and generalized the Crusoe story to one of survival in a distant wilderness and, less frequently, also to themes associated with colonial mastery. Moreover, Ian Watt pointed out over half a century ago that Defoe's narrative "hardly supports some of the symbolic uses" to which the Crusoe myth has been put, adding by way of explanation that a defining feature of myths is that they are shaped by the "unconscious needs" of the society that invokes them at least as much as by the contents of the original story.[9] This is unsurprisingly borne out by the many Crusoe illustrations, which, as David Blewett has explained, at times "distort or travesty" Defoe's work. The many visual representation and interpretations of *Robinson Crusoe* have nevertheless generated an "Iconic Crusoe," to use Blewett's phrase. In what follows I will read this phrase literally: leaving to one side the images that are commonly associated with Defoe's famous book and that continue to give life to the Crusoe myth, I will explore how the name, that is, the linguistic sign "Robinson Crusoe," has assumed iconic status in modern Western culture as well as the connotative range of this name.

The motivation for this path of inquiry emerges at least partly out of the observation that many recent screen versions do not explicitly signal their indebtedness to Defoe's novel: for example, the big-budget Hollywood movies *Cast Away* (2000) and *The Martian* (2015) do not make explicit their connection with *Robinson Crusoe*, and viewers unfamiliar with Defoe's book would not necessarily have realized that they were watching screen Robinsonades.[10] In fact, Andy Weir, who wrote the book on which the 2015 film is based, has explained that he was not consciously inspired by Defoe's novel.[11] Even when there is an explicit link, as in the case of Patrick Keiller's documentary film *Robinson in Ruins* (2010) or the recent Netflix update of the 1960s TV series *Lost in Space* (2018), which narrates the adventures of the Family Robinson, we cannot assume that the high-brow musings of a Defoe-Crusoe observer or the images of space travel and a wealth of futuristic equipment perpetuate the cultural ubiquity of Defoe's iconic protagonist, especially when the novel is no longer widely read outside of universities and colleges.[12] And yet the name "Robinson Crusoe," in its entirety or in one of its two parts, has retained its resonance in popular culture, as *Lost in Space* and the range of examples presented below will illustrate. I will suggest that, after three hundred years, and beyond the many Crusoe illustrations and screen Robinsonades, the linguistic sign "Robinson Crusoe" for the most part continues to perform effectively as a signifier that connotes aspects of the Crusoe myth in a manner that corresponds recognizably, and sometimes surprisingly, to the original story. Occasionally, however, the name "Crusoe" is used in a manner entirely detached from Defoe's story and the Crusoe myth: the word functions as a stand-alone cultural icon without an apparent intention to evoke any specific connotations. Ultimately, my examples will suggest that, alongside still or moving images that perpetuate the popularity of the Crusoe myth, if not the novel itself, it is the name "Robinson Crusoe" that has assumed, especially over recent decades, an iconic function that keeps alive Defoe's character in the Western collective consciousness and culture.

In one of the most comprehensive recent theorizations of the formation of cultural icons, Michael Parker has identified as their defining features that they are "always images" that are "distinct, durable, and reproducible" in the "collective memory of large groups of people." Moreover, in order to attain lasting cultural iconicity, Parker repeatedly emphasizes that, while cultural icons "can take many forms such as, objects, fictional characters, cartoons, and buildings," they have to be connected to "a tragic, or at least a highly dramatic, human narrative."[13] However, extending this list of possibilities, Parker explains that "real people, given extraordinary conditions, are the ones most likely to attain primary iconic status. Personal experience narratives, related through the dramatic biography of the iconic image, or through a singular tragic event, are the sources of meaning contained in distinct iconic phenomena."[14] While the case-study basis of Parker's overarching theorization as well as his focus on post-1900 examples (a brief section on David Garrick is the conspicuous exception) necessarily yield some questionable generalizations, the typical features of modern iconicity can be harnessed to signal the iconicity of the figure of Robinson Crusoe. Presented to its readers as a real autobiography, *Robinson Crusoe* undoubtedly offers a dramatic, and in parts tragic, personal narrative of survival under extraordinary conditions. The central image that feeds the iconic status of Robinson Crusoe has been that of the individual figure in a desolate landscape far away from civilization. Given its three-hundred-year history, the durability of the Crusoe phenomenon across countless generations will hardly be questioned: Defoe's character Robinson Crusoe doubtlessly demonstrates all of the defining features of a primary cultural icon.

To test Crusoe's iconic status in this way contributes little to our understanding of the name's function in modern popular culture, however. Rather, it is Parker's comment that the durability of a cultural icon applies not only to its dominant image(s) but also to its name that will be of greater utility to the present discussion: "the name prompt and the iconic image should be cross-referential, so that the name, for example 'Che Guevara,' should initiate a distinct image and vice versa."[15] While Robinson Crusoe clearly qualifies as a primary cultural icon and while Defoe's story gave birth to a central Western myth, in our case the associated iconic image is rather less distinct and singular than that of Parker's example, Che Guevara. The Crusoe story has yielded many different iconic images, ranging from a lonely goat-skin-clad Crusoe on the shore to a single footprint in the sand, from Crusoe facing a submissive Friday to Crusoe, accompanied by his dog, brandishing one or two guns. The example of Robinson Crusoe will demonstrate that a primary cultural icon does not necessarily have to emerge from and initiate one distinct image, or refer to one specific event, but can also trigger a range of associations of a more abstract nature and be motivated by several different events that are nevertheless connected through the biography of the individual. Moreover, the manner in which the Crusoe myth operates at an iconic level suggests that the name "Robinson Crusoe" as a linguistic sign is at least as important to the perpetuation of the myth as the images that have traditionally been associated with the story.

Before we consider recent manifestations of the iconicity of the name "Robinson Crusoe," we should remember that Defoe himself emphasized the symbolic power of names in his novel, certainly with regard to Friday, but also repeatedly in relation to his protagonist. Unlike the similarly myth-generating literary characters of Faust, Don Juan, and Don Quixote, Crusoe offers his readers an onomastic account of his name in the novel's first paragraph:[16]

> I Was born in the Year 1632, in the City of York, of a good Family, tho' not of that Country, my Father being a Foreigner of Bremen, who settled first at Hull. He got a good Estate by Merchandise, and leaving off his Trade, lived afterward at York, from whence he had married my Mother, whose Relations were named Robinson, a good Family in that Country, and from whom I was called Robinson Kreutznear; but by the usual Corruption of Words in England, we are now called, nay we call our selves, and write our name Crusoe, and so my Companions always call'd me. (5)

An Anglicization of the German surname Kreutznaer, "Crusoe" instantly gains symbolic weight by incorporating the German word for the most powerful of all Western icons, the Christian cross (*Kreuz* in modern German spelling). By situating the composite structure of his name in relation to larger familial, regional, and national communities and identities, Crusoe's early words emphasize the function of his name as a signifier that refers to something bigger than himself, as a symbol that points to structures and ideas beyond the individual.[17] David Marshall has drawn our attention to the iconic resonance of Crusoe's surname by identifying the "cross" Crusoe erects on the island's shore for time-keeping purposes "as a representation of his name. It is a symbolic or even hieroglyphic signature, a kind of literal self-portrait."[18] Defoe thus abstracts Crusoe's name in a material manifestation that connects his identity as an individual to the universal meanings and iconography Western culture has assigned to the cross.

The movement toward abstraction caused by Crusoe's history of his name and the erection of the cross on the shore is continued in an uncanny episode that sees the parrot Poll repeatedly vocalize the protagonist's name. Alone on the island, Crusoe is awoken from a deep sleep "by a Voice calling me by my Name several times, *Robin, Robin, Robin Crusoe,* poor *Robin Crusoe,* where are you *Robin Crusoe*?" (121). Crusoe explains that, in an initially semiconscious state, he "thought I dream'd that some Body spoke to me: But as the Voice continu'd to repeat *Robin Crusoe, Robin Crusoe*, at last I began to wake up more perfectly, and was at first dreadfully frighted" (121), until he realized that his parrot was simply uttering the words he had been taught. Extending his reading of the cross on the shore, Marshall plausibly suggests that Poll's mimicry of Crusoe's voice and words becomes "in a sense Crusoe's talking signature," while the nonhuman voice also positions "Crusoe as an *other* rather than *himself*."[19] One might add that the repeated vocalization of Crusoe's name causes a process of defamiliarization in the same way in which a repeatedly uttered word becomes strange to the speaker. Crusoe's "talking signature" is not entirely his own anymore, and while the connection between signifier and signified remains largely intact, the distance between the verbal sign and its referent is increased through a process of alienation. The idea of "poor Crusoe," the Englishman lost on a desert island, rather than the actual individual is moved center-stage through the intense focus on the verbal sign "Robin Crusoe." Importantly, even within the novel the linguistic sign "Robinson Crusoe" assumes an existence that is ultimately detached from the individual to which it refers: explaining that he has heard that parrots can live up to a hundred years, Crusoe imagines at the time of writing, years after he has left the island, that "perhaps poor Poll may be alive there still, calling after *Poor Robin Crusoe* to this Day" (152). The reader also learns that Crusoe "had two more Parrots which talk'd pretty well, and would call *Robin Crusoe*" (153). Not only does Defoe consistently draw his readers' attention to the symbolic power of his protagonist's name, but the name as a verbal linguistic sign has its own independent existence on the island and, by Crusoe's reckoning, likely beyond the earthly existence of its referent. In a sense, then, Crusoe predicts the emergence of his own "Poor Robin Crusoe" myth through the iconic power of his name.

In the event, the name of "Robinson Crusoe" has gone on to be called out "to this day" and well beyond Crusoe's island. There is evidence that by the middle of the following century the name had become increasingly detached from the specific images generated by the novel to signify more generally the idea of an adventurous if solitary life in a desolate location.[20] In 1868, the reviewer of a new Macmillan edition of *Robinson Crusoe*, the Globe Edition edited by Henry Kingsley, offered a revealing comment concerning the fully established iconic status of the name as part of his lament that an otherwise excellent edition lacks a reproduction of the novel's original title page: "Something more than a mere bibliographical interest is attached to these parts of the book in its earliest shape. The title-page to 'Robinson Crusoe' is in itself an instance of Defoe's emphatic manner. It is indeed almost what would be now called sensational. To us the mere name is enough. It comes to us already clothed with all necessary ideas of adventure and solitude. But when 'Robinson Crusoe' was born into the world of fiction, 'nudus intravit,' and preparations had to be made for his reception by a bold advertisement of his 'strange surprising adventures.'"[21] By the late 1860s, then, the linguistic sign "Robinson Crusoe" was invested with such iconic power that its mere mention universally generated "ideas of adventure and solitude." There was no longer a need for illustrative images or plot summaries to perpetuate the Crusoe myth; the name alone held the necessary evocative charge. That the name "Robinson Crusoe" predominantly came to signify a specific experience is readily apparent from later nineteenth- and early twentieth-century newspaper reports. Here, the notion of a "modern Robinson Crusoe" was especially dominant: in 1894 the *Guernsey Star* ran a story titled "A Modern Robinson Crusoe" about a certain Henry Nilford who had undertaken a wager to live for twelve months on a small uninhabited island near Guernsey, with "a donkey, a dog, and two pigs as his companions."[22] In 1898 the *Edinburgh Evening News* labeled a certain M. De Rougement a modern Crusoe for "astonishing the British Association by his yarns about his residence among the cannibal blacks in Australia."[23] The *Evening Telegraph* reported in 1910 of a modern Crusoe "by choice" on an island near Algoa Bay off the coast of South Africa, while the *Western Gazette* ran a story in 1932 of a "new" Robinson Crusoe who had survived for two to three years on an uninhabited island near the equator after his ship caught fire.[24] More recently, the New Zealander

Thomas Neale chose to make himself a modern Robinson Crusoe when he lived in the Cook islands for sixteen years in the 1950s and 1960s, while David Glasheen became "Australia's Robinson Crusoe" by relocating to the tiny Restoration Island in the early 1990s after he lost his fortune.[25] While the connection to Defoe's story is never entirely lost in these reports, from the mid-nineteenth century to the present day the Crusoe myth is reduced to the absolute minimum of, and has become universally applicable to, survival in a remote, uncivilized location. The reports rarely focus on specific Crusoe images—it is the name that performs all of the associative work.

And yet, while one may plausibly claim that "we all love Robinson Crusoe stories,"[26] the presence of the name in the world of moving images, the main medium of popular culture for perpetuating the Crusoe story, has been minimal over the last two decades. With recent screen Robinsonades largely eschewing explicit links to Defoe's book, one might surmise that the strictly reduced connotative range of the name Robinson Crusoe evident in the late nineteenth century has found a continuation over recent years. As the examples below shall demonstrate, however, in combination the various uses to which the iconic name of Robinson Crusoe has been put suggests a, perhaps surprisingly, multifaceted perpetuation of the Crusoe myth in recent popular culture: the companies and products discussed below range from the more predictable, such as a virtual reality computer game, to those that might not be quite so obvious, such as a research-facilitating software application. While imagery still plays a role in the various marketing strategies, it will become apparent that it is largely the iconic power of the name "Robinson Crusoe" that is at the forefront of the ongoing appeal of Defoe's protagonist

Given that *Robinson Crusoe* is a self-proclaimed adventure story, there can be little surprise that the Crusoe myth has appealed to game makers. The most recent example is the virtual reality computer game *Robinson: The Journey* (2016) for the Sony PlayStation (figure 10.2), which one reviewer has described as "a not-so-subtle futuristic/prehistoric take on Robinson Crusoe."[27] Anticipating the Netflix remake of *Lost in Space*, the game places players in the role of young Robin, who, after his spacecraft has crash-landed on an alien planet populated by dinosaurs, "must rely on his wits—and HIGS, one of the ship's AI units—to survive" and to find other human survivors, which is, in fact, the central goal of the game.[28] *Robinson: The Journey* clearly borrows several story elements from Defoe's novel—the shipwreck and sole survivor plotline, the desolate and threatening environment, and the desire for human company—but beyond these basic narrative building blocks, the perhaps most noteworthy effect of the game that ties it to Defoe's original story is its realism: according to one reviewer, young Robin's makeshift home

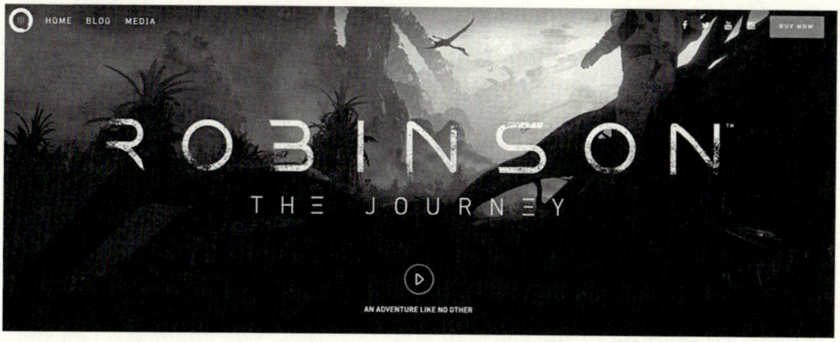

Figure 10.2. Robinson: The Journey. Homepage image. © by Crytek.

"feels like a space that has been lived in by a real, lonely human being just trying to get by."[29] However, the most appealing aspect of *Robinson: The Journey* is, it seems, that it gives gamers an immersive 3D experience of "a beautiful place" in which the "massive dinosaurs are even more impressive."[30] Indeed, that the game's celebrated virtual environment has been "lifted straight out of Jurassic Park,"[31] rather than Defoe's books, seems to be a dominant sentiment among reviewers. This raises an interesting question regarding the marketing strategy for the game: the game's creators might alternatively have promoted the game's virtual environment as a new Jurassic Park and named the game after its setting, the planet Tyson III, for example. That Robinson was ultimately chosen suggests that the iconic power of the name and the story associated with it were considered more representative than a marketing focus on the carefully rendered prehistoric environment that has fascinated the gamers.

The attraction of a beautiful place is also at the heart of the next example, albeit in a rather more peaceful fashion. The travel company Robinson, a TUI group subsidiary that offers luxury club holidays, harnesses the name's common association with a "natural" desert island life to promote its product. Holiday makers are promised "scenic surroundings" that include "lagoons teeming with wildlife, unspoilt beaches and coral-filled waters," locally sourced "fresh, wholesome and delicious food," and a wide range of activity classes to keep at bay the boredom that Defoe's Robinson undoubtedly suffered.[32] Moreover, an interest resignification is evident with regard to the company's logo, which features a somewhat abstracted representation of the single footprint Crusoe finds on the beach (figure 10.3).[33] The lone footprint—an iconic image in its own right—seems intended to signify the company's focus on an individualized holiday experience to distinguish it from the packed beaches and hotels of mass tourism. Of course, in *Robinson*

ROBINSON

Figure 10.3. Robinson Club. Company logo. © by Robinson Club GmbH.

Crusoe the single footprint on the shore induces extreme anxiety and paranoia in Crusoe, which is presumably not the state of mind that a TUI Robinson holiday is intended to cause in the consumer. Nevertheless, one might say, at a slight stretch perhaps, that the company's appropriation of the footprint nevertheless speaks to an aspect of Defoe's original story, namely Crusoe's subsequent desire not to have direct contact with the humans who left the mark in the sand. A luxury version of relative isolation thus becomes a key selling point in this holiday version of a Robinsonade.

The upmarket experience offered by TUI Robinson of course stands in stark contrast to the primitive, if well-fortified, housing that Defoe's Crusoe creates for himself on the island. And while the construction of shelter features centrally in both *Robinson Crusoe* and many Robinsonades, the episode concerning Crusoe's "Bower" or "Country-House" (87) is not usually a focus in stories inspired by Defoe's novel. Crusoe, after having invested much time and effort in constructing his main habitation, the cave and tent he labels his "Sea-Coast-House" (87), has very specific reasons for seeking out alternative accommodation in an inland location: while his main home's shore location is strategically necessary for detecting passing ships in order to escape the island, Crusoe realizes that it "was by far the worst Part of the Country" (86). In contrast, the location of his new country house "appear'd so fresh, so green, so flourishing, everything being in a constant Verdure, or Flourish of *Spring*, that it looked like a planted Garden" (85). Importantly, Crusoe's garden bower not only offers him ready access to an abundance of fruit, but also brings much needed visual variety and "a secret Kind of Pleasure" (85) that his main shore habitation cannot generate. Crusoe's pleasure at an alternative living space in a garden setting appears to have inspired a British manufacturer to brand itself "Crusoe Garden Rooms." The company produces a range of "handcrafted Western Red cedar-clad timber framed buildings" that, it is claimed, make an "ideal addition to your home."[34] The names of the various models are prefixed by "The Crusoe," for example, "The Crusoe Classic" or "The Crusoe Retreat," and the simplicity of the logo's outline of what seems to be a basic shed belies the rather luxurious nature of the anything-but-rustic garden rooms (figure 10.4). Nevertheless, the descriptions of each garden room as "a home from home

Figure 10.4. Crusoe Garden Rooms. Company logo. © by Crusoe Garden Rooms.

with amazing views" and a "sleepover heaven"[35] closely align with Crusoe's sentiments concerning his garden bower in the "delicious Vale" (85). What is perhaps most noteworthy with regard to the utilization of the iconic resonance of Crusoe's name here is that it is not predicated on the name's culturally dominant connotations of adventure and survival, even if it still seems to reference the notion of isolation or, at least, of a separation from the everyday.

If the previous example draws on the less commonly referenced story element of Crusoe's country retreat, the next example harnesses a feature of Defoe's novel that does not represent a standard element of the popular Crusoe myth as we know it. This most modern of products, a software application, has the name of Crusoe emblazoned across its homepage in a signature style font that appears to suggest something of an authentic connection between the product and the novel's protagonist (figure 10.5).[36] In the context of the common association of Robinson Crusoe with adventure and isolation, the application's highly ambitious central purpose is rather surprising: it "gives you the ability to recall everything you've ever wanted to remember."[37] This ambition is to be realized by allowing

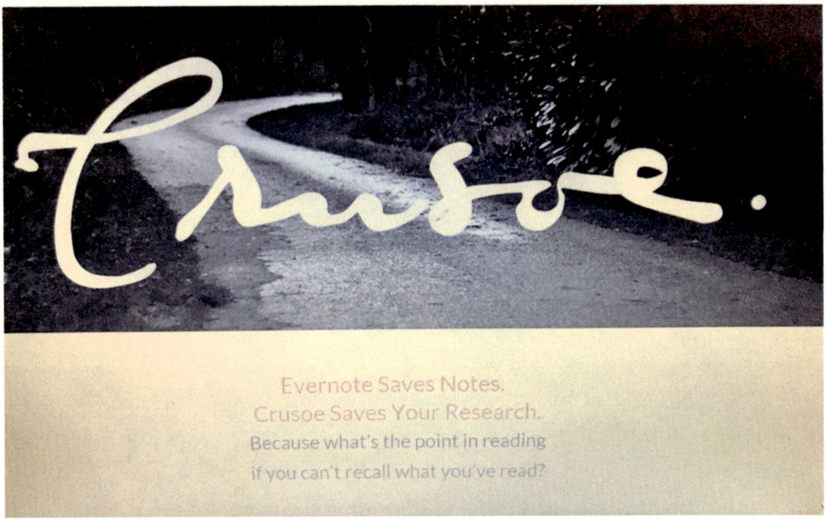

Figure 10.5. Crusoe App. Homepage image. © by J Douglas Johnson.

researchers to record not only their individual ideas but also the "connection-pathways," that is, the various trains of thought that link two or more ideas. This, the creators explain, allows users to issue a key command to the Crusoe application: "When I see this note, make sure I see these notes too." The application is thus designed to enable users to create a personal web of knowledge, with the perhaps slightly disconcerting result that, with each added connection, a virtual version of one's thinking processes will gradually come into existence: "Crusoe will think like you."

It is perhaps not readily apparent why an application of this type should bear the name of Crusoe, and the product's website offers no explanation for a connection with Defoe's protagonist. However, a direct enquiry to the application's creators concerning their rationale for naming their product Crusoe yielded a response that shows a relatively deep engagement with Defoe's novel:

> The story of Robinson Crusoe is a journey plot, a journey plot of conscience and faith. His path is worn mostly by recollection and contemplation of past memories connected to new experiences. And this is also how the act of recall works. Ideas don't just pop into our heads randomly. Rather, we see, hear, or read something that recalls something else. That link creates a synapse and as long as that synapse holds together we can recall information. All of Crusoe's learning on the island is a process of present experience connected to old memories. The Crusoe app saves these

> links between memories so that you can have perfect recall of anything you've ever read, and you can build memory pathways just like Robinson Crusoe did.[38]

While it is questionable that Defoe's Crusoe in any meaningful way represents a model of memory characterized by "perfect recall," the combination of Crusoe's prior knowledge and his empirical charting of his island experiences and observations undoubtedly allows him to generate a better understanding of his environment to ensure his survival, and, within limits, even to prosper in his isolation.[39] In that sense Crusoe does establish a web of knowledge about his island and naming the application after him therefore does not appear unduly far-fetched, although, admittedly, one might make an equally good case for using the name of Mnemosyne, the Greek goddess of memory, for example. What the creators' choice and rationale indicate is that even when the name "Crusoe" is employed in a manner that does not directly echo the established thematic pillars of the Crusoe myth, the iconic weight of the name surpasses that of other at least equally appropriate choices. It also shows that aspects of the novel that are not at the forefront of the traditional Crusoe myth have not slipped from recent popular culture.

This undiminished presence of the name Crusoe in contemporary popular culture is further evidenced by a graffiti tag that adorns various locations in the German capital Berlin (figure 10.6). Tourists who embark on a river cruise around the city will chance upon a "Cruzoe" signature that is placed, oddly fittingly, above a gated "cave" in the jungle that is the sprawling metropolis. It seems hard to imagine that "Faust" or "Don Juan" would appeal to the imagination of both the graffiti artist and those gazing upon the name in quite the same way here. How much of the Crusoe myth motivated the use of the name in this instance is impossible to say, and its placement above the fortified entrance may not be intentional, but, at the very least, the Berlin tag illustrates the ongoing iconicity of the name Crusoe, even in less mainstream popular culture.[40] Moreover, this more broadly iconic appeal of the name is also evident in my final examples: two Crusoe restaurants in the city of St. Louis, Missouri. There is nothing unusual about these examples per se: a brief internet search shows that, across the globe, there are many bars, public houses, and restaurants that bear the name of Defoe's protagonist. The real point of interest here is that two restaurants in the same city have claimed the name for themselves and that, in order to distinguish themselves from each other, one restaurant has added the adjective "original" to its name.

Reflecting the promise of its name, "The Original Crusoe's Restaurant" explicitly emphasizes its tradition and longevity: the logo advertises its year of establishment as 1979, while the website points out that it is "one of South St. Louis'

Figure 10.6. Cruzoe graffito in Berlin. © by Andreas Mueller.

oldest restaurants" (figure 10.7).[41] The restaurant's focus on Southern American comfort food is confirmed in the restaurant's video commercial, which confidently declares that patrons can enjoy "homestyle meals so good, you'll think we kidnapped your mom."[42] Neither the Original Crusoe's menu nor its décor suggest any obvious links to Defoe's novel: there is a "Crusoe's Special Salad," but no other meals are linked to the novel—one could imagine a "Friday's Meat Lovers Pizza" or "Poll's Fried Pickle Chips," for example—and the design of the restaurant is perhaps best described as "early twentieth-century retro." However, the restaurant's loyalty program, the Reward Club, features an image that establishes a clear connection to *Robinson Crusoe*: an "old" beige map of "Lost Island," with the edges duly torn and depicting images of what is presumably Crusoe's island, the masts

Figure 10.7. The Original Crusoe's Restaurant. Company logo. © by The Original Crusoe Restaurant.

and sails of an otherwise obscured ship, palm trees, and a compass (figure 10.8). Why the Reward Club is linked to the island is not apparent, but then Defoe's story itself is obviously not the driving force behind the choice of Crusoe for the restaurant's name. Rather, the general iconicity of the word "Crusoe" is evidently the overriding motivation here, which is further illustrated by the existence of a second restaurant in South St. Louis named after Defoe's protagonist.

Serving American bar food that is "sure to please even the most finicky eater,"[43] in this case there is absolutely no connection to Defoe's novel beyond the restaurant's name (figure 10.9). One would have to take quite an interpretative leap to read the phrase "From Humble Beginnings" on the restaurant's homepage as connected to the trajectory of Crusoe's life. Nevertheless, here too the iconic power of the name Crusoe is evidently great enough for this establishment to adopt the name in spite of the existence of a Crusoe rival in the same city. Thus, in a manner reminiscent of Crusoe's fantasy of his parrots still calling out his name on the island long after he has left, the name of Crusoe can be heard around St. Louis without a meaningful link to Defoe's book. The linguistic sign lives on, but its referent has all but vanished: detached from images associated with the myth of survival and isolation, the iconic name Crusoe has truly developed a life of its own.

Figure 10.8. The Original Crusoe's Restaurant. Reward card. © by The Original Crusoe Restaurant.

Figure 10.9. Crusoe's Restaurant & Bar signage. © by Rosalyn Rapp.

The above selection of examples offers a sense of the wide variety of commercial purposes that the name "Robinson Crusoe" has been made to serve. What we learn from these examples is that while the traditional images associated with the Crusoe myth have not disappeared from popular culture, the popular familiarity with Defoe's protagonist and at least some aspects of the Crusoe story is not exclusively dependent on those images. Instead, the primary iconic status of the name "Robinson Crusoe" itself does much of the work of cultural transmission, often with little to no support from conventional Crusoe images. To be sure, some of the novel's central themes are gestured toward by the developers of the various products discussed above, in some cases in a way that does not adhere to the conventions of the established myth, but if Robinson Crusoe lives on in contemporary popular culture, it does so predominantly through the iconicity of the name. The assessment of the mid-nineteenth-century reviewer thus continues to hold true in the twenty-first century: "To us the mere name is enough."

NOTES

1. Ian Watt, "*Robinson Crusoe* as Myth," *Essays in Criticism* 1, no. 2 (April 1951): 95.
2. Louis James, "Unwrapping Crusoe: Retrospective and Prospective Views," in *Robinson Crusoe: Myths and Metamorphoses*, ed. Lieve Spaas and Brian Stimpson (Basingstoke: Macmillan, 1996), 1.
3. John Richetti, *The Life of Danie Defoe* (Oxford: Blackwell, 2005), 185.
4. Andrew O'Malley, *Children's Literature, Popular Culture, and* Robinson Crusoe (Basingstoke: Palgrave Macmillan, 2012), 1–2; Evan R. Davis, "Introduction," in Daniel Defoe, *Robinson Crusoe*, ed. Davis (Peterboro: Broadview, 2010), 9.
5. David Blewett, "The Iconic Crusoe: Illustrations and Images of *Robinson Crusoe*," in *The Cambridge Companion to Robinson Crusoe*, ed. John Richetti (Cambridge: Cambridge University Press, 2018), 159, 186n2. Blewett's article analyzes the interpretative range of these illustrations across the centuries.
6. See chapter 2 in the present volume.
7. Robert Mayer, "*Robinson Crusoe* in the Screen Age," in Richetti, *Cambridge Companion*, 221, 223–224.
8. James, "Unwrapping Crusoe," 8.
9. Watt, "*Robinson Crusoe* as Myth," 97.
10. One exception is the Belgian-French-produced animated adventure-comedy movie *Robinson Crusoe* (2016), which was, at best, only moderately successful. However, even this production was ultimately marked by a somewhat odd turn away from Defoe's novel: when the entertainment company Lionsgate purchased the U.S. distribution rights to the movie in 2015, the company's president Steve Beeks rejoiced that "*Robinson Crusoe* is a timeless adventure classic that has enthralled families since it was first published," claiming that the new "animation will help introduce the story to a new generation." See Ali Jaafar, "Lionsgate Nabs U.S. Rights to StudioCanal's 3D 'Robinson Crusoe,'" *Deadline Hollywood*, November 10, 2015, https://deadline.com/2015/11/lionsgate-finds-dry-land-with-studiocanals-robinson-crusoe-1201616914/. In a move that rather jarred with Beeks's claim, Lionsgate then decided to market the movie under the alternative title *The Wild Life* in North America.
11. Andy Weir, comment on "Was Andy Weir Inspired by Robinson Crusoe while Writing His Novel?," *Quora*, February 16, 2016, https://www.quora.com/Was-Andy-Weir-inspired-by-Robinson-Crusoe-while-writing-his-novel.
12. Robert Mayer has pointed out that, while *Robinson in Ruins* as well as Keiller's earlier *London* (1994) and *Robinson in Space* (1997) are characterized by a newly invented method called "Robinsonism," the three productions are also "inspired by myriad texts" not by Defoe. See "Defoe's Cultural Afterlife, Mainly on Screen," in *The Afterlives of Eighteenth-Century Fiction*, ed. Daniel Cook and Nicholas Seager (Cambridge: Cambridge University

Press, 2015), 242. While Keiller's documentaries certainly contribute to the perpetuation of the name Robinson in nonmainstream circles, I am not convinced that there has been a significant popular audience for these films. With regard to Keiller's target audience, Paul Dave explains that, due to funding issues, *Robinson in Space* had to be reconfigured "in terms of 'collaborative research in an academic context'" and, tellingly, Dave's extended discussion of the film does not engage with Defoe's novel at all. See "Robinson in Ruins: New Materialism and the Archaeological Imagination," *Radical Philosophy* 169 (September/October 2011): 19.

13. Michael Parker, "Cultural Icons: A Case Study Analysis of their Formation and Reception" (PhD diss., University of Central Lancashire, 2012), 10–13, 23.
14. Parker, "Cultural Icons," 23–24.
15. Parker, "Cultural Icons," 18.
16. Robert W. Ayers, "*Robinson Crusoe*: 'Allusive Allegorick History,'" *PMLA* 82 (October 1967): 404–405n28.
17. Jacob Sider Jost has identified a tension at the center of Robinson Crusoe's name: "Robinson's given name suggests continuity, while his family name has changed" from the German original. The name of Defoe's protagonist "points to stability across time (the name of a man who will spend twenty-six years on an island) and to mobility across space (the name of a man with irresistible wanderlust)." See "The Interest of *Crusoe*," *Essays in Criticism* 66, no. 3 (2016): 304. Taking a different angle, Wolfgang Streit, in his German-language postcolonial study of Defoe's novel, argues that the lack of a conventional first name constitutes a deficiency: "Damit ist der Name 'Robinson Crusoe' defizitär, weil er der Hauptfigur nur Merkmale der Sippenschaft und keine der Individualität zuweist, wie es ein Vorname tun würde." Ultimately, Streit regards the name Robinson Crusoe as a "Signatur der Instablilität des Individuums und von dessen Identität," that is, as a signature of the instability of the individual and his identity. See *Freitags Widerstand und die Unterwanderung von Crusoes Vorherrschaft* (Norderstedt: BoD, 2014), 9–10.
18. David Marshall, "Autobiographical Acts in *Robinson Crusoe*," *ELH* 71, no. 4 (2004): 902.
19. Marshall, "Autobiographical Acts," 908.
20. The images Geoffrey Sill reproduces in his discussion of nineteenth-century pantomime Crusoes suggest that the original engraving remained a dominant image in relation to popular knowledge of the Crusoe story.
21. "Robinson Crusoe," *Pall Mall Gazette*, February 20, 1868, 11.
22. "A Modern Robinson Crusoe," *Guernsey Star*, January 23, 1894, n.p.
23. "The Modern Robinson Crusoe," *Edinburgh Evening News*, September 14, 1898, 4.
24. "Modern Robinson Crusoe," *Evening Telegraph*, March 31, 1910, 4; "New Robinson Crusoe," *Western Gazette*, January 1, 1932, 14.
25. Jonathan Pearlman, "Australia's Robinson Crusoe May Be Forced to Leave His Island Paradise," *Telegraph*, August 24, 2012, https://www.telegraph.co.uk/news/worldnews/australiaandthepacific/9497391/Australias-Robinson-Crusoe-may-be-forced-to-leave-his-island-paradise.html.
26. Sider Jost, "Interest of *Crusoe*," 315.
27. Brian Albert, "Robinson: The Journey Review," *IGN*, November 8, 2016, http://www.ign.com/articles/2016/11/09/robinson-the-journey-review.
28. "The End of a Voyage: The Start of an Adventure," http://www.robinsonthegame.com/.
29. Albert, "Robinson: The Journey Review," http://www.ign.com/articles/2016/11/09/robinson-the-journey-review.
30. Jason D'Aprile, "Walking with Dinosaurs," *Gamespot*, December 5, 2016, https://www.gamespot.com/reviews/robinson-the-journey-review/1900-6416584/.

31. Tom Regan, "Review of Robinson: The Journey," *Trusted Reviews*, November 11, 2016, http://www.trustedreviews.com/reviews/robinson-the-journey.
32. Robinson Club GmbH, www.robinson.com/en. On the topic of boredom in *Robinson Crusoe*, see Pat Rogers's "Life Gets Tedious: Crusoe and the Threat of Boredom," chapter 7 in the present collection.
33. Robinson Club's brand manager, Martina Lotsch, explained to me after this essay was completed that I had misinterpreted the company's logo: "Our logo shows a parrot and not a footprint. You can see that it's a bird when you look to the right side (=beak) and the small circle on the left side is the eye" (email to author, April 2, 2020). In a subsequent email, Lotsch added that it is not uncommon for the logo to be read as something other than a parrot, with a coffee bean featuring as another example. These repeated "misinterpretations" of the logo neatly illustrate the associative range of the name Robinson Crusoe, which is why I have chosen not to adjust my reading. I would maintain that, to those familiar with the actual story, the single footprint on the beach represents the most iconic image created by Defoe, one that speaks directly to the type of up-market holiday offered by Robinson Club.
34. Homepage, Crusoe's Garden Rooms, https://www.crusoegardenrooms.co.uk/.
35. See the company's promotional video, https://www.crusoegardenrooms.co.uk/the-world-of.
36. Crusoe Application Homepage, http://crusoe.co/.
37. "What Is Crusoe?," http://crusoe.co/what-is-crusoe.
38. J Douglas Johnson, email to the author, April 30, 2018.
39. William T. Hastings, "Errors and Inconsistencies in Defoe's *Robinson Crusoe*," *Modern Language Notes* 27, no. 6 (1912): 161–166.
40. Further examples of the Cruzoe/Crusoe tag may be found on the following website: https://itsallabouttags.tumblr.com/post/154376650390/berlin-itsallabouttags-handstyles-graffiti.
41. "About Us," Original Crusoe's Restaurant, http://www.dineocr.com/about-us.html.
42. "Home," http://www.dineocr.com.
43. Crusoe's Restaurant & Bar, http://www.crusoesrestaurantstl.com/home.

ACKNOWLEDGMENTS

The editors wish to thank the University of Northern Colorado and the University of Louisville for their support of this project, as well as all at Bucknell University Press, where the volume first took shape with the help of Greg Clingham and then Suzanne E. Guiod and Pam Dailey. As is the case with all publications of this nature, we are indebted to those behind the scenes, including the anonymous readers for the Press, copyeditor Joseph Dahm, and Cheryl Hirsch at Westchester for their engagement with our manuscript.

BIBLIOGRAPHY

Abunasser, Rima. "Daniel Defoe and the Economic Production of English National Identity." *New Perspectives on the Eighteenth Century* 5, no. 1 (Spring 2008): 3–12.

Adorno, Theodore. "The Handle, the Pot, and Early Experience." In *Notes to Literature*, vol. 2, edited by Rolf Tiedeman, translated by Shierry Weber Nicholson, 211–219. New York: Columbia University Press, 1992.

Alaimo, Stacy. "States of Suspension: Trans-corporeality at Sea." *Interdisciplinary Studies in Literature and the Environment* 19, no. 3 (2012): 476–493.

Allen, Robert C. *Horrible Prettiness: Burlesque and American Culture*. Chapel Hill: University of North Carolina Press, 1991.

Allston Brown, T. *The History of the American Stage, from 1733 to 1870*. New York: Dick and Fitzgerald, 1870.

———. *A History of the New York Stage*. 3 vols. New York: Benjamin Blom, 1903.

Armstrong, Nancy. *Desire and Domestic Fiction*. New York: Oxford University Press, 1987.

Ayers, Robert W. "*Robinson Crusoe:* 'Allusive Allegorick History.'" *PMLA* 82 (1967): 399–407.

Baer, Joel H. "'The Complicated Plot of Piracy': Aspects of English Criminal Law and the Image of the Pirate in Defoe." *The Eighteenth Century: Theory and Interpretation* 23, no. 1 (Winter 1982): 3–26.

Baird, Ilena, and Christina Ionescu, eds. *Eighteenth-Century Thing Theory in a Global Context: From Consumerism to Celebrity Culture*. Farnham: Ashgate, 2013.

Beesemyer, Irene Basey. "Crusoe the Isolato: Daniel Defoe Wrestles with Solitude." *1650–1850: Ideas, Aesthetics, and Inquiries in the Early Modern Era* 10 (2004): 79–102.

Benedict, Barbara M. *Curiosity: A Cultural History of Early Modern Inquiry*. Chicago: University of Chicago Press, 2001.

Bennett, Jane. "The Force of Things: Steps toward an Ecology of Matter." *Political Theory* 32, no. 3 (2004): 347–372.

———. *Vibrant Matter: A Political Ecology of Things*. Durham, NC: Duke University Press, 2009.

Bingham, Clifton. *The Strange and Surprising Adventures of Jumbo Crusoe: As Told by Himself*. Buffalo: Berger, 1905.

Blackburn, Timothy C. "Friday's Religion." *Eighteenth-Century Studies* 18, no. 3 (1985): 360–382.

Blackwell, Jeannine. "An Island of Her Own: Heroines of the German Robinsonades from 1720 to 1800." *German Quarterly* 58, no. 1 (Winter 1985): 5–26.

Blewett, David. "The Iconic Crusoe: Illustrations and Images of *Robinson Crusoe*." In *The Cambridge Companion to Robinson Crusoe*, edited by John Richetti, 159–190. Cambridge: Cambridge University Press, 2018.

———. *The Illustration of* Robinson Crusoe, *1719–1920*. Gerrards Cross: Colin Smythe, 1995.

———. "The Retirement Myth in *Robinson Crusoe*: A Reconsideration." *Studies in the Literary Imagination* 15, no. 2 (Fall 1982): 37–50.

Booth, Michael R. *English Plays of the Nineteenth Century*. Oxford: Clarendon, 1976.

Boyce, Benjamin. "The Question of Emotion in Defoe." *Studies in Philology* 50, no. 1 (January 1953): 45–58.
Brown, Bill. *Other Things*. Chicago: University of Chicago Press, 2015.
———. "Thing Theory." *Critical Inquiry* 28 (2001): 1–22.
———, ed. *Things: A Critical Inquiry Book*. Chicago: University of Chicago Press, 2004.
Brown, Tony C. *The Primitive, the Aesthetic, and the Savage*. Minneapolis: University of Minnesota Press, 2012.
Burgess, Mark. *C.A.T. Crusoe*. London: Orion, 1993.
Cahill, Samara Anne. "Realist Latitudes: Textilic Nationalism and the Global Fiction of the 1720s." *Digital Defoe: Studies in Defoe & His Contemporaries* 7, no. 1 (Fall 2015): 66–91.
Carroll, Siobhan. *An Empire of Air and Water*. Philadelphia: University of Pennsylvania Press, 2015.
Chow, Jeremy. "Crusoe's Creature Comforts." *Digital Defoe* 10, no. 1 (2018). http://digitaldefoe.org/2018/11/01/crusoes-creature-comforts/.
Coats, Karen. *Looking Glasses and Neverlands: Lacan, Desire, and Subjectivity in Children's Literature*. Iowa City: University of Iowa Press, 2004.
Cole, Lucinda. *Imperfect Creatures: Vermin, Literature, and the Sciences of Life, 1600–1740*. Ann Arbor: University of Michigan Press, 2016.
Coole, Diana, and Samantha Frost, eds. *New Materialisms: Ontology, Agency, and Politics*. Durham, NC: Duke University Press, 2010.
Coppola, Al. *The Theater of Experiment: Staging Natural Philosophy in Eighteenth-Century Britain*. Oxford: Oxford University Press, 2016.
Corbin, Alain. *The Lure of the Sea: Discovery of the Seaside in the Western World, 1750–1840*. Translated by Jocelyn Phelps. Berkeley: University of California Press, 1994.
Damrosch, Leopold, Jr. *God's Plot and Man's Stories: Studies in the Fictional Imagination from Milton to Fielding*. Chicago: University of Chicago Press, 1985.
Dave, Paul. "Robinson in Ruins: New Materialism and the Archaeological Imagination." *Radical Philosophy* 169 (September/October 2011): 19–35.
De Beauvoir, Simone. *The Second Sex*. New York: Vintage, 1989.
Defoe, Daniel. *The Novels of Daniel Defoe*. 8 vols. Edited by P. N. Furbank and W. R. Owens. London: Pickering & Chatto, 2008.
———. *The Political and Economic Writings of Daniel Defoe*, 8 vols. Edited by W. R. Owens and P. N. Furbank. London: Pickering & Chatto, 2000.
Derrida, Jacques. *The Sovereign and the Beast*. Vol. 2. Chicago: University of Chicago Press, 2011.
Dharwadker, Aparna. "Nation, Race, and the Ideology of Commerce in Defoe." *Eighteenth Century* 39, no. 1 (Spring 1998): 63–84.
Dittmer, Jason. "Colonialism and Place Creation in Mars Pathfinder Media Coverage." *Geographical Review* 97, no. 1 (2007): 112–130.
Domingo, Darryl P. *The Rhetoric of Diversion in English Literature and Culture, 1690–1763*. Cambridge: Cambridge University Press, 2016.
Dowdell, Colby. "'A Living Law to Himself and Others': Daniel Defoe, Algernon Sidney, and the Politics of Self-Interest in Robinson Crusoe and Farther Adventures." *Eighteenth-Century Fiction* 22, no. 3 (Spring 2010): 415–442.
Downie, J. A. "Defoe, Imperialism, and the Travel Books Reconsidered." *Yearbook of English Studies* 13 (1983): 66–83.
Earle, Peter. *The World of Defoe*. New York: Atheneum, 1977.
Ellis, Markman. "Crusoe, Cannibalism and Empire." In *Robinson Crusoe: Myths and Metamorphoses*, edited by Lieve Spaas and Brian Stimpson, 45–61. New York: St. Martin's, 1996.
Encyclopedia Britannica. 11th ed. Edited by Hugh Chisholm et al. New York: Horace Everett Hooper, 1910–1911.

Fairholt, F. W. *Tobacco; Its History and Associations; Including an Account of the Plant and Its Manufacture; with Its Mode of Use in All Ages and Countries.* London: Chapman & Hall, 1859.

Fallon, Ann Marie. *Global Crusoe: Comparative Literature, Postcolonial Theory and Transnational Aesthetics.* Farnham: Ashgate, 2011.

Flint, Christopher. "Orphaning the Family: The Role of Kinship in *Robinson Crusoe.*" *ELH* 55, no. 2 (Summer 1988): 381–419.

Free, Melissa. "Un-erasing Crusoe: Farther Adventures in the Nineteenth Century." *Book History* 9 (2006): 89–130.

Furbank, P. N., and W. R. Owens. *A Critical Bibliography of Daniel Defoe.* London: Pickering & Chatto, 1998.

———. "Defoe and the 'Improvisatory' Sentence." *English Studies* 67, no. 2 (1986): 157–166.

———, eds. *Religious and Didactic Writings of Daniel Defoe.* 10 vols. London: Pickering & Chatto, 2012.

Gänzl, Kurt. *Lydia Thompson, Queen of Burlesque.* New York: Routledge, 2002.

Ghosh, Peter. "Max Weber's Idea of 'Puritanism': A Case Study in the Empirical Construction of the Protestant Ethic." *History of European Ideas* 29, no. 2 (2003): 183–221.

Golinski, Jan. *British Weather and the Climate of the Enlightenment.* Chicago: University of Chicago Press, 2007.

Gould, Marty. *Nineteenth-Century Theatre and the Imperial Encounter.* New York: Routledge, 2011.

Grapard, Ulla, and Gillian Hewitson, eds. *Robinson Crusoe's Economic Man: A Construction and Deconstruction.* New York: Routledge, 2011.

Green, Martin. *The Robinson Crusoe Story.* University Park: Pennsylvania State University Press, 1990.

Guardini, Romano. *Sacred Signs.* St. Louis: Pio Decimo Press, 1955.

Guerrini, Anita. *Obesity and Depression in the Enlightenment.* Norman: University of Oklahoma Press, 2000.

Hamblyn, Richard. "Introduction." In *The Storm.* New York: Penguin, 2005.

Hastings, William T. "Errors and Inconsistencies in Defoe's *Robinson Crusoe.*" *Modern Language Notes* 27, no. 6 (1912): 161–166.

Heidegger, Martin. "The Thing." Translated by Albert Hofstader. In *Poetry, Language, Thought,* 161–180. New York: Harper & Row, 1971.

Hindmarsh, D. Bruce. *The Evangelical Conversion Narration.* Oxford: Oxford University Press, 2005.

Horne, Jackie C. Review of *Children's Literature, Popular Culture, and "Robinson Crusoe,"* by Andrew O'Malley. *Digital Defoe: Studies in Defoe & His Contemporaries* 5, no. 1 (Fall 2013): 161–165.

Houlihan Flynn, Carol. *The Body in Swift and Defoe.* Cambridge: Cambridge University Press, 1990.

Hulme, Peter. *Colonial Encounters.* New York: Methuen, 1986.

Hunter, J. Paul. *The Reluctant Pilgrim: Defoe's Emblematic Method and Quest for Form in Robinson Crusoe.* Baltimore: Johns Hopkins University Press, 1966.

Hutchins, Henry C. *Robinson Crusoe and its Printing 1719–1731: A Bibliographical Study.* New York: Columbia University Press, 1925.

Jacques, Zoe. *Children's Literature and the Posthuman: Animal, Environment, Cyborg.* New York: Routledge, 2015.

James, Louis. "Unwrapping Crusoe: Retrospective and Prospective Views." In *Robinson Crusoe: Myths and Metamorphoses,* edited by Lieve Spaas and Brian Stimpson, 1–9. Basingstoke: Macmillan, 1996.

Joseph, Betty. "Capitalism and Its Others: Intersecting and Competing Forms in Eighteenth-Century Fiction." *Studies in Eighteenth-Century Culture* 45 (2016): 157–173.

Keenleyside, Heather. *Animals and Other People: Literary Forms and Living Beings in the Long Eighteenth Century*. Philadelphia: University of Pennsylvania Press, 2016.

Kelly, James. "The Worcester Affair." *Review of English Studies* 51 (2000): 1–23.

Kripke, Saul. *Wittgenstein on Rules and Private Language*. Oxford: Blackwell, 1982.

Kuhn, Reinhard. *The Demon of Noontide: Ennui in Western Literature*. Princeton: Princeton University Press, 1976.

Lamb, Jonathan. *The Things Things Say*. Princeton: Princeton University Press, 2011.

Le Guin, Ursula. *Cheek by Jowl*. Seattle: Aqueduct, 2009.

Lewis, C. S. *On Stories: And Other Essays on Literature*. Orlando: Harcourt, 1966.

Liu, Lydia H. "Robinson Crusoe's Earthenware Pot." *Critical Inquiry* 25 (1999): 728–757.

———. "Robinson Crusoe's Earthenware Pot: Science, Aesthetics, and the Metaphysics of True Porcelain." In *Romantic Science: The Literary Forms of Natural History*, edited by Noah Heringman, 139–171. Albany: State University of New York Press, 2003.

Lloyd, T. O. *The British Empire, 1558–1983*. New York: Oxford University Press, 1984.

Loar, Christopher. "How to Say Things with Guns: Military Technology and the Politics of Robinson Crusoe." *Eighteenth-Century Fiction* 19, nos. 1–2 (2006): 1–20.

Logan, Olive. *Before the Footlights and Behind the Scenes: A Book about "The Show Business" in All Its Branches*. Philadelphia: Parmelee, 1870.

Lovett, Robert W. *Robinson Crusoe: A Bibliographical Checklist of English Language Editions (1719–1979)*. New York: Greenwood Press, 1991.

Loxley, Diana. *Problematic Shores: The Literature of Islands*. New York: St. Martin's, 1990.

Markley, Robert. "'Casualties and Disasters': Defoe and the Interpretation of Climatic Instability." *Journal for Early Modern Cultural Studies* 8, no. 2 (2008): 102–124.

———. *The Far East and the English Imagination, 1600–1700*. Cambridge: Cambridge University Press, 2006.

Marshall, David. "Autobiographical Acts in *Robinson Crusoe*." *ELH* 71, no. 4 (2004): 899–920.

Marx, Karl. *Capital*. Translated by Samuel Moore and Edward Aveling, 1906. Reprint, Mineola, NY: Dover, 2011.

Mayer, Robert. "Defoe's Cultural Afterlife, Mainly on Screen." In *The Afterlives of Eighteenth-Century Fiction*, edited by Daniel Cook and Nicholas Seager, 233–252. Cambridge: Cambridge University Press, 2015.

———. "*Robinson Crusoe* in the Screen Age." In *The Cambridge Companion to Robinson Crusoe*, edited by John Richetti, 221–233.Cambridge: Cambridge University Press, 2018.

McKeon, Michael. *The Origins of the English Novel, 1600–1740*. Baltimore: Johns Hopkins University Press, 1987.

McMullin, Ernan. *Newton on Matter and Energy*. Notre Dame: University of Notre Dame Press, 1979.

McVeagh, John. "*Robinson Crusoe*'s Stage Début: The Sheridan Pantomime of 1781." *Journal of Popular Culture* 24, no. 2 (Fall 1990): 137–152.

Meyer Spacks, Patricia. *Boredom: The Literary History of a State of Mind*. Chicago: University of Chicago Press, 1995.

Moore, John Robert. *Checklist of the Writings of Daniel Defoe*. Bloomington: Indiana University Press, 1960.

Neill, Anna. *British Discovery Literature and the Rise of Global Commerce*. New York: Palgrave Macmillan, 2002.

Nikolajeva, Maria. "The Identification Fallacy: Perspective and Subjectivity in Children's Literature." In *Telling Children's Stories: Narrative Theory and Children's Literature*, edited by Mike Cadden, 187–208. Lincoln: University of Nebraska Press, 2010.

Nineteenth Century Collections Online: British Theatre, Music, and Literature: High and Popular Culture. https://www.gale.com/c/ncco-british-theatre-music-and-literature-high-and-popular-culture.

Norton, Marcy. *Sacred Gifts, Profane Pleasures: A History of Tobacco and Chocolate in the Atlantic World.* Ithaca, NY: Cornell University Press, 2008.

Novak, Maximillian E. *Daniel Defoe: Master of Fictions.* Oxford: Oxford University Press, 2001.

———. *Defoe and the Nature of Man.* Oxford: Clarendon, 1963.

———. *Economics and the Fiction of Daniel Defoe.* Berkeley: University of California Press, 1962.

———. "Robinson Crusoe's Original Sin." *Studies in English Literature, 1500–1900* 1, no. 3 (1961): 19–29.

———. *Transformations, Ideology, and the Real in Defoe's* Robinson Crusoe *and Other Narratives: Finding the Thing Itself.* Newark: Delaware University Press, 2014.

O'Brien, John. *Harlequin Britain: Pantomime and Entertainment, 1690–1760.* Baltimore: Johns Hopkins University Press, 2004.

O'Malley, Andrew. *Children's Literature, Popular Culture, and* Robinson Crusoe. Basingstoke: Palgrave Macmillan, 2012.

———. "Crusoe's Children: *Robinson Crusoe* and the Culture of Childhood in the Eighteenth Century." In *The Child in British Literature: Literary Constructions of Childhood, Medieval to Contemporary,* edited by Adrienne E. Gavin, 87–100. New York: Palgrave Macmillan, 2012.

O'Toole, Fintan. *A Traitor's Kiss: The Life of Richard Brinsley Sheridan.* New York: Farrar, Straus and Giroux, 1997.

Owen, C. M. *The Female Crusoe: Hybridity, Trade and the Eighteenth-Century Individual.* Amsterdam: Rodopi, 2010.

Parker, Michael. "Cultural Icons: A Case Study Analysis of Their Formation and Reception." PhD dissertation, University of Central Lancashire, 2012.

Pearl, Jason. "Desert Islands and Urban Solitudes in the Crusoe Trilogy." *Studies in the Novel* 44, no. 2 (Summer 2012): 125–143.

Pisani, Michael V. *Music for the Melodramatic Theatre in Nineteenth-Century London & New York.* Iowa City: University of Iowa Press, 2014.

Pivetti, Kyle. "The King of Mars: *The Martian*'s Scientific Empire and *Robinson Crusoe.*" In *The Cinematic Eighteenth Century: History, Culture, and Adaptation*, edited by Srividhya Swaminathan and Steven W. Thomas, 118–138. New York City: Routledge, 2018.

Potter, Beatrix. *The Tale of Little Pig Robinson.* 1930. Reprint, New York: Penguin, 1988.

Pullen, Kirsten. *Actresses and Whores: On Stage and in Society.* Cambridge: Cambridge University Press, 2005.

Ratelle, Amy. *Animality and Children's Literature and Film.* London: Palgrave Macmillan, 2015.

Regunathan, Swetha. "An Incongruous Monster: Idolatrous Aesthetics in Crusoe's China." *Digital Defoe: Studies in Defoe & His Contemporaries* 5 (2013): 45–64.

Richards, Jeffrey. *The Golden Age of Pantomime: Slapstick, Spectacle and Subversion in Victorian England.* London: Tauris, 2015.

Richetti, John. *The Life of Danie Defoe.* Oxford: Blackwell, 2005.

———. "Secular Crusoe: The Reluctant Pilgrim Re-visited." In *Eighteenth-Century Genre and Culture: Serious Reflections on Occasional Forms,* edited by Dennis Todd and Cynthia Wall, 58–78. Cranbury: Associated University Presses, 2001.

Rønning, Anne Birgitte. "Female Robinsonades—A Bibliography." https://www2.hf.uio.no/tjenester/bibliographfi/Robinsonades.

Rowe Townsend, John. *Written for Children: An Outline of English-Language Children's Literature.* London: Lothrop, Lee, and Shepard, 1965.

Schmidgen, Wolfram. *Eighteenth-Century Fiction and the Law of Property*. Cambridge: Cambridge University Press, 2002.

———. "The Metaphysics of *Robinson Crusoe*." *ELH* 83 (2016): 101–126.

———. "*Robinson Crusoe*, Enumeration, and the Mercantile Fetish." *Eighteenth-Century Studies* 35, no. 1 (Fall 2001): 19–39.

Schofield, Robert E. *Mechanism and Materialism: British Natural Philosophy in an Age of Reason*. Princeton: Princeton University Press, 1970.

Schonhorn, Manuel. *Defoe's Politics: Parliament, Power, Kingship and "Robinson Crusoe."* Cambridge: Cambridge University Press, 1991.

———. "Weber, Watt, and Restraint: Robinson Crusoe and the Critical Tradition." In *Approaches to Teaching Defoe's Robinson Crusoe*, edited by Maximillian E. Novak and Carl Fisher, 55–60. New York: Modern Language Association of America, 2005.

Sherman, Stuart. *Telling Time: Clocks, Diaries, and English Diurnal Form, 1660–1785*. Chicago: University of Chicago Press, 1996.

Shields, David S. *Still: American Silent Motion Picture Photography*. Chicago: University of Chicago Press, 2013.

Sider Jost, Jacob. "The Interest of *Crusoe*." *Essays in Criticism* 66, no. 3 (2016): 301–319.

Sill, Geoffrey. *The Cure of the Passions and the Origins of the English Novel*. Cambridge: Cambridge University Press, 2001.

Smith, Chloe Wigston. "'Callico Madams': Servants, Consumption, and the Calico Crisis." *Eighteenth-Century Life* 31, no. 2 (Spring 2007): 29–55.

Spielman, David W. "The Value of Money in *Robinson Crusoe, Moll Flanders*, and *Roxana*." *Modern Language Review* 107, no. 1 (January 2012): 65–87.

Starr, G. A. "Defoe and China." *Eighteenth-Century Studies* 43, no. 4 (2010): 435–454.

———. *Defoe and Spiritual Autobiography*. New York: Gordian Press, 1971.

Steig, William. *Abel's Island*. New York: Square Fish, 1976.

Steinberg, Phillip. *The Social Construction of the Ocean*. Cambridge: Cambridge University Press, 2001.

Stevenson, James. *The Castaway*. Hong Kong: Greenwillow Books, 2002.

Streit, Wolfgang. *Freitags Widerstand und die Unterwanderung von Crusoes Vorherrschaft*. Norderstedt: BoD, 2014.

Todd, Dennis. *Defoe's America*. Cambridge: Cambridge University Press, 2010.

Turley, Hans. "Protestant Evangelicalism, British Imperialism, and Crusonian Identity." In *A New Imperial History: Culture, Identity, and Modernity in Britain and the Empire, 1660–1840*, edited by Kathleen Wilson, 176–193. Cambridge: Cambridge University Press, 2004.

Turrell, James F. "Anglican Liturgical Practices." In *A Companion to the Eucharist in the Reformation*, edited by Lee Palmer Wandel, 273–292. Leiden: Brill, 2014.

Vickers, Ilse. *Defoe and the New Sciences*. Cambridge: Cambridge University Press, 1996.

Wallace, Ivy L. *Getup Crusoe*. London: Collins, 1948.

Watt, Ian. *The Rise of the Novel: Studies in Defoe, Richardson, and Fielding*. Berkeley: University of California Press, 1957.

———. "*Robinson Crusoe* as Myth." *Essays in Criticism* 1, no. 2 (April 1951): 95–119.

Weber, Max. *The Protestant Ethic and the Spirit of Capitalism*. Translated by Stephen Kalberg. New York: Oxford University Press, 2011.

———. "The Social Psychology of the World Religions." In *From Max Weber: Essays in Sociology*, edited by H. H. Gerth and C. Wright Mills, 267–301. New York: Oxford University Press, 1946.

———. *The Sociology of Religion*. Translated by Talcott Parsons. Boston: Beacon, 1963.

Weir, Andy. *The Martian*. New York: Broadway Books, 2014.

Wenzel, Siegfried. *The Sin of Sloth: Acedia in Medieval Thought and Literature.* Chapel Hill: University of North Carolina Press, 1967.

Wheeler, Roxann. "The Complexion of Desire: Racial Ideology and Mid-Eighteenth-Century British Novels." *Eighteenth-Century Studies* 32, no. 3 (1999): 309–332.

———. "'My Savage,' 'My Man': Racial Multiplicity in *Robinson Crusoe.*" *ELH* 62, no. 4 (1995): 821–861.

Wilkinson, Andrew M. "The 'Meditations' of Daniel Defoe." *Modern Language Review* 46, nos. 3/4 (1951): 349–354.

Wittgenstein, Ludwig. *The Philosophical Investigations.* Edited by George Pitcher. London: Macmillan, 1968.

Woolf, Virginia. *The Second Common Reader.* 1932. Reprinted in *Robinson Crusoe: A Norton Critical Edition*, 2nd ed., edited by Michael Schinagel. New York: Norton, 1975.

Yolton, John W. *Thinking Matter: Materialism in Eighteenth-Century Britain.* Minneapolis: University of Minnesota Press, 1984.

NOTES ON CONTRIBUTORS

LAURA BROWN (PhD, University of California, Berkeley) is the John Wendell Anderson Professor of English at Cornell University. She has published widely in eighteenth-century studies, and has served as president of the American Society for Eighteenth-Century Studies and as vice provost at Cornell University. She studies "feminization" and gender, slavery and imperialism, species and racial difference, the portrayal of animals, and the counter-human force of "things" in eighteenth-century literary culture. Her current book project—*Storms, Pots, and the Power of Detritus: The Counter-Human Imaginary in Modern Literary Form*—builds upon the contributions of her most recent monograph on *Homeless Dogs and Melancholy Apes: Humans and Other Animals in the Modern Literary Imagination.*

JEREMY CHOW is assistant professor of English at Bucknell University. His research and teaching interweave eighteenth-century studies, gender and sexuality studies, and the environmental humanities. His work has appeared in or is forthcoming from *Eighteenth-Century Fiction*, *Digital Defoe*, *Journal of Eighteenth-Century Studies*, *English Language Notes*, *Resilience: A Journal of the Environmental Humanities*, *Atlantic Studies*, and *Camera Obscura: Feminism, Culture, & Media Studies*, in addition to several edited collections. His chapter here draws from his current monograph, *The Queerness of Water: Aqueous Violence & Bodies in Water, 1719–1818.*

AMY HICKS received her PhD in English studies, with a specialization in children's and young adult literature, from Illinois State University. She has taught a variety of courses on such topics as the children's castaway novel, space and place in children's literature, retellings and adaptations in children's literature, as well as survey courses in literature for young children, middle readers, and adolescents. Her previous publications include essays on nineteenth- through twenty-first-century girl's castaway novels and *Robinson Crusoe*–inspired toys. Her current research project traces the historical trajectory of children's Robinsonades to explore how girl characters construct modes of femininity through their connections with other people, animals, and nature.

ANDREAS K. E. MUELLER is professor and chair of English at the University of Northern Colorado. He is the author of *A Critical Study of Daniel Defoe's Verse* (2010) and editor of *Daniel Defoe's Non-Fiction: Form, Function, Genre* (2011). He has published several essays on Defoe and on the eighteenth-century Bishop of Worcester, Richard Hurd. His current book project is concerned with the social and political functions of gratitude in eighteenth-century literature and culture.

MAXIMILLIAN E. NOVAK is distinguished research professor (emeritus) at University of California, Los Angeles. He has written widely on the literature of the Restoration and eighteenth century, especially on its drama and fiction. He edited several volumes of the works of John Dryden and is one of the general editors of the Stoke Newington Edition of the Writings of Daniel Defoe, having also co-edited several volumes in that series. He has also written a number of books on Daniel Defoe, including his biography, *Daniel Defoe Master of Fictions*, which first appeared in 2001, and *Transformations, Ideology, and the Real in Defoe's Robinson Crusoe and Other Narratives* in 2015.

BENJAMIN F. PAULEY is professor of English at Eastern Connecticut State University. He has published essays on Defoe, Samuel Johnson, and William Godwin. He was the founding secretary of the Defoe Society, and is a member of the faculty of Rare Book School at the University of Virginia.

SCOTT PYRZ is a PhD candidate at Illinois State University specializing in children's and young adult literature and technical communications manager at TuSimple, Inc., a San Diego–based autonomous trucking startup. His research interests include children's animal stories, children's and young adult adaptations, narrative theory, and technical writing. His current research project investigates the ideological role of anthropomorphic animals in children's chapter books and films.

GLYNIS RIDLEY is professor and chair of English at the University of Louisville, Kentucky. She is the author of the books *Clara's Grand Tour. Travels with a Rhinoceros in Eighteenth-Century Europe* (2004), winner of the Institute of Historical Research Prize, and *The Discovery of Jeanne Baret. A Story of Science, the High Seas, and the First Woman to Circumnavigate the Globe* (2010), and has published widely in eighteenth-century studies. Her current book project is using an original album from 1824 to 1827 to build a biography of its owner, Thomasina Gleadowe-Newcomen, a history of the unconventional Anglo-Irish family to which Thomasina belonged, and to reconstruct the family's lost Dublin estate—all against the backdrop of the high and low culture represented in the album's pages.

PAT ROGERS, distinguished professor emeritus at the University of South Florida, has previously published two editions of Defoe's *Tour of Great Britain*, and a monograph on the book, a study of *Crusoe*, and an edition of *Moll Flanders*, as well as editing the Critical Heritage volume. Has contributed to several essay collections, most recently *The Cambridge Companion to Robinson Crusoe* (2018), and two forthcoming books, *The Oxford Handbook to Daniel Defoe* and *Defoe in Context*. Latest articles include discussions of Defoe's place in early modern historiography and his pioneering survey of the turnpike system. Current research involves Defoe and economic geography, with consideration of his possible role in *Atlas Maritimus* (1728).

GEOFFREY SILL is a professor emeritus of English at Rutgers University in Camden, New Jersey. He is the author of *Defoe and the Idea of Fiction* (1983), *The Cure of the Passions and the Origins of the English Novel* (2001), and articles on Walt Whitman, Daniel Defoe, and Frances Burney. He is working on a new edition of *Memoirs of Publick Transactions in the Life and Ministry of . . . the Duke of Shrewsbury* (1718).

DANIEL YU is a visiting assistant professor of English at St. Mary's College of Maryland. He studies gifts and reciprocity as expressed in eighteenth-century literature, using a combination of critical theory and sociology of religion. His work on *Robinson Crusoe* is also found in *Eighteenth-Century Fiction*. Aside from scholarship, he writes poetry, having received a PhD from Emory University and an MFA from the University of California, Irvine.

INDEX

Page numbers in italics refer to figures.